Sine Die

A Guide to the Washington State
Legislative Process

1997 Edition

Sine Die

A Guide to the Washington State
Legislative Process

1997 Edition

EDWARD D. SEEBERGER

University of Washington Press

Seattle and London

The original edition of *Sine Die: A Guide to the Washington State Legislative Process* was published in 1989 by the Institute for Public Policy and Management and the Graduate School of Public Affairs of the University of Washington and distributed by the University of Washington Press.

Library of Congress Cataloging-in-Publication Data
Seeberger, Edward D.
    Sine die : a guide to the Washington State legislative process /
Edward D. Seeberger. — 1997 ed.
        p. cm.
    Includes bibliographical references and index.
    ISBN 0–295–97572–5
    1. Washington (State). Legislature. 2. Legislation—Washington
(State) 3. Budget—Washington (State)   I. Title
JK9271.S44   1996   96–36855
328.797'077—dc21

The paper used in this publication meets the minimum requirements of American National Standard for Information Sciences—Permanence of Paper for Printed Library Materials, ANSI Z39.48–1984. ∞

Contents

FIGURES

Page

Acknowledgments

The 1997 edition of *Sine Die* owes a great debt to six friends who agreed to read a first draft and make suggestions for improvements. They are former State Representative, Utilities and Transportation Commission member, lobbyist, and current chair of the Public Disclosure Commission **Don Brazier,** who in his retirement has made himself the single most knowledgeable person about the history of the Washington State Legislature; my long-time associate and the best overall legislative staff person I have known, Secretary of the Senate **Marty Brown**; my former political science professor at Seattle University, a wonderful teacher and enduring friend, now at Gonzaga University, **Frank Costello, S.J.**; the person who prodded me into writing a new edition of this book and who amazes me at every encounter with his knowledge, **Dr. Ronald B. Dear**, professor at the University of Washington; my companion and wife for thirty-three years, **Joan E. Seeberger**; and the best pure legislator I encountered during my twenty-two years in Olympia, current Supreme Court Justice **Phil Talmadge**.

Ginny Spadoni edited for substance and form and took charge of getting a camera-ready manuscript to the Press. She is that rare jewel of an employee who insists on getting things right. Thanks also to Ginny's two co-workers in Senate Word Processing, **Darilyn Sundstrom** and **Betty Higgins,** for their help on the first edition as well as this current one.

I am grateful to several other people who provided valuable comments and suggestions and material for selected parts of the book. They include former Senator **Jeannette Hayner** for her help on the Gender Revolution chapter, as well as the description of the 1991-1992 sessions; former House staffer **Tim Burke** for assistance on the ethics issues; current Senate Ways and Means economist **David Schumacher** for material concerning the accuracy of revenue forecasts; Department of Transportation Systems Planning Branch Manager **Brian Ziegler** for his excellent memo explaining the transportation budget process; and Chief Clerk of the House **Tim Martin** for his general comments.

Thanks to those from the University of Washington Press who encouraged and assisted in various ways, especially **Julidta Tarver, Pat Soden,** and **Pam Chaus.**

Former Senator **George Fleming** offered me the job as Senate Committee Services Director I held for fourteen years which made it possible for me to write this book. Thanks to **Marty Brown** and to **Senator Sid Snyder** and **Senator Dan McDonald** for creating a wonderful work environment in the Senate and for giving me the flexibility to complete the 1997 version of *Sine Die*.

Edward D. Seeberger
October 1996

Introduction to the 1997 Edition

Since the first edition of *Sine Die* in 1987-88, there have been dramatic changes in the Legislature and in state politics. Limits have been placed on campaign contributions; campaign finance reporting requirements were expanded; ethics laws were passed following revelations of improper use of caucus staff; Initiative 601 was passed by the voters, imposing limitations on state taxing and spending powers; the legislative process has been computerized, making information easily and quickly electronically accessible to all; and term limits, passed in 1992, start taking their toll on state legislators in 1998. Even more significant, there has been a gender revolution in the Washington State Legislature. Women are on the verge of having an equal place in numbers and power and are having a dramatic effect on the legislative climate and on state policy.

This 1997 edition of *Sine Die* is not an update. It is a new book that resembles the original only in name and subject matter.

Chapter 1 attempts to give the reader a sense of the beauty, majesty and history of the state capitol and its surrounding buildings and grounds.

Chapters 2, 3 and 4 provide background about the frequency of legislative sessions, where bills come from, their component parts, legislative terminology, the public hearing process accomplished by legislative committees, and a list of helpful publications and where they can be obtained. After providing extensive material about length and purpose of sessions, I present a thumbnail summary of special sessions for the last seven years. In the section on Origin of Bills in Chapter 3, I present my own findings on the sources of bills. In the same chapter, I speculate about some modifications in state law caused by rapid technological changes.

Chapter 5 is the heart of the book. Using cutoffs as a guide, it walks the reader through the various steps and pitfalls in the legislative process, complete with examples and illustrations.

Chapter 6 deals with the three major budgets. I give considerable emphasis to budget forecasting and to Initiative 601, which limits overall spending, because they are the two constants in an evolving and changing process. I hope the discussion of the capital and transportation budgets is simplified and improved.

In the original book, I gave the governor only a few paragraphs. He or she deserves more. In Chapter 7, I give full coverage to the various ways the governor interacts with the Legislature, with particular emphasis on gubernatorial appointments, confirmations, and use of the veto. Hopefully, the reader will find comparisons of the last five governors as interesting as I did.

Chapter 8 is about the stars, the celebrities, the legislators. I try to dissect them in terms of politics, number, background, experience, age, and ethnic diversity. I've added material on term limits and on the controversial residency requirement, and dug up historical data about two expulsions. I try to convey a sense of what legislators' lives are like during those long, dark, damp winter days in Olympia during session.

In the first edition, I treated gender in the same chapter as age, race, and other characteristics of legislators. Since then, however, the number of women legislators has grown so they are now a majority in the Democrat party and are on the verge of becoming a majority in the entire Legislature. To my way of thinking, that is revolutionary. It deserves a full chapter to itself. I attempt to give a brief history of women gaining the right to vote, getting elected, and finally gaining power, with brief descriptions of several of the most prominent early female legislators. I illustrate the "revolution" with a longer description of the remarkable former Senate Majority Leader Jeannette Hayner. Lastly, I offer an answer to the question of so what? My contention is that women have already had a major influence on the kinds of laws passed in this state, and

I offer evidence to support that view and give a glimpse of what is to come.

Chapter 10 is a description of the various legislative staff, those who work directly for the Legislature and some who have more indirect contacts. This, too, is greatly expanded from the earlier version.

Chapter 11 on ethics, financial disclosure and political campaigning is all new since 1989 and is critical to an understanding of the legislative process.

Throughout the first eleven chapters, I have highlighted key words and phrases used in the legislative process. These terms are either defined in their context and/or can be found in the glossary.

Chapter 12 is a detailed case study of the 1991 and 1992 legislative sessions. It could as easily be the first chapter. It serves to illustrate how the process, which looks rather neat and tidy in earlier analyses, is often messy and undisciplined. Why 1991-1992? Partly because those years were marked by strong external events in the Gulf War and the teachers' strike, partly because the regular and special sessions were quite typical, and partly because enough time has passed to give some perspective to what happened. The 1991-92 biennium was significant as well because it marked the end of the careers of three dominant state political figures of the decade of the 1980s: Governor Booth Gardner did not seek reelection to a third term, Speaker Joe King ran for governor and lost in the primary, and Senate Majority Leader Jeannette Hayner retired.

While I liberally used data from sources both inside and outside the Legislature, and gave appropriate credit, the work is entirely my own. No one, including my employer, the State Senate, attempted to censor me or guide my thinking. Good or bad, I take full responsibility for all material presented.

After twenty-two years as a member and staff, I view the Legislature as a dynamic and creative institution, constantly adapting to changing situations and personalities. The legislative process is at heart merely a mechanism for identifying problems and reaching solutions. I believe that, for the most part, it works well. The citizens of this state can generally be proud of the efforts of the men and women they send to Olympia to represent them and, assuming an adequate level of citizen vigilance, can be confident about the future of state government.

Edward D. Seeberger
October 1996

Sine Die

A Guide to the Washington State
Legislative Process

1997 Edition

1

The State Capitol

The village of Olympia was founded in 1850 by Edmund Sylvester. So sudden was the migration that within three years the area boasted a newspaper, customs house, steamboat landing and mercantile community, and was the largest town on Puget Sound. Sylvester had an even greater vision, though. In 1853 when Washington territory was established, Sylvester platted the town and donated twelve acres of land on the hill overlooking what is now Budd Inlet for construction of a state capitol building.

There seemed to be no dispute that the first territorial Legislature would meet in Olympia. They used a frame building later known as the Gold Bar Restaurant near Capitol Way and Second Street. In 1856, thanks to a $5,000 appropriation from Congress, a small wooden structure was built on the present site of the capitol to serve as a temporary seat of government.

In 1889 Washington became the forty-second state in the Union, and voters chose Olympia as the site of the state capital. In his proclamation of statehood, President Harrison also announced the donation of 132,000 acres of federal land, to use the income for construction of a state capitol. In 1893 a competition was held to pick a design for a permanent capitol structure. Ernest Flagg of New York was selected from 188 entries, and excavation and foundation work was begun in 1894. However, work soon stopped due to a lack of funds and continued jealousy by the cities of Yakima, Ellensburg, Vancouver and Tacoma over the location of the state capital.

In 1901 the state took advantage of Thurston County's financial woes and purchased the grand but unfinished courthouse at Legion Way and Washington Street, currently the offices of the superintendent of public instruction, and added a wing to house the Legislature. The building was still viewed as too small, however, and was only a temporary solution. It served as the state capitol from 1905 until 1928. In 1909 the Legislature authorized completion of the Flagg design for the capitol building on Sylvester's donated twelve acres but appropriated no funds. It did, however, authorize construction of the governor's mansion, still in use today.

Following another competition to complete the Flagg design, in 1911 New York architects Walter R. Wilder and Harry K. White were chosen. They followed the classical Roman architectural style and the "City Beautiful" movement of the time. The challenge as they viewed it was "how to split the usual massive Capitol Building up into six or more components without diminishing each part so as to make it seem comparatively insignificant." (*American Architect,* November 1915.)

The Temple of Justice was the first building completed (except for the exterior facing). Governor Ernest Lister's Inaugural Ball was held there in 1913. Work on the current Legislative Building (the capitol) resumed in 1919. Wilder and White enlarged the old footings and designed a dome twice the height of Flagg's original concept. They first considered making the dome 307 feet, the same height as the national capitol in Washington, D.C., but settled instead on 287 feet as the correct proportion to the other buildings and, perhaps, out of deference to the central government.

The Insurance Building was the second of the group to be completed, in 1921. The Legislative Building was completed third, in 1928; the Institutions Building, not part of the original plan and clearly of a different architectural style, was completed in 1934; the Public Lands Building, now named the John A. Cherberg Building, was finished in 1937; and the Public Health Building, now called the John L. O'Brien Building, was completed in 1940. Senate committee meetings and staff are currently located in the Cherberg Building, and House committee meetings and staff are in the O'Brien Building. A sixth structure, identical to the Insurance

Building, was planned for the west side of the Legislative Building where the governor's mansion sits, but has not yet been built.

The Legislative Building is the central structure in the capitol design and dominates the entire region. It is the equivalent of twenty-eight stories at its highest point and, at the time of completion, was the fourth highest dome in the world. The arched dome is a rarity in that it contains no steel reinforcements. It is built entirely of 1,400 cut stones taken from a quarry about forty miles east of Olympia. None of the stones has a straight line on any edge or face. The stones are cut so precisely that upon completion on October 13, 1926, there was exactly three-eighths of an inch projection on all sides, just as is called for in the architectural drawings. The building has six massive bronze external doors, weighing 2,000 pounds each, depicting various scenes from Washington early history.

Major earthquakes occurred in 1949 and in 1965 but did little serious damage to the capitol building. As a precaution, however, following the 1949 quake, workers built an inclined railway to the top of the dome, took the lantern apart piece by piece (1,500 pieces), redesigned them and put them back together in order to lighten the load from 180 to 110 tons. Following the 1965 quake, twenty-two of the thirty windows in the colonnade were filled with reinforced concrete to give the dome more rigidity.

Washington State's capitol campus is one of the most beautiful in the world. Not only did early leaders show vision in planning on such a grand scale, but subsequent leaders showed resolve in maintaining the area in such a manner as to show the magnificent buildings in their best light. One of the features that sets Olympia apart from many other capitals is the luxuriant spacing between the buildings.

John A. Cherberg, who served thirty-two years as lieutenant governor and much of that time as chair of the State Capitol Committee, believed that the wide expanses of green lawn and trees did as much to enhance the beauty of the campus as the buildings. He resisted attempts to place various state offices near the capitol inside the original campus. Thanks to Cherberg and other leaders of vision, the grounds today are broad and spacious, interspersed only with tasteful memorials to war dead and commemorative plaques and gardens.

The current capitol campus runs from Capitol Lake east to Jefferson Street, bounded on the north by 11th Street and on the south by 15th and Maple Park. There are over 1,700 trees, 900 rose bushes, and 26,000 shrubs and bushes located on over 33 acres. Many of the trees and bushes have been donated in memory of various dignitaries and historic figures. For example, there is the Dixy Lee Ray tree donated by Dolph Price of

Kelso and dedicated in 1980 in honor of the state's first woman governor. Her tree is actually a Dawn Redwood from China. It is the only redwood tree that is deciduous.

A grove of Yoshino cherry trees was donated by Mitsuo Mutai, head of the Shimbun newspapers in Tokyo, in 1984. The trees are located on lawns between the Cherberg and O'Brien buildings and the capitol and are just coming to maturity. Their blossoms are a delicate whitish pink. More famous was the grove of Kwanzan cherry trees planted in 1932 that grew to form a canopy stretching from both sides over Water Street between the capitol and the Insurance Building. They were remarkable for their lush deep pink double-ruffle blooms that would carpet the street and sidewalk west of the capitol in early spring. Unfortunately, they had to be removed in 1995 due to disease, but new ones have been planted for the enjoyment of future generations.

There are plans to add thirty-four additional acres of land stretching from behind the Temple of Justice, down the wooded slope, around Capitol Lake, to Budd Inlet. Called Heritage Park, it would complete the capitol campus plan envisioned eighty-five years earlier.

Early spring in Olympia is generally cold and wet and gray. But in some years nature will surprise with a gift of sun and blue sky. When that occurs, the variegated pink flowering cherry trees, joined by yellow daffodils and purple magnolias set against the familiar green conifers, create a scene of beauty that is only outdone when the flaming red rhododendrons bloom a few weeks later.

The Saucer Magnolia tree outside the southeast entrance to the Legislative Building was dubbed the "sine die tree" by Jack Pyle, long-time correspondent for the Tacoma *News Tribune,* during the 1960s. It is often mistaken for a tulip tree because of its large tulip-like white flowers. It usually blooms in early March, thus coinciding with the end of the sixty-day session. Pyle insinuated that when the tree blooms, it is nature's way of signaling time for the legislators to finish their business and go home. A new sidewalk was built in 1975 and the original sine die tree was cut down by mistake. Senators Gordon Sandison (D-Port Angeles) and Charles Newschwander (R-Tacoma) felt so strongly that the tradition should not die that a new tree was found and planted. It continues to bloom to this day, although its signal for the end of session is usually ignored.

The interior of the Legislative Building is predominantly faced with light gray Tokeen and Gravina marble from Alaska. A five-ton Tiffany-made bronze chandelier dangles 185 feet down from the interior of the dome. Beneath it in the center of the rotunda is the four-foot polished brass Great

Seal of the state of Washington featuring George Washington encircled by oak leaves. The location of the state seal on the floor was a concern since people could and did walk on it. According to a 1929 letter from E. L. Gale to A. C. Martin, Secretary of the Capitol Committee, "George Washington's nose is already badly worn off by thousands having walked over his face." In the late 1930s, Governor Hartley had a rope enclosure installed around the seal, which remains today.

The Legislative Building is home to a number of state offices including the governor, secretary of state, auditor, and treasurer, all on the second floor. However, the largest rooms are the legislative chambers and despite the presence of these other important officials, there is little doubt that the primary function and design of this magnificent building is to accommodate a bicameral legislature.

The first things one notices on entering the House chamber are the ninety-eight walnut desks standing stiffly at attention before an ornately hand-carved mahogany two-step elevated rostrum. The desks are in pairs, with the rows slightly rounded and there is an aisle down the center, roughly separating members of the two political parties. The floor is carpeted in gray with a rhododendron pattern and trillium background. There is a slight rise in elevation from the rostrum to the rear of the chamber. Above the rostrum is a large electronic voting machine. The walls are lined with French Escalette marble, with a background of cream and veins of yellow, pink and red. It is warmer and cheerier than the gray Alaskan marble in the rotunda. Columns separate the chamber itself from aisles along the two sides, with heavy goldish-pink drapes that are sometimes closed during late-evening sessions to keep out the noise.

The Senate chamber is located on the opposite side of the rotunda on the third floor. It is the same size as the House chamber but seems more spacious since there are only forty-nine desks (of mahogany rather than walnut), each sitting singly. There is a second row of columns in the Senate, creating a ten-foot antechamber on each side between the chamber proper and the aisle. Like the House chamber, the Senate, too, is divided by an aisle which separates members of the two parties and faces an ornate, hand-carved, tiered mahogany rostrum. The wall marble in the Senate is German Rose Formosa with graded tones from almost black to pearly gray and veins of rose and yellow. There is more of a patrician feeling coming off the darker shading in the Senate as opposed to the populist lighter hue in the House. There is no electronic voting machine in the Senate, but small electronic signboards sit incongruously in front and to the side of the rostrum to indicate the business at hand.

Between the chambers is the state reception room described by Wilder as "intended to be the most ornate in the building." It is faced with Bresche Violet marble from Italy with a cream background and veining of red, lavender and green. There is a fireplace at each end of the room (blocked off). The room is finished with teak floors and two Tiffany chandeliers from Czechoslovakia. There is a seven-foot-diameter table in the center of the room and heavy lined velvet drapes with matching valances and silk tasseled ties at the large floor-to-ceiling windows.

Recessed visitor galleries above the chambers can be entered from the fourth floor and face down from both sides. Gallery pews, wainscoting and most of the furniture is a dark highly polished mahogany.

At the rear of both chambers are massive double doors. When opened wide, the presiding officers on the respective rostrums can see one another across the rotunda. It is a long-standing tradition that the final act of a legislative session occurs when the two officers simultaneously bang their gavels and announce they are now adjourned **sine die;** that is, without setting a time to reconvene.

A person entering the chambers cannot help but be awed at the surroundings, a feeling similar to that on entering a great cathedral or museum. The effect is surely deliberate. It is to remind those selected by their fellow citizens to sit on the floor of these chambers of the importance of their actions and responsibilities. In almost sixty years of legislative meetings inside these chambers, there have been incidents of unruliness and alcohol abuse and intemperance and boorishness, but these have been relatively rare. The norm is a feeling of honor for having been chosen by the people for this high office, of respect for the institution and its traditions, and of courteousness toward others involved in the important process of making laws.

The Washington State Capitol Building and grounds are open to the public most of the year. Information is available from the State Capitol Tour Office, the Secretary of State's Office, the Washington State Capital Museum, or the Washington Room of the Washington State Library, all located in Olympia.

2

Legislative Sessions

REGULAR AND SPECIAL

Under the original state Constitution, regular sessions of the Washington State Legislature after the first one were to be held for up to sixty days every odd-numbered year. The first legislative session in 1889 took 143 days and legislators needed to come back in 1890 for another nine days. But for the next fifty-eight years, from 1890 through 1948, there were only five special sessions, despite two world wars and the Great Depression.

The Constitution specifically exempted the first legislative session from the sixty-day provision. It also provided that the first session would begin on the first Wednesday after the first Monday in January, not on the second Monday of January as was later decided.

According to the official records in the Journals of the House and of the Senate, regular sessions in every odd-numbered year from 1891 through 1979 lasted exactly sixty days. But that was only officially. Unofficially, sessions could last days and even weeks longer. For example, the 1935 session actually lasted sixty-six days; the 1937 session lasted sixty-one

7

days; the 1939 session went sixty-three; the 1941 session lasted sixty-two; the 1943 session ended at five hours past midnight of the sixtieth day; in 1945 the session lasted sixty-four days; and in 1949, the Regular Session wasn't adjourned until 2:30 P.M. on Sunday, March 3, the seventieth day. But one must read the newspapers from those days to determine the actual count. Officially, according to the Journals of the House and of the Senate, all these sessions lasted exactly sixty days.

Sometimes the Speaker of the House or the President of the Senate would literally stop the clock at midnight on the sixtieth day. Members would occasionally poke fun at the presiding officer. Here is an exchange from the *Senate Journal,* March 9, 1961, p. 1192:

> Senator Riley: "Mr. President, would you please give me the time on your wrist watch?"
> The President: "Senator Riley, my watch is wrong. My timing has been bad for years!"
> Senator Riley: "According to my time, it is exactly midnight on Thursday, March 9, 1961."
> The President: "The President believes you are pretty close."

The Senate then continued to work on a variety of matters that took several more hours before it finally adjourned sine die.

Beginning in 1949, special sessions became more frequent and lasted longer. Between 1949 and 1979, when the Constitution was changed to provide for annual sessions, there were special sessions in all but five of the nineteen two-year legislative cycles.

In 1972 the Supreme Court addressed the question of the length of sessions in *Distilled Spirits Institute v. Kinnear,* 80 Wn. 2d 175 (1972). The Distilled Spirits Institute objected to Substitute Senate Bill 897, which raised liquor taxes, on the ground (among others) that the bill was passed after the sixtieth day of a special session. Since regular sessions are constitutionally limited to sixty days, they reckoned that the same applies to special sessions. There were Attorney General Opinions on both sides of the question.

The court unanimously held that "inherent in the power to enact laws is the power to deliberate, and deliberation necessarily requires time." The court held that since there was no specific constitutional limitation on special sessions, the court would not imply one. Therefore, once a special session is called by the governor, it has no time limit. By implication, this same decision seems to say that where there is a specific limitation it must be adhered to. Since adoption of the 68th Amendment in 1979, both the regular and special sessions now have specific time limits and these presumably must be obeyed.

In 1979 Washington voters adopted the 68th Amendment to the state Constitution providing for annual sessions of 105 days in odd-numbered years, and of sixty days in even-numbered years. The days are consecutive, so Saturdays and Sundays count. The amendment took effect in 1980.

Both the original Constitution and the change adopted in 1979 prescribe the length of session but allow the Legislature itself to decide when to meet. The Washington Legislature could meet in March, as Florida does; or April, as Louisiana does; or May, as North Dakota does. Instead, Washington stays safely with the majority of other states and meets beginning on the second Monday in January. During the 1980s there was some discussion about delaying sessions until February in odd-numbered years in order to have in hand the latest revenue projections on which to base the budget. One proposal was to have a short organizational session early in the year, then come back for the full session later. Several states including Alabama, California, Florida, Idaho, Kentucky, Missouri and Utah do this. However, Initiative 601 took most of the mystery out of revenue projections, so that discussion has died down.

Perhaps the main argument for adopting the annual session amendment was to provide certainty to the legislative meetings. The problem for legislators was that only the governor could call a special session, thus giving her/him some leverage over the agenda. The governor could and often would extract promises from legislators in return for calling a special session. Keep in mind that the Constitution provided for only sixty days every two years. As a way around the governor, legislators not only stopped the clock but resorted to other means to avoid adjourning. For example, the Legislature stayed in session from July 18, 1975, until March 26, 1976 by taking very long recesses. It started as a special session, but once called (prior to the 1979 change), it could go on and on until the next regular session convened.

Since the adoption of regular annual sessions in 1979, the total amount of time spent in session has averaged about 195 days per biennium, split between 165 days of regular session and 30 days of special sessions. During the nine bienniums prior to 1980, the average was 138 days in session per biennium, split between 60 days of regular session and 78 days of special session. Thus, since the change of 1980, time spent in special session has diminished but total time in session has increased. In fact, there has not been a biennium without a special session since 1957-58 (see Fig 2.1).

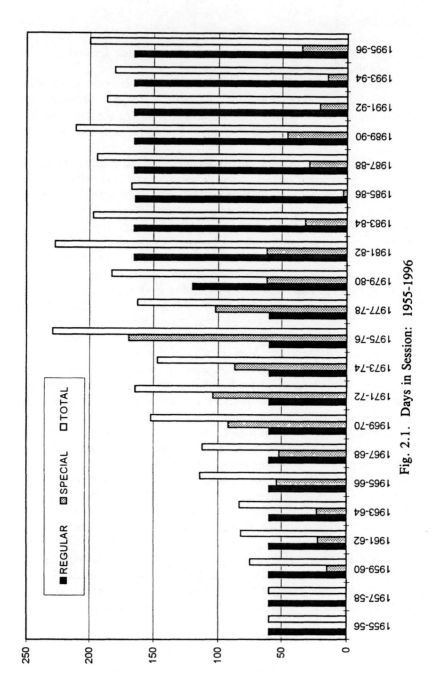

Fig. 2.1. Days in Session: 1955-1996

According to a National Conference of State Legislatures 1992 study, Washington State fits into the middle group of states which have some of the characteristics of a full-time legislature, such as a large staff, but some traits of a part-time legislature, such as low member compensation and limited regular sessions. Washington, with an average of just over three months of session per year, is slightly below the average session time of just under four months per year for the twenty-three states which comprise this middle group. States with full-time legislatures, like California and New York, meet an average of nine months per year in session and true part-time states like Idaho and Montana average about five months of session per biennium.

SHIFT OF POWER IN 1979

The constitutional amendment of 1979 represented a major shift of power from the executive to the legislative branch of government. Before 1980, legislators were limited to meeting only sixty days every other year on their own. If they wanted more, they had to persuade the governor to call a special session. This was never easy to do because once called, the governor lost control—legislators could stay on and on, as shown in 1975. There was no way the governor could limit the length or subjects of a special session. In an article for the Tacoma *News Tribune* of March 11, 1996, Peter Callaghan recounts how Governor Dixy Lee Ray refused to call a special session in 1978 despite pleas from many quarters of a need to address flaws in the juvenile justice system. It was the first year without a special session in a decade. He says that led legislators to put the 1979 constitutional amendment for annual sessions on the ballot.

No governor likes to have the Legislature in session for long. Legislators are a nuisance to the governor: they are always asking for help of one kind or another for their districts or constituents, or asking for jobs for themselves or others, or embarrassing the governor by holding hearings on executive mismanagement, or refusing to confirm the governor's appointments. There are hundreds of ways legislators make a governor's life miserable. Under the friendliest of circumstances, coaxing a governor into calling a special session isn't easy, as Governor Ray showed.

It can work the other way, with the Legislature resisting and the governor wanting a special session, although that would be fairly unusual. In happened in the late spring of 1996 when Governor Lowry, in his last few months in office, tried to coax legislators into a special session in order to confirm some gubernatorial appointments and into spending additional money for capital projects. Neither made much sense to legislators in an election year. Governor Lowry could, of course, have called a special session anyway, but legislative leaders made it clear that they would quickly adjourn or take up issues not much to the governor's liking.

The constitutional change adopted in 1979 gave legislators annual sessions. They would henceforth be in session for at least 165 days per biennium, an increase of 105 days. And the best part for them was that they would no longer have to go to any governor, hat in hand, begging for the call.

There were also some changes in the terms for special sessions. Special sessions are limited to thirty days, not open-ended as before. They are called by the governor issuing a proclamation (see copy of Governor Lowry's Proclamation of May 24, 1995, page 14) which is required to set out the purpose of the special session, although this is not binding on the Legislature. Governors often list topics or even specific bills for the Legislature and even try to limit the number of days, as in the example (notice that Governor Lowry says "not more than two consecutive days"). Neither has any force of law. They are just suggestions. Once called, the Legislature can stay as long as it wants up to thirty days and take up any matters it chooses.

On the first day of the first special session of 1983, the question of whether the governor could limit the length of special sessions to something less than thirty days was discussed in a colloquy between Senate Majority Leader Ted Bottiger and Senate President John Cherberg. At least as far as the Legislature is concerned, it resolved the issue. It is reported in the *Senate Journal* for that year as follows:

> Senator Bottiger: "Mr. President, in his proclamation, the Governor lists those subject areas to be considered by the Legislature and states that the first special session shall not last longer than thirty days. My point of inquiry is, may the Governor limit this Senate to subject and/or time?"
>
> President Cherberg: "Senator Bottiger, Article II, Section 12 of our State Constitution, as amended by the 68th Amendment, provides that special legislative sessions may be convened for a period of time not more than thirty consecutive days by a proclamation of the Governor. It also provides that the resolution concerning the legislature shall specify purpose or purposes for the convening of the special session and notes that specification of purpose shall be considered by the legislature, but shall not be mandatory.

"In answer to your point of parliamentary inquiry, the President would rule that in accordance with the State Constitution, the Governor may not limit the subject matter this body may consider and may not restrict the legislature's time to act to less than thirty days given to the legislature by the Constitution." *(Senate Journal, 1983, p. 1629)*

There is one other change in the 68th Amendment that hasn't surfaced yet but doubtless will someday. After setting out how the governor calls a special session, the constitutional amendment goes on to provide an alternative which allows the Legislature to call itself into special session. By vote of two-thirds of the members of each chamber, while still in session or during the interim, the Legislature may call a special session of not more than thirty days. The form required is a resolution which sets out the purpose for the special session. Unlike when the governor calls a special session, a special session called by the Legislature itself would be limited to the purpose or purposes in the resolution. It could take up other matters only with another two-thirds vote of each house.

WHAT WAS SO SPECIAL?

In the last ten years (1987 through 1996) there have been fourteen special sessions. Nine of these began immediately following or within a few days of the conclusion of a regular session or a first special session. The majority of special sessions are called because legislators do not complete work on some major item(s) in the time allotted for the regular session. The most common unresolved issue is the operating budget. Below is a description of the special sessions over the past seven years, beginning with the most recent, to give the reader a flavor of what special sessions are about.

Third Special Session, October 12-14, 1995. There was an agreement beforehand that the only business would be how to fund an outdoor stadium for the Seattle Mariners baseball team. Legislators took three days to work out details and pass EHB 2115.

Second Special Session, May 24-25, 1995. Governor Lowry called this second special session immediately after the first special session expired. Legislators reached agreement on all three biennial budgets and adjourned in two days.

STATE OF WASHINGTON
OFFICE OF THE GOVERNOR
P.O. Box 40002 • Olympia, Washington 98504-0002 • (206) 753-6780

PROCLAMATION BY THE GOVERNOR

WHEREAS, in accordance with Article II, Section 12 (Amendment 68) of the Washington State Constitution, the 1995 First Special Session of the legislature adjourned May 23, 1995, the 30th day, without completing its work; and

WHEREAS, it is therefore necessary for me to convene a Second Special Session for the purpose of addressing matters related to the Budgets;

NOW, THEREFORE, I. Mike Lowry, Governor of the state of Washington, by virtue of the authority vested in me by Article II, Section 12 (Amendment 68) and Article III, Section 7, of the State Constitution, do hereby convene the Legislature of the State of Washington on Wednesday, the 24th day of May, 1995 at 10:00 a.m. in Special Session in the Capitol in Olympia for a period of not more than two consecutive days.

IN WITNESS whereof. I have hereunto set my hand and caused the seal of the State of Washington to be affixed at Olympia this 24th day of May, A.D.. nineteen hundred and ninety-five.

Governor of Washington

BY THE GOVERNOR

Secretary of State

First Special Session, April 24-May 23, 1995. First Special Session started 10:00 A.M. on the day following the end of the Regular Session. Governor Lowry proclaimed the special session was needed to address "the budgets, the Puget Sound Water Quality Authority, Juvenile Justice Reform, Personnel System Reform, and the Presidential Primary." Legislators disagreed. In Senate Concurrent Resolution 8412 they said that "neither house may consider any bills ... except budgets, matters necessary to implement budgets, and matters incident to the interim and ... closing."

First Special Session, March 11-March 14, 1994. Governor Lowry called this special session to start at 10:00 A.M. the day following the end of the Regular Session "for purposes of completing the business of the 1994 session." There were a variety of issues from an anti-violence package to tax breaks to unemployment insurance rate reductions to collective bargaining for state employees. It took four days.

First Special Session, April 26-May 6, 1993. Special session immediately following 1993 Regular Session "for purposes ... related to the 1993-95 Operating, Capital and Transportation Budgets." This one lasted eleven days.

There was no special session in 1992.

First Special Session, June 10-June 30, 1991. The 1991 special session was called by Governor Gardner "for the purpose of adequately addressing ... tasks not completed." Unlike most years when the special follows immediately on the regular, this year they waited to get the latest revenue projections. State law requires that there be a budget by the end of June. Legislators just made it, passing both the operating and transportation budgets on June 30, the latest finish ever. This special session lasted twenty-one days.

Second Special Session, June 5, 1990. Legislators worked out details of an anti-crime aid package for cities and counties beforehand, then came in for an efficient one-day special session called by Governor Gardner.

First Special Session, March 9-April 1, 1990. Governor Gardner called the First Special Session immediately following the end of the Regular Session. In his proclamation, he listed a dozen topics plus any bills still in dispute at the end of the Regular Session. Legislators listed fourteen specific bills in their concurrent resolution. This one lasted twenty-four days.

3

Bills

BILLS, MEMORIALS AND RESOLUTIONS

A variety of instruments are used to accomplish specific legislative purposes.

A **bill** is a proposed law introduced into the Legislature for consideration. Bills are numbered consecutively in the order in which they are introduced. Since 1987 it has been the practice to number House bills starting with 1000 at the beginning of the legislative biennium and Senate bills starting at 5000. Numbering continues in a consecutive fashion throughout the two-year period. When used alone, a bill may mean bill, joint memorial, joint resolution and/or concurrent resolution (Senate Rule 54).

A **substitute bill** is one which replaces the original bill. It is a new bill in every way except the title. When several amendments are adopted to a bill, it is common practice to "roll them together into a substitute."

A **companion bill** is a bill introduced in the same form in both the House and the Senate.

An **engrossed bill** is one that includes all the amendments attached by the originating body. It becomes an **enrolled bill** when it has passed both bodies, incorporates all amendments, and has a certificate of enrollment indicating the date passed, votes cast, and signature of certifying officer (Chief Clerk of the House or President of the Senate). It is then ready for presentment to the governor.

An **executive request** or **agency request** or **department request bill** is one introduced at their request.

A **title-only bill** is a bill which contains nothing more than a title and a number. It is introduced in order to have a vehicle on which to amend substance at a later time.

A **joint memorial** is a request directed at some outside body or person such as Congress and/or the President. Joint memorials can originate in either the House or the Senate. Numbering begins at 4000 for House joint memorials and 8000 for Senate joint memorials.

A **joint resolution** is an instrument which proposes an amendment to the state Constitution. It must receive the approval of two-thirds of the elected members of both the House and the Senate and is then submitted to a vote of the people. Joint resolutions are numbered starting with 4200 in the House and 8200 in the Senate.

A **concurrent resolution** is one relating to business between the two houses and may originate in either body. Joint rules and cutoffs are examples of matters dealt with by concurrent resolution. They require approval of a majority in each body. Concurrent resolutions are numbered starting with 4400 in the House and 8400 in the Senate.

A **resolution**, usually called a **floor resolution**, may be adopted by either the House or the Senate and is typically used to commemorate or congratulate. Resolutions are also used for internal matters such as adopting rules for the body. They are one-body actions. Floor resolutions are numbered starting with 4600 in the House and 8600 in the Senate.

Gubernatorial appointments are names of persons designated by the governor to fill an office or position. Some require confirmation by a majority of senators elected. These are referred to the Senate as they are made by the governor and numbered starting with 9000.

A **measure** means a bill, joint memorial, joint resolution, or concurrent resolution.

DRAFTING, FILING AND SPONSORSHIP OF MEASURES

Tucked away in the northeast corner of the Legislative Building, on the
first floor, is a small but amazing group of attorneys and word processors
called the Code Reviser's Office. These people play a very important part
in the legislative process. They draft the various measures that are
introduced in the Legislature, including many of the amendments and
substitute bills. In effect they are the guardians of the **Revised Code of
Washington** (RCW), the compilation of the laws of the state. State law
(RCW 1.08) guarantees the nonpartisanship of the Code Reviser's Office.
Confidence in them is so high that they are authorized to make technical
corrections to laws already passed in order to accomplish what was
intended.

Bills are created for a member or staff, on behalf of a member, by
request to the Code Reviser. A member may also specifically authorize
other persons (i.e. constituents, lobbyists, etc.) to receive Code Reviser
assistance in drafting a bill for that member. The request may be anything
from an idea written on the back of an envelope to a complete draft
prepared by a section of the Bar Association, for example. It doesn't
matter. The Code Reviser puts the idea or draft into proper form and
attaches a **member signature sheet.** Only about half of all the bills
drafted by the Code Reviser are actually introduced.

To be introduced, a measure must be sponsored by a member of the
House or the Senate. The first name on the signature sheet becomes the
prime sponsor. A measure needs only one signature to be introduced.
Other signatories are **co-sponsors.** Only House members may sponsor
measures introduced in the House and only Senate members may introduce
measures introduced in the Senate. Incidentally, this is not universally
true. Some states allow or even require members of both bodies to
sponsor bills. Colorado's joint rules, for example, say: "A bill may be
introduced in either house by one or more members of that house and the
joint sponsorship of one or more members of the other house." (Colorado
Joint Rule 24 (a)) In other words, it takes both a House and a Senate
sponsor to introduce a bill in Colorado.

Once a measure has a sponsor or sponsors, it is returned to the Code
Reviser's Office and "dropped in the hopper." This is a wire basket where
bills with signature sheets can be left. The bill is then delivered to the
Chief Clerk of the House or Secretary of the Senate where it receives a
number. Here the procedure differs slightly between the two bodies. In
the House, bills filed with the Chief Clerk by 10:00 A.M. are introduced
at the next day's session, except during the last ten days of session when

it takes a two-thirds vote of the members to introduce a bill. In the Senate, bills filed by noon with the Secretary of the Senate are introduced at the next day's session. There is the same constitutional two-thirds requirement for bill introductions during the last ten days of a regular session.

The House allows bills to be **prefiled** within twenty days of the start of a regular session. Senators and senators-elect may prefile bills beginning on the first Monday in December or twenty days prior to a special session. Prefiled bills are introduced on the first day of the session (SR 55-56).

After bills are introduced, the list of bill introductions is distributed among the members of the body. Secretary of the Senate Marty Brown in an e-mail dated January 18, 1994, explains what happens next and the mechanics involved. "Members wishing to add their names as sponsors of bills have until 2:00 P.M. the day a bill is introduced to do so. Please do not send sign up notes with pages. It is best to have your staff or yourself hand deliver them to the Workroom by 2:00 P.M." And here is part of a memo from Secretary of the Senate Gordon Golob dated January 30, 1992: "For the past several years we have adhered to a 2:00 P.M. cutoff for members who wished to be added as sponsors of bills. The reason for this is administrative. The Senate Workroom must proof all introductions and transmit the bills to the state printer. Unless the sponsor requests are submitted by 2:00 P.M. it is very difficult to insure that all bills will be published and made available to the committees, members, and the public in a timely fashion." The key point is that any member may add his or her name as a co-sponsor of any bill introduced. Permission of the prime sponsor is not required. Think of it in terms of the expression, "A good idea belongs to everybody."

During the summer of 1996 there were daily reports of battles between Republicans and Democrats in the United States Congress and between congressional Republicans and President Clinton over a variety of issues. At one point, Democrats were pushing for a hike in the minimum wage, which enjoyed popular support, and Republicans wanted to lower the federal gas tax, also popular. In the United States Senate these two very separate issues were joined in one bill along with a proposal to allow employers to meet with employees without going through unions. A number of legislators who favored one or two of these ideas, but not the third, called for these proposals to be voted on separately. They bemoaned the fact they could not get a "clean" vote on these three different issues. In the United States Senate it is a common practice to attach totally unrelated amendments to measures. Fortunately, this practice is prohibited in the Washington State Legislature.

Our state Constitution requires that "No bill shall embrace more than **one subject,** and that shall be expressed in the **title**" (emphasis added). (Article II, Section 19) Titles can be very broad, such as "AN ACT Relating to education," but at least they are limited to that one subject so our state legislators generally get "clean" votes on issues. Procedurally, it has been the practice of the presiding officers of the two houses in our state not to rule on constitutional issues. Therefore, it would not be appropriate for members to raise the one subject objection on second reading. Rather, this objection would be raised in court in testing the constitutionality of a law after it has taken effect and there is an aggrieved party.

It is easy to confuse the one subject constitutional requirement with the **scope and object** provision which states that "No amendment to any bill shall be allowed which shall change the scope and object of the bill." (Article II, Section 38) While these two may overlap, the scope and object provision generally applies to the amendatory process rather than the title of the original bill and is a common objection raised and ruled upon during second reading. In deciding whether a particular amendment is beyond the scope and object of a bill, the presiding officer will look to the subject matter of the entire bill and not just the title.

ORIGIN OF BILLS

For several decades now, in every two-year Washington State legislative cycle, over 3,000 bills are introduced in the Legislature and about 20 percent of them become law. Where do the ideas for these bills come from? How do they get into the system? Why are there so many bills introduced every year?

Ideas and Causes

There are two ways to look at the origin of bills. There is the first cause, such as the event or thing which gives rise to the idea that a change in state law is needed. The second way to look at origins is to look at the person or entity which suggests the change (this is a distinction not made in the earlier edition of this book). Here are some categories for first causes of legislation:

Dramatic Events or Tragedies. In 1986 in Snohomish County a three-year-old boy named Eli Creekmore was beaten to death by his father. There was evidence that the father had been abusing Eli for most of his short life. Child Protective Services was involved. The father was convicted of second-degree murder and given a life sentence. The Creekmore killing shocked Washingtonians both for its incomprehensible brutality and for the inability of the state agency that had received notice of problems to protect little Eli. It gave rise to several bills, among them one passed in 1987 to create the new enhanced crime of first degree homicide by abuse.

A common problem in prosecuting child abuse cases is showing the adult involved actually intended to kill the child. Prosecutors often reduce the charge to manslaughter. Under the law passed in 1987, in order to gain a first degree murder conviction, prosecutors need only show a pattern of abuse or torture and death of a child or dependent under circumstances indicating an extreme indifference to human life.

In 1996 in another case involving the murder of a three-year-old, the new law was used. The mother became the first person in Washington State to be convicted of the new crime of homicide by abuse. Unfortunately, changes in the law are more easily made than changes in people's behavior or in the state agency that failed both Eli Creekmore and Louria Grace.

External Crises or Acts of God. The floods of 1996 and the eruption of Mount St. Helens in 1980 were natural disasters. Legislators who represent districts affected by these acts of God, whether Democrat or Republican, are quick to look for help from the government. The public generally supports the use of state resources to help those who suffer from natural disasters so legislation in the form of loans or grants is usually forthcoming (a fact not lost on national politicians who attach all sorts of pork to federal emergency legislation).

Internal Crises. These are things which are man-caused problems of a general sort, such as the 1995 "crisis" over the potential loss of the Seattle Mariners baseball team. When King County voters turned down a local sales tax increase to fund a new stadium, the Mariners threatened to leave town. A special session of the state Legislature was called by Governor Lowry to create state legislation which would lead to the construction of an outdoor baseball stadium.

Changing Societal Attitudes. The flood of legislation providing for tougher penalties for violent crime reflects a new no-tolerance attitude by the public toward criminals. This is especially true in crimes such as rape and domestic abuse which primarily involve men against women. See the chapter on the gender revolution for more examples of laws resulting from a change in the attitudes of society.

Government Efficiency. This is probably the single largest source of legislative proposals. Government employees at all levels from police officers and prosecutors to sewer district directors to heads of state agencies seem to spend a good deal of time thinking up ways to enhance and perfect the laws governing what they do. They usually present these ideas to legislators as executive, department, local government or agency request bills. Many of these bills are actually the result of legislative requests or mandated studies. For example, studies of the need for a separate state energy office were mandated and paid for in bills passed by the Legislature in 1993 and 1994. Subsequent legislation passed in 1995 and 1996 eliminated this agency and delegated its responsibilities to other state agencies.

Special Causes. Special causes is a softer term for special interests. People who represent special causes aren't necessarily the fat, greedy "Boss Tweed" characters portrayed by editorial cartoonists. They are mostly ordinary folks who want a little break or help or just recognition of their particular endeavor. Perhaps a group representing disabled kids wants a law enabling them to fish license-free any time of year; or a hunters group wants a law requiring all hunters to wear bright orange for added safety; or truckers want legislation to speed up the process at weigh stations; or nurses want to be able to administer certain prescription drugs; or a group wants a law declaring state hobby train day; or a church organization wants an exemption from taxation on bingo games and garage sales; or a veterans group wants a state law preventing local cities and counties from passing ordinances against their sale of fireworks; or a group wants a law designating the square dance as the official state dance.

Turf Battles. Some bills are really little more than a disguised battle between two or more groups for economic survival or supremacy. The area of medicine and health care seem particularly rife with turf battles. Medical doctors, nurses, social workers, naturopaths, optometrists, chiropractors, massage therapists and others in the health care field have become politically active and savvy. Battles rage over who can prescribe which drugs or perform which procedures, over whether they must be included in health plans, and over licensing requirements.

For a time the state's four-year institutions of higher education battled over which would serve various parts of the state, and even directly competed in some cities. This matter has now been largely resolved with branch campuses in the prime areas of Vancouver, Tri-Cities, Tacoma, and Woodinville.

Federal Law Changes/Requirements. States now must spend a large amount of time just trying to find out about and reacting to federal laws that are entangled with state laws. As an example, in April of 1996 Congress passed and the President signed House Resolution 3136. This act changes federal law so that persons who are disabled by reason of alcoholism and/or drug addiction are no longer eligible to receive disability benefits. According to some estimates, there may be as many as 10,000 persons in Washington State who could lose benefits as of January 1, 1997, under this law. Without the federal benefits, the incomes of some of these persons may drop low enough to qualify for state-funded drug and alcohol programs or general assistance. The fiscal impact on Washington State could be as much as $60 million per year in cash and medical assistance.

This is just one program. Nearly everything Congress does impacts the states and is related to state programs which either build on it, or rely on it or administer it. In the above case, for example, the 1997 state Legislature will probably be asked to do everything from setting up its own cash benefit program for those disabled by alcohol and drug addiction to prohibiting addicts and alcoholics from receiving any state assistance. These are tough, complicated decisions for state legislators, the kind that get little publicity and are rarely discussed in political campaigns, and that do not lend themselves to short, simple explanations.

Technological Changes. Technology is changing everything from the way we communicate to the way we work and even the way we think. Most government agencies are embracing technology and are changing too. Many police already have portable breathalyzer machines so they can get a quick reading for an alcohol level right on site. There are hand-held electronic devices that print out parking tickets and citations for moving violations. Optical equipment at truck weigh stations can "read" license plates. In Kentucky, every social worker will soon be equipped with a laptop computer that integrates a staff directory, directory of schools and attorneys, a word-processing program, case notes and policy manuals. Gone are index cards, notebooks, typewriters and paper forms. All eighty members of the California State Assembly now have laptop computers at their desks in chamber reducing the blizzard of paper that collected in the past.

Many changes need statutory modifications to clear the way or to preserve the public interest or just to recognize them after the fact. We are just at the beginning of this technological revolution. Here are some more developments just around the corner:

Crime. DNA identification and the breathalyzer have already prompted changes in state law. Readings on the breathalyzer are considered presumptive proof of intoxication and shift the burden of proof. DNA identifications are almost universally accepted as evidence. In Los Angeles County all 16,000 welfare applicants coming into the department each month must place both index fingers on an electronic scanner which matches them against a database to prevent fraud or duplication. But DNA, the breathalyzer and fingerprints may be minor compared to what lies ahead.

There are eighty cities in England that have tiny surveillance cameras mounted at every street corner. Police sit at stations monitoring screens and can instantly contact other officers in patrol cars, making detection of crime quicker and conviction of criminals more certain. Surveillance cameras are already present in many stores in this country and are being introduced into workplaces. Legislators will have to decide between privacy and security on many fronts.

What if it were possible through genetic testing to determine criminal traits from an individual's blood or a skin scraping? Should we test all children to determine the dangerous ones? Does society have a superior interest in finding potential Ted Bundys before they begin to kill innocent victims?

Higher Education. Money was included in the 1996 supplemental budget to move Washington toward a statewide electronic educational network. Soon, all of education from kindergarten through college may be linked together. But why stop there? Technology is available to make the link truly interactive. A student at any level may attend class not just by watching a monitor but by asking questions and giving responses as well with the teacher and student visible to one another. Classes could be in the evening so parents could be actively involved. It raises lots of policy questions including whether it is wise for the state to spend billions of dollars on branch campuses for a limited number of college students when a fraction of that money could provide education to everyone who wants it—tough decisions that will have to be made by legislators.

Licensing. The idea of a driver's license or a library card or a fishing license is to identify the holder as authorized to do a particular thing. But why do we need a little plastic card with a picture? Why do we need anything at all? Technology can already identify individuals by a variety of other means. In the 1983 James Bond movie *Never Say Never Again*, a character's identity was established by a machine that recognized the pattern of his iris. It turns out this is not so farfetched after all. By the end of 1996, the Japanese had Automatic Teller Machines that operate on iris-identification technology (see *Forbes* magazine, May 20, 1996, p.18).

The technology exists today for a grocery clerk, when he finishes scanning your groceries, to scan your iris (or some other form of identification), push a button and automatically debit your bank account. Perhaps it will soon be possible to simply scan the back of a person's hand. There has been much discussion about the introduction of a national identification card to help in the illegal immigration problem, among others, but who needs it? What if instead there was a computer bank which contained some sort of identification key (iris, DNA, fingerprints, etc.) for every American citizen? We could do away with all forms of identification. But do we really want such a system? This issue generates lots of close questions between privacy and efficiency, between the public good and individual rights, and many of them will be decided in the state legislatures of this country.

The Advocates

We've been discussing some root causes of legislation in terms of challenges to society. Another way to look at the origin of bills is to see where they came from, who proposed the bill.

It has been part of my job in the Senate for many years to read bill reports. In 1995 I decided to add a little detective work to the mix. I tried to determine the source of the 550 bills that were signed out of Senate committees, roughly half of all the bills introduced during the 1995 session in the Senate. The half I looked at all had complete bill reports because they had passed out of committees. They fell generally into six categories (see Fig. 3.1).

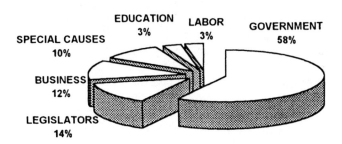

Fig. 3.1. Sources of Legislative Proposals

Government was the largest source, accounting for 58 percent of the bills that were signed out of Senate committees. This is using government in the broadest sense to include everything from the largest agency to the smallest water district. These bills were usually clearly identified as agency or executive request bills or bills that came from some branch of local government.

One interesting thing I noticed early was that most of these government-sponsored bills had a companion bill, a House bill identical to the one introduced in the Senate. That showed a slightly more sophisticated knowledge of the process plus good contacts in both houses.

Business interests seemed to be responsible for about 12 percent of the bills. Labor interests accounted for about 3 percent. Education interests (lumping together teachers and administrators) were also at 3 percent. However, this latter figure may be low because many of the education and higher education advocates also fall in the government category. Special causes such as veterans or sportsfishers seemed to be behind about 10 percent. Legislators either acting on their own or from meetings with constituents accounted for about 14 percent of the bills.

I indicated earlier that the number of bills introduced each year is relatively constant, no big swings up or down. This would seem to confirm that the majority of bills originate from within government because bureaucracies tend to be constant, repetitive, to do things in an established way. It is reasonable to assume that most state and local agencies have some sort of annual process regarding legislation. They typically assess the impact of new laws, promulgate rules and regulations, plan implementation, evaluate how new legislation works, and make recommendations for changes, hence, new bills. As regular as the seasons. Multiply this process by hundreds of state and local agencies and departments and there is a constant stream of proposals awaiting legislators at the beginning of each session.

The Council of State Governments publishes a record of the number of bills introduced and enacted in every state legislature. Washington's totals are about average for the country. During the 1992-93 biennium, there were 3,382 bills introduced in the Washington Legislature and of these, 783 were enacted. Texas, in just 1993 alone, had 4,380 introductions and 1,075 enactments. That's a lot but it pales compared to the 32,263 bills that were introduced in New York in those two years. Only 1,566 of the New York bills were enacted, however, so one assumes most were throwaways. On the other hand, in North Dakota during 1993 there were 1,062 bills introduced but 648 of those were enacted. That seems reasonable compared to New York even if the success rate is pretty high. However, when one considers that the North Dakota Constitution requires that every bill introduced must have a hearing, things don't look so unbalanced after all. Every state has its own variations.

Is there a correlation between the number of government proposals and the number of lobbyists employed by public agencies?

A 1995 Associated Press survey found that 441 public employees from 153 state and local governments and agencies were registered to lobby the Washington State Legislature. The agencies reported spending over $2.4 million on this effort but that may be only a part of it. How many state employees "monitor" legislative hearings, then attend discussions of the proceedings back at the agency with other state employees? How many others watch the proceedings live on TVW or listen on the squawk boxes? And is there anything wrong with that?

Some would argue that taxpayers should be alarmed that many legislative hearings are packed with "agency liaison" or other public employees who have a clear advantage over the public and even private lobbyists both in information and access. While state agencies may generally be advocating for the public interest as they see it, there are certainly differing opinions.

On the other hand, every good agency director is going to stay fully informed about what the Legislature is doing and actively engaged with state legislators. Legislators need to understand an agency's mission and its programs in order to determine whether to support its programs. Outstanding agency heads like Christine Gregoire, the state attorney general, and Mary Riveland, former head of the Ecology Department, spend hours of their own time "on the hill" meeting with legislators, getting input and explaining programs.

Some legislators think it is wrong for the state to pay hundreds of people to lobby the state for more money for their own state agencies. At the least, some think there should be limits. Representative Dale Foreman (R-Wenatchee) introduced a bill in 1996 that in its original form would have restricted public employee lobbying to elected officials, college presidents, agency heads, and a small number of others. Foreman may have been influenced by the budget negotiation meetings he attended where the audience consisted largely of "legislative liaisons" from state agencies. His bill, HB 2289, passed the House but died in the Senate (see House Bill 2289 on pp. 28-29).

This is an issue that will not go away. Some kind of balance needs to be struck so the flow of necessary information from expert state officials can freely take place without the agencies sending an army of lobbyists to meet with and monitor legislators' every move. Agency heads need to learn what Gregoire and Riveland practiced: that legislators want to hear from agency heads, not their "liaisons;" and that legislators sitting behind raised daises can just as easily watch the audience as the audience can watch them.

H-3865.3 _____

HOUSE BILL 2289
_____

State of Washington   54th Legislature   1996 Regular Session

By Representatives Foreman, Crouse, Backlund, Goldsmith, L. Thomas, Elliot, Mulliken, McMahan, Johnson, Thompson, Hargrove, Carrell, Lisk and Boldt

Read first time 01/09/96. Referred to Committee on Government Operations.

1   AN ACT Relating to restricting lobbying activities by taxpayer-
2 supported entities; adding a new section to chapter 41.04 RCW; creating
3 a new section; and prescribing penalties.

4 BE IT ENACTED BY THE LEGISLATURE OF THE STATE OF WASHINGTON:

5   NEW SECTION. Sec. 1. (1) The legislature affirms that the
6 legislative authority of the state of Washington is vested in the
7 legislative branch of government and that the legislative body alone is
8 given the constitutional duty and power to establish public policy
9 through the enactment of state law.

10   (2) The legislature affirms that the executive authority of the
11 state of Washington is vested in the executive branch of government,
12 that the executive branch is given the constitutional duty and power to
13 see that the laws enacted by the legislature are faithfully executed,
14 and that the supreme executive power of state government is vested in
15 the office of the governor.

16   (3) The legislature finds that to ensure responsible and
17 accountable government, lobbying activities at public expense to
18 influence the public decision-making process in the legislative branch
19 of government should be restricted.

1   (4) The legislature further finds that restrictions on lobbying
2 activities at public expense by individuals employed by taxpayer-
3 supported agencies or units of government will reduce the cost of
4 maintaining efficient government, increase public confidence in the
5 integrity of government, and assist in restoring representative
6 government to the people.

7   (5) It is therefore the intent of the legislature to restrict
8 lobbying activities at public expense by taxpayer-supported agencies or

9   units of government to influence the public decision-making process in
10 the legislative branch of government and to consolidate such activities
11 within the office of the governor.

12   NEW SECTION. **Sec. 2.** A new section is added to chapter 41.04 RCW
13 to read as follows:
14   (1) Representatives of taxpayer-supported agencies or units of
15 government may not participate in lobbying activities.
16   (2)(a) As used in this section, "representatives of taxpayer-
17 supported agencies or units of government" includes any employees of
18 these agencies or units of government and any nonemployees of these
19 agencies or units of government who have entered into a contractual
20 agreement to represent these agencies or units of government for
21 financial remuneration.
22   (b) As used in this section, "representatives of taxpayer-supported
23 agencies or units of government" does not include state-wide elected
24 officials or a designated representative of a state-wide elected
25 official if the designated representative is employed in the office of
26 the state-wide elected official.   "Representatives of taxpayer-
27 supported agencies or units of government" does not include elected
28 local officials, but does include employees of elected local officials.
29   (3)(a) As used in this section, "lobbying activities" means any
30 oral or written communication, including electronic communication, to
31 members of the legislature or legislative staff with regard to the
32 advocacy or opposition to the formulation, modification, or adoption of
33 state legislation, including legislative proposals.   "Lobbying
34 activities" includes measures taken by representatives of taxpayer-
35 supported agencies or units of government to motivate others to contact
36 members of the legislature or legislative staff with regard to the
37 advocacy or opposition to the formulation, modification, or adoption of
38 state legislation, including legislative proposals.

1   (b) As used in this section, "lobbying activities" does not include
2   providing factual information to members of the legislature or
3   legislative staff in response to specific requests made by members of
4   the legislature or legislative staff.
5   (4) The state and each of its political subdivisions shall report
6   to the office of financial management on expenditures associated with
7   lobbying activities.
8   (5) A representative of a taxpayer-supported agency or unit of
9   government who authorizes, directs, or participates in lobbying
10 activities in violation of this section is subject to a civil fine of
11 not more than ten thousand dollars for each violation.

--- **END** ---

Severability Clause, Emergency Clause, Effective Date and Expiration Date

A **severability clause** is a sentence inserted into a measure which instructs a court that if any part of the measure is found unconstitutional, the remainder is to be unaffected.

State v. Anderson, 81 Wn. 2d 234 (1972), involved an appeal from a conviction for professional gambling. Anderson and others were convicted under a statute which also contained a provision to legalize bingo games and raffles by charities. The latter part was found to be unconstitutional and the defendants argued that their conviction should be dismissed because it was part of the same bill. The trial court found the portions of the new statute related to gambling unseverable from what was conceded to be an unconstitutional attempt to legalize bingo. The Supreme Court overruled, saying:

> An act of the legislature is not unconstitutional in its entirety because one or more of its provisions is unconstitutional unless the invalid provisions are unseverable and it cannot reasonably be believed that the legislature would have passed the one without the other, or unless the elimination of the invalid part would render the remainder of the act incapable of accomplishing the legislative purposes. (p. 236)

That would have made severability clauses in bills unnecessary, except Justice Utter in his unanimous opinion, went on to add:

> The presence of a severability clause ... offers to the courts the necessary assurance that the remaining provisions would have been enacted without the portions which are contrary to the constitution. (p. 236)

So, to be safe, it is standard practice in the Washington State Legislature to put a severability clause in all major bills. The latest wording for such a clause is:

> If any part of this act or its application to any person or circumstance is held invalid, the remainder of the act or the application of the part to other persons or circumstances is not affected. (Memorandum from Code Reviser, April 2, 1996, p. 10)

There is another concern related to severability which is that a part of a bill would be found to be in conflict with federal law, jeopardizing either the remainder of the bill or federal funding. Many federal statutes contain financial penalties if a state does not do one thing or another. In fact there are so many federal requirements that it now seems prudent to put a standard clause in many bills to make sure that the state doesn't do something unknowingly that will result in the loss of federal funding. Thus, a second severability clause:

> If any part of this act is found to be in conflict with federal requirements that are a prescribed condition to the allocation of federal funds to the state, the conflicting part of this act is inoperative solely to the extent of the conflict and with respect to the agencies directly affected, and this finding does not affect the operation of the remainder of this act in its application to the agencies concerned. The rules under this act must meet federal requirements that are a necessary condition to the receipt of federal funds by the state. (Memorandum from Code Reviser, April 2, 1996, p. 11)

An **effective date** tells when a bill, after it has passed the Legislature and has been signed by the governor, becomes a law.

If a bill is silent on the subject, the effective date of a bill is ninety days after sine die of the session in which the bill was passed (Washington Constitution, Article II Section 41). The reason for the ninety-day delay for a bill to become a law is to give the people time to file a referendum and gather the necessary signatures to stop a bill they do not want. When a referendum is filed, the new law is held in abeyance until after the vote in the next general election.

There are two exceptions to the usual ninety-day effective date. Bills, or parts of bills, may include specific effective dates. For example, many of the provisions of the Tort Reform Act of 1986 were delayed to August 1 of that year rather than the normal (meaning ninety days after adjournment of the 1986 Regular Session) effective date of June 11. Bills may contain different effective dates for different sections or provisions.

Suppose one action depends on another. For example, the Legislature passes (by two-thirds of each body) a constitutional amendment guaranteeing that every citizen who graduates from a high school in this state shall be entitled to a free four-year public college education. It is submitted to the people. At the same time, the Legislature passes a three-cent increase in the sales tax which contains these words: "This act takes effect if the proposed 89th Amendment to the state Constitution is validly submitted to and is approved and ratified by the voters at the next general election." What we have in the tax bill is a **contingent effective date** that depends on passage of the constitutional amendment.

The second exception to the ninety-day rule is for bills that contain an **emergency clause.** This clause states: "This act is necessary for the immediate preservation of the public peace, health or safety, or support of the state government and its existing public institutions, and takes effect immediately." (Washington Constitution, Article II, Section 1(b)) A bill with an emergency clause takes effect when the governor signs it. No referendum is possible on a bill with an emergency clause.

Bills may specify effective dates other than the normal ninety days after session or immediately upon signature of the governor. If the effective date specified is less than ninety days after adjournment, however, it must contain an emergency clause, as well as the specific date.

Some legislators like to put emergency clauses in almost all legislation, especially if controversial, in order to prevent attempts at a referendum. Governors generally don't like unnecessary emergency clauses, though, and have often vetoed them out of bills. In fact, emergency clauses probably account for more partial vetoes than anything else. Typical was the 1995 partial veto by Governor Lowry of HB 1790. In his veto message he said in part:

> This legislation includes an emergency clause in section 2. In contacting the principal proponents of this measure, my office has been informed that, although this new language will prove of great importance, no jurisdiction faces an immediate issue due to this change as was the case earlier. (*1995 Final Legislative Report*, p. 128)

About 14 percent of all the bills passed during the 1996 legislative session contained an emergency clause. Another 18 percent had specific effective dates (usually the start of the next biennium) and none had contingent effective dates, leaving 68 percent with the normal effective date of ninety days after adjournment of session.

On a related note, bills may also contain **expiration dates**, indicating when the measure ends. If one is included, the law will be removed from the code (RCW) on the specified date. Few bills contain such provisions, however, perhaps because the Legislature meets every year. The language of an expiration clause is very simple: "This act expires December 31, 1999."

INITIATIVE AND REFERENDUM

The Washington State Constitution could not be clearer about where the ultimate power to make laws resides. Article II deals with the Legislative Department, but in the very first section, after stating that the legislative authority is vested in a house of representatives and a senate, it goes on: "but the people reserve to themselves the power to propose bills, laws, and to enact or reject the same at the polls, independent of the legislature, and also reserve power, at their own option, to approve or reject at the polls any act, item, section, or part of any bill, act, or law passed by the legislature." (Article II, Section 1)

The **initiative** is a process whereby the voters of the state may enact new laws or change existing laws themselves. The only limit is that initiatives cannot change the state Constitution. A **referendum** is a process whereby voters must approve a legislative act before it becomes law. There are two kinds of referenda: one is a provision attached by the Legislature to a bill which bypasses the governor and goes directly to a vote of the people. The second is an action by voters which stops a bill enacted by the Legislature and signed by the governor from taking effect until it has been approved by the people.

Any registered voter, acting individually or on behalf of an organization, may propose an initiative or a referendum simply by filing a copy with the office of the secretary of state. A copy is sent to the Code Reviser who reviews it in terms of proper drafting and advises the proposer of any problems and recommend changes to correctly accomplish the purpose. It is the same assistance offered to legislators in drafting bills. When the proposer is satisfied, the secretary of state assigns a number to the initiative or referendum and sends it to the attorney general to write the ballot title and summary.

The attorney general has seven days to create a **ballot title** that is impartial and nonargumentative, phrased as a question, and has no more than twenty words. The attorney general also writes a **ballot summary** for the initiative or referendum which must be impartial and nonargumentative and no more than seventy-five words. The proposer is notified by telephone of the title and summary.

Anyone dissatisfied with the title or summary has five days to take the matter to Thurston County Superior Court. The court is required to act expeditiously and its decision is final. For example, in 1996 there was a proposal, Initiative 671, to allow Indian tribal casinos to have slot and other gambling machines that were previously illegal. Opponents of the initiative objected to the ballot title written by the state attorney general's office because it used the term "electronic gaming" rather than "slot machines." The group, Citizens Opposed to Addictive Gambling, filed an appeal in Thurston County Superior Court, asking the judge to change the title of the initiative (*The Olympian*, May 9, 1996).

Armed with an official number, ballot title and summary, initiative or referendum sponsors are ready now to have **signature petition sheets** printed (at their own expense) and gather signatures.

Initiatives to the people must have the signatures of 8 percent of the total votes cast for governor in the last election. They must be filed with the secretary of state no later than four months before the date of the next general election. If the proper number of signatures are certified, the initiative goes directly onto the ballot in the November general election.

Initiatives to the Legislature need the signatures of 4 percent of the total votes cast for governor in the last election. They must be filed with the secretary of state no later than ten days before a regular session of the Legislature. If the proper number of signatures are certified, this initiative would effectively be introduced into the Legislature. The Legislature can either pass it and it becomes law; pass an alternative to the initiative which goes on the next November general election ballot along with the initiative; or do nothing, in which case the initiative goes on the ballot in November by itself. The governor plays no role in the initiative process.

Referendum petitions from the people must be filed with the secretary of state no later than ninety days after adjournment of the session in which the act referred was passed. It is necessary to gather the signatures of 4 percent of the total number of ballots cast in the last gubernatorial election. If the signatures are certified, the act is held in abeyance and goes on the next general election ballot.

The Legislature may attach a referendum clause to any bill it passes except ones that deal with budgets or taxes or have an emergency clause. The language used is:

The secretary of state shall submit this act to the people for the adoption and ratification, or rejection, at the next general election to be held in this state, in accordance with Article II, Section 1 of the state Constitution and the laws adopted to facilitate its operation. (Memorandum from Code Reviser, April 2, 1996, pp. 8-9)

Washington is one of twenty-four states, mostly in the West, that permits initiative and referendum. And it has had an effect. There is a direct correlation between states with the initiative and states with term limits, for example. Fiscal questions are also favorite targets. In 1996 alone, Florida, Missouri, Montana and Oregon voters decided whether to require voter approval for all future tax increases.

Washington State has had initiatives on the ballot since 1914. Many hundreds have been submitted to the secretary of state's office, but relatively few have garnered enough signatures to move forward. There have been twenty-two **initiatives to the Legislature** (through 1995). Three were approved by the Legislature and thus became law. Of the remaining nineteen, voters rejected eight, approved nine, and voters approved two alternatives which had been placed on the ballot by the Legislature along with the proposed initiatives.

Washington State has had ninety-four **initiatives to the people** on the ballot since 1914. Of these, forty-six were approved and forty-eight rejected. In 1914 alone there were seven initiatives on the ballot, including statewide prohibition of alcohol and abolishing employment offices, which were approved, and an eight-hour workday law, a blue sky law (regulating fly-by-night investment companies), abolishing the Bureau of Inspection, First Aid to Injured, and a Convict Labor Road Measure, which were all rejected.

The most popular topic for Washington initiatives is taxes. Next come schools, alcohol, electric power, redistricting (before our state adopted the Redistricting Commission), and various aspects of fishing.

In 1996 the use of paid signature gatherers was a subject of controversy. Representative Helen Sommers (D-Seattle) was quoted in a January 25, 1996, article by Michael Paulson for the *Seattle Post-Intelligencer* as saying: "A number of us feel that our populist, grass-roots initiative process has been perverted and distorted by the payment for signatures." Both school initiatives which appeared on the 1996 ballot used paid signature gatherers. So did a property rights measure and a tribal gambling initiative in 1995. In his article, Paulson says that the most egregious example of the use of paid signature gatherers was in 1994 when denture makers taxed themselves to come up with the funds for a successful initiative to legalize denturism.

In 1993 the Legislature passed a law banning the use of paid signature gatherers (RCW 29.79.490 (2)), but that law was overturned by a federal court as an infringement on the freedom of political speech. Sherry Bockwinkel, who has managed several initiatives, and who led the successful federal court challenge, says that paying initiative signature gatherers is a legitimate tactic that dates back to 1929 in this state.

The 1996 Legislature had several initiative "reform" measures before it including a requirement for a warning on petitions that signature-gatherers are paid; a requirement for a fiscal note on any measure that makes the ballot; a requirement that the voter's pamphlet disclose whether initiative proponents employed paid signature gatherers; a bill to increase penalties for fraudulent signatures; and a prohibition against any initiative which would offer money to voters (as an unsuccessful 1995 Indian gambling measure did). None of these proposals passed the Legislature.

4

Committees

The Washington State Constitution contains no requirement for number, names or composition of legislative committees. Committees are only referenced in the 68th Amendment, adopted in 1979, which says: "Standing and special committees of the legislature shall meet and conduct official business pursuant to such rules as the legislature may adopt." (Article II, Section 12 (3)) A **standing committee** is one that continues for the two-year life of a legislature. Numbers of committees and total membership of committees is set out in the rules of each house adopted at the beginning of the odd-numbered regular session. During the first half of every regular session, most of the business of the Legislature is conducted in these standing committees. The committees are crucial to the process because they provide the only opportunity for members of the public to speak directly and publicly about specific legislative proposals.

The standing committee meeting times are typically divided into four two-hour blocks per day, such as 8:00–10:00 A.M., 10:00 A.M.–noon,

1:30–3:30 P.M., and 3:30–5:50 P.M. Multiplied by five days that equals twenty meeting slots in a week. A few of the slots are given over to floor time or caucus but the bulk are assigned to standing committees during the first half of a legislative session. Both the House and the Senate publish generic committee meeting times before each session as well as specific weekly and daily meeting schedules with agendas.

Standing committees tend to reflect the contemporary concerns of society. It is interesting to note the changes since statehood as illustrated by agriculture. Listed below are the various Senate standing committees dealing with agriculture-related topics since statehood. Notice that in some years the Legislature had as many as three separate committees handling various aspects of agriculture. One can see the evolution of agriculture from horticulture and forestry to irrigation and reclamation and livestock to the current emphasis on international trade in agricultural products.

Agriculture and Agricultural Trade and Development (1995-96)
Agriculture and Water Resources (1991-92)
Agriculture (1889-1943, 1973-1990)
Agriculture and Horticulture (1961-1972)
Agriculture and Livestock (1945-1953, 1957-1960)
Horticulture, Irrigation and Reclamation (1957-58)
Agriculture, Livestock, Reclamation and Irrigation (1955-56)
Reclamation and Irrigation (1927-1934, 1945-1954)
Reclamation, Irrigation, Dikes and Ditches (1943-44)
Dairy and Livestock (1905-1944)
Reclamation, Irrigation, Dikes, Drains and Ditches (1935-1942)
Horticulture (1921-1940)
Rural Credits and Agricultural Development (1915-1940)
Reclamation, Irrigation and Logged-off Roads (1921-22)
Irrigation and Arid Lands (1889-1920)
Horticulture and Forestry (1903-1920)

Other committees have also undergone changes. The word "ecology" didn't appear in a committee title until 1973. Before that, there were parks, capitol grounds and recreation. "Energy" didn't appear until 1977 and may soon be overshadowed by telecommunications. The Health and Long-Term Care Committee has its origins in the Medicine, Dentistry, Surgery and Hygiene Committee (1889). The Human Services and Corrections Committee emerged from the Public Welfare and Unemployment Relief Committee (1935) which traced its roots to the State Schools for Defective Youth Committee (1889). Gone are separate standing committees on Flood Control (1933), Game (1909), Internal Improvements (1889), Liquor Control (1933), Public Morals (1909 through 1954), State Insane (1889), Compensation and Fees for State and County Officers (1923), Elections and Privileges (1889-1944), Aeronautics (1945), Post War Planning (1945), Federal Relations and Immigration (1923-1934), and Purchase and Supplies (1907).

In 1995-96, the Senate had fifteen standing committees (SR 41) and the House had eighteen (HR 23). These numbers are fairly close to the average in the two bodies for several decades now, but at one time there were many more committees. In 1951, for example, there were thirty-two standing committees in the Senate, so many in fact that the majority Democrats allowed Republicans to chair some. During legislative sessions from 1933 until 1940, there were fifty-three standing committees in the Senate at a time when there were only forty-six senators (see Fig. 4.1).

The Washington Legislature's tendency to reduce the number of standing committees is counter to the national trend. According to a Council of State Governments 1996 study, the number of standing committees in the lower houses of state legislatures ranges from a low of six in Massachusetts and Rhode Island to a high of forty-three in Missouri. In the upper houses, the low is four in Maine and the high is thirty in Mississippi. The national average in lower houses is eighteen and in upper houses it is fifteen.

There are several other committees created by or used by the Legislature for special purposes. A **conference committee** is one appointed by the presiding officers of the two bodies to discuss differences in bills passed by the two bodies. A **special committee**, used interchangeably with **select committee**, is one appointed to consider a particular topic within a limited period of time, such as the Joint Select Committee on Water Policy, and may include non-legislative members. **Joint committees** have members from both houses.

Legislative members of the above committees are appointed by the presiding officers of the two bodies and then confirmed by the whole body. In the House that duty is fairly uncomplicated since the presiding officer is also the leader of the majority party. It is potentially a bit more complicated in the Senate because the presiding officer, the lieutenant governor, may be a member of the minority party. An example will illustrate.

In the 1987 Regular Session, Senate Democrats had a one-vote majority. Democrat John A. Cherberg was lieutenant governor and presiding officer. After the Senate Democrats' budget failed to pass the Senate, three Democrats joined the twenty-four Senate Republicans and passed a "coalition budget." The heavily Democratic House amended this coalition budget and asked for a conference committee with the Senate to resolve the differences. The Joint Rules in 1987 prescribed that the three members from each body assigned to conference committees were to represent "the majority and minority positions as relates to the subject matter, and to the extent possible the majority and minority political parties." Since Senate Republicans made up the majority on the budget bill, Senate Republican Minority Leader Jeannette Hayner recommended two members from her caucus. Senate Democrats nominated Senator Jim McDermott (D-Seattle), their budget chair, as their lone representative.

But Lieutenant Governor Cherberg saw it differently. He observed that there were actually three groups in the Senate, the third being the coalition Democrats. So instead of following the usual procedure and simply naming the members suggested by the two caucus leaders, he named Senator Frank "Tub" Hansen (D-Moses Lake), a coalition Democrat, along with Senator Jim McDermott, the mainstream Democrat, and Senator Dan McDonald, representing the Republicans. Senate Republicans smelled a rat and wondered aloud if Hansen had voted for their budget as part of a grand scheme to stack the conference committee (as Democrats had stacked other committees that year). It would have been a clever plot, indeed, but well beyond the ability of a divided Democratic caucus. The appointment of a representative from the dissident Democrats was purely Cherberg's idea as the proper interpretation of the rules and his right as presiding officer. "Tub" Hansen may have been the most surprised member in the body that day when the President made his announcement.

The incident in 1987 with Lieutenant Governor John Cherberg and Senator "Tub" Hansen was a rare exception. The tradition in our state is for the Senate presiding officer to appoint those persons nominated by the respective caucus leaders. This is not true in other states. Georgia, for example, like Washington, has a separately-elected President (lieutenant governor) who presides over the Senate. While Georgia Senate rules name the standing committees and their numbers, again like Washington's Senate rules, they are unambiguous about the appointing authority. Georgia Senate rules provide that "The President shall appoint a chairman, a vice chairman and a secretary for all standing committees and a chairman of standing subcommittees." (Georgia State Senate Rule 185) The Georgia Senate President guards this appointment power jealously. Washington Senate rules are much weaker. They provide for the President to appoint members to committees, but make the appointments subject to Senate confirmation and provide for election of committee members in the event of refusal to confirm (SR 41). Thus, in Washington, the rules provide for the majority to overrule the Senate President on committee appointments should he or she go contrary to the majority leader's recommendations.

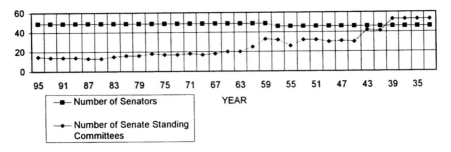

Fig. 4.1. Number of Washington State Senators
and Senate Standing Committees: 1933-1995

COMMITTEE CHAIRS AND MEMBERSHIP

Within two weeks after the general election in November of even-numbered years, the four caucuses hold **reorganization meetings** to elect or reelect their leaders for the upcoming Legislature. For the two caucuses with majorities, the question of committees and committee chairs may also be considered. Sometimes the promise of a chairmanship or a seat on a powerful committee is part of the process of soliciting votes for Speaker or Senate majority leader.

The method of selection of committee chairs may be provided for in caucus rules, done by the caucus leader, or left to a committee. In most cases the putative committee chair is obvious from seniority or prior claim or having been the vice chair of the committee earlier. On fewer occasions, it may be awarded to a losing candidate for a leadership position or bigger committee. Or, it may be the result of strong interest or superior qualifications.

The process of determining committee membership is to first solicit from each member his or her top choices. This is usually done confidentially and in writing and given to the Committee on Committees, often chaired by the Speaker in the House and the majority leader in the Senate. The committee brokers the appointments to reward friends and punish foes or, more common today, to keep all members of the majority party content. While this is usually possible, the author remembers one year when the majority leader had to make a very difficult choice between two qualified members for chair of a major committee. He consulted with numerous members of his caucus and made his decision. The winning candidate went on to be a distinguished chair. The losing candidate refused all offers of a second committee or leadership position and left the Legislature at the end of her term. It was unusual in two respects: that no way could be found to satisfy the losing candidate and that the loser didn't stick around to seek revenge.

The majority party determines what the committee structure will be and how many members of each party will be on each committee. These are made part of the rules of the body. One year the majority party in the House decided it would also determine which members of the minority party would serve on committees. Needless to say, minority party leaders balked and the majority relented. However, the majority party does have the historical right—perhaps one should say the votes—to determine total membership on various committees and this can be critical.

The 1987 session illustrates the advantages and disadvantages of the power of the majority over committee membership. Senate Democrats had a one-person majority. To compound their problem, three of their members shared the more conservative Republican philosophy about the size of the budget. Being in the majority, Democratic leaders were nevertheless responsible for organizing the Senate and passing a budget. While there was little they could do about the number of votes on the floor, they could and did make sure the budget would have no trouble getting that far. Despite having only a one-vote majority, they gave themselves a fourteen to nine majority on the Ways and Means Committee and a nine to six majority on the Rules Committee, the two committees that must pass the budget to get it to the floor. They could do this because these matters are enumerated in the rules and it takes a simple majority to adopt the rules. And it worked. The budget flew through the two committees, over the howls of the Republicans. But that was as far as the Democrats' plan went. Their budget was defeated on the floor and a coalition of Republicans and Democrats ended up writing the Senate budget.

To be fair, it should be noted that when the Republicans took over in 1989 and had a similar one-vote majority, they also stacked the committees. They gave themselves a thirteen to ten majority on Ways and Means and a ten to seven majority on Rules, and this time the Democrats cried foul.

Efforts by both sides to use a one-vote majority to adopt rules which enhance the majority's membership on committees are short-sighted, counterproductive and waste valuable time. One of the purposes of the committee system is to produce bills which reflect the thinking of the body. Committees that are "stacked" misrepresent the body. Their legislation is doomed to fail when the full body comes into play. It is far better to have committees which accurately reflect the full membership and are thus likely to produce bills which are acceptable. Looking back again at the 1987 session, it seems clear to the author that it would have been better for the Senate Democrats to have had a Ways and Means Committee that truly represented the will of the body to amend, discuss and work the budget in committee. The product of a representative committee would not have been as much to some leaders' liking, but it likely would have passed the body. Instead, the committee passed a budget which represented only a minority and, as expected, it failed on the floor. Worse, the Democratic leadership was so heavy-handed in their tactics that they literally forced some of their members to form a coalition with the minority Republicans and they were taken out of the game. In hindsight, it seems clear that the better approach is let the process work rather than trying to find ways around it.

COMMITTEE HEARINGS AND PROCEDURES

The purpose of committees is to disperse the workload, to break the full body into smaller parts—committees, which take more time to hear and perfect measures. It is in committees that public testimony is heard, amendments offered, the merits of measures debated, and votes taken. However, keep in mind that committees cannot substitute for the full house. Committee action is more akin to a recommendation as to what the full body should do. A committee cannot by itself advance a bill to the other house.

House committee meetings are held in the John L. O'Brien Building, and Senate committee meetings in the John A. Cherberg Building. Rules Committee meetings are usually held in the Legislative Building (the Senate has also used the first-floor conference rooms in the Cherberg Building at times). Hearing rooms have capacities from fifty to 250 and are all located on the first floors of the O'Brien and Cherberg buildings. All hearing rooms are laid out in similar style: there is a dais in front, usually raised and sometimes in tiers, for committee members. There are tables and chairs directly in front of and facing the dais for testimony, and rows of chairs behind that for the audience. There is also a table along the side for committee staff and, sometimes, a table on the opposite side for the press. Usually only members, identified by nameplates, are seated at the dais, but a few committee chairs will have staff at the dais as well. The committee chair typically sits in the front row center (sometimes in the back row center) where there is a control panel for the sound system. Materials germane to the meetings are available at the entry.

Committee meetings are required to be held in public with at least five days' notice of the date, time, place, and title and number of bill(s) or subject matter to be considered (SR 44, HR 24). House rules provide that the Speaker may grant an exception to the notice provisions if there are less than eight days remaining for action on a bill (HR 24(A)). Senate rules allow a majority of committee members present to waive the notice requirements, making a record of the reasons (SR 45(1)). It is common for committees to use these exceptions in the days just prior to one of the cutoffs.

Standing committee meetings are recorded, with tapes available at cost. Meetings generally start when the chair turns on the sound system, bangs the gavel, calls the meeting to order, and announces the order of business. The chair will often ask staff to summarize the bill or matter under consideration, referring to the appropriate place in the notebook of material distributed to each member. The chair then may take public testimony based on the **sign-up sheets** located near the main entry. It is entirely up to the committee chair as to who may testify and in what order. Chairs generally try to hear from all interested parties, often calling those who had to travel the farthest first. To save time, chairs may call individuals to the testimony table in groups of three or four in order to save time.

When giving notice of hearings, most committees will distinguish between a hearing for the purpose of taking **public testimony** on a bill and one in which **executive action**, i.e., a vote, may be taken and no further public testimony permitted. There is no requirement in the rules of either body to make this distinction, however. Some committees may further designate **work sessions** at which a number of parties, including members, will gather around tables and exchange ideas on a particular subject or bill.

Senate rules prohibit a committee from taking executive action during the interim (SR 44). This rule came out of a dispute between the House and Senate some years ago when House leaders decided to get a head start on the session by allowing their standing committees to pass bills in the week prior to the start of session. The Senate insists that the Legislature must be in session before executive action can be taken. Legally, the issue is still unresolved.

A majority of a committee equals a **quorum** (HR 24). Under Senate rules there is a presumption of a quorum unless a member raises the issue (SR 45). Thus, it is not improper in the Senate to hold a hearing with only the chair present. House rules require a quorum of the committee to actually be present in order to transact business. In both the House and Senate, committees are precluded from meeting when their respective chambers are in session. In the Senate, committees are also prohibited from meeting during any scheduled caucus (SR 46).

To be technically correct, one should say bills are **reported out** of committees, not passed by committees. This is because the operative action is the signatures of a majority of the committee members on the committee majority report, not the votes in committee.

In the Senate, recorded votes are often not taken at all and the chair will simply announce, "The bill is out subject to signatures." Staff then find the committee members either at the meeting or later and ask if they wish to sign the majority report. However, there is a provision that one-sixth of committee members may demand an oral roll call (SR 22 (7)), although this is rarely done.

Bills reported out must have a **majority report**, signed by a majority of the committee members. The report may contain a recommendation of "do pass" or "do not pass" or no recommendation. Depending on the action taken by the committee, the majority report may also make the same recommendations on a substitute bill and on amendments. Committee members may request and sign a **minority report** designating a different recommendation from the majority. These terms are somewhat misleading in that there is no actual written report either by the majority or minority. The report simply means the signatures of committee members recommending a certain action on a bill.

The Senate majority report designates where the bill is to be sent next, usually to the Rules Committee or to the Ways and Means Committee. If this designation is wrong, for example because the bill has a large fiscal impact but was sent directly to the Rules Committee, then the bill is **rereferred** to another committee by motion on the floor. In the absence of a designation, Senate bills are sent to the Rules Committee.

In the House, recorded committee votes are required and a majority of the members of the committee must sign the majority report at a regular meeting (HR 24). House members are not permitted to sign committee reports other than at committee meetings. Also unlike Senate committees, when a House committee passes a bill, there is no designation as to where it is being sent. House bills signed out of committees are reviewed by the majority floor leader who determines whether they should go to the Rules Committee, one of the fiscal committees, or another policy committee.

From a public policy viewpoint, the House rules on passing bills out of committee are superior. Everything is done in the open and there is no gap between the vote and the signature. The Senate has had instances in the past when members voted for a bill in committee but refused to sign the majority report; when a committee chair killed a bill by locking the committee report, signed by a majority of members, in his desk until after the cutoff; and when the majority report was carried across the state so an absent member could provide a needed signature.

FISCAL NOTES

A **fiscal note** is an estimate of the cost of a measure to state and/or local governments within a given time period. In 1977 the Legislature made the Office of Financial Management (OFM) the lead executive agency to work with the Legislature in setting up a process for determining the predicted fiscal impact of bills on state revenues or expenditures. In 1984 the Legislature added **judicial impact notes**, which are the same as fiscal notes except they predict the impact legislation will have on the workload and administration of the courts of this state (RCW 2.56.120). Fiscal notes are required to identify the financial impact of a bill in the biennium it takes effect and for the subsequent two bienniums. Legislators may also request fiscal notes on proposals not yet put in bill form (see sample form).

OFM receives a fiscal note request form on a bill from a legislator, legislative staff, or as an executive request. OFM forwards the bill and request form to affected agencies to determine the fiscal impact and return the results to OFM, which reviews for accuracy and completeness, and forwards the fiscal note to the requestor and to the fiscal committees of the House or Senate. The Legislature also established a fiscal note system to determine the cost of bills to local governments (RCW 43.132). As with state notes, OFM coordinates the process but the actual task of preparing the notes falls to the Department of Community, Trade, and Economic Development (CTED). CTED consults with local governments based on a random selection process and/or the Department of Revenue.

Statutes provide that local government fiscal notes are to be prepared within seventy-two hours of the request (RCW 43.132.020). State fiscal notes are to be provided prior to the first hearing on a bill "whenever possible." (RCW 43.88A.030(3))

Fiscal notes were requested on about 40 percent of all the bills introduced in 1995. Since measures are changed as they wind through the process and many measures affect multiple agencies, the total number of fiscal notes processed and distributed by OFM that year was 4,386. That accounts for a very large amount of state employee time and cost.

FISCAL NOTE REQUEST

BILL NUMBER _____ DATE REQUIRED _____

HEARING DATE _____ HEARING TIME _____

FISCAL NOTE TYPE: STATE _____ LOCAL _____

REQUESTED BY _____

COMMITTEE: HOUSE _____ SENATE _____

BUILDING/ROOM # _____ PHONE # _____ DATE _____

STAFF CONTACT (REGARDING BILL CONTENTS) _____

_____

PRELIMINARY IDENTIFICATION OF AFFECTED STATE OR LOCAL GOVERNMENT AGENCIES _____

_____

_____

_____

COMMENTS OR SPECIAL INSTRUCTIONS _____

_____

_____

_____

**TWO COPIES OF THE CODE REVISER DRAFT OR BILL
MUST ACCOMPANY THIS REQUEST**

Rev 1/8/96

Members and staff have a dilemma on fiscal notes. If there is even a hint of a fiscal impact and no fiscal note is requested, the bill may be held up or seriously jeopardized. Thus, the prudent thing is to order more fiscal notes than really needed. Members may not trust the notes, but they want to see them before voting on a bill. OFM and agencies properly complain that there are too many requests for fiscal notes. They can't keep up. They would like requests to be limited to important bills or at least to bills that clearly have a fiscal impact. They also claim that the intent of many proposed bills is too vague to provide an accurate estimate of costs.

Members have many complaints about fiscal notes. They say that agencies slant their fiscal estimates for their own purposes. There is a suspicion that if an agency likes a bill, it gives it a low cost estimate in order to improve its chances of passage. If an agency doesn't like a bill, a high cost estimate can decrease likelihood of passage. Fiscal notes are often late and, some say, inaccurate. Members have sought a better method or source to determine true costs of measures. Ultimately, though, whether the lead agency is OFM or a legislative committee or even a group outside government, someone is still going to have to ask agencies themselves about the impact of legislation affecting them.

During the 1995 interim, OFM and legislative fiscal staff did a thorough study of fiscal notes and held a series of meetings to try and improve the process. A new form was created to provide more information about the bill in order to make a fiscal estimate sounder and to establish easier contact between the requestor and the author of the fiscal note. From the legislative side, there were promises to try to reduce unnecessary requests and from the agency budget staff, pledges to do a better and more timely job.

INFORMATION AVAILABLE

There are many materials published during and after legislative sessions and a variety of means available to aid in staying up to date and understanding the content and progress of bills.

At the time a bill is introduced, the same attorney in the Code Reviser's Office who helped draft the bill prepares a **bill digest.** This contains the number of the bill, sponsor(s), title, and a section-by-section summary of its contents. Bill digests are printed daily in the **Bill Digest Supplements** and at the end of each session in the **Final Digest and History of Bills,** which contains not only a digest/summary of each bill introduced but a history of every action that impacts it, a list of bills introduced or sponsored by each member during the two-year legislative period, and a table for determining which current state laws are affected by each bill. Both publications are available from the **Bill Room** on the first floor of the Legislative Building in Olympia.

After a bill is read into the record and is assigned to a House or Senate standing committee, one of the committee staff prepares a **bill report.** The timing of the bill report varies somewhat from committee to committee, but generally in the Senate the bill report is available at the bill's first committee hearing, and in the House it is available after the bill is signed out of committee. The format for House and Senate bill reports is very similar and contains the sponsor name(s), short title of the bill, committee hearing dates, name of the committee staff assigned to the bill, date of the report, background of the bill, summary of the bill, appropriation, date of fiscal note request, effective date, and the names and a summary of the testimony of those who spoke for or against the bill in committee. Bill report summaries differ from bill digest summaries in that digests are strictly section-by-section summaries while bill reports are written more like newspaper articles with the most important things first. Bill reports are updated each time a bill is changed or any action is taken. Bill reports are used in the House and Senate floor calendars published during session, although the amount of information contained varies from House to Senate and year to year.

After session, the bill reports for all bills that passed the Legislature appear in the **Final Legislative Report.** This document is prepared by the committee staff of the House and Senate and is a summary of all the bills passed for the year. It is available about a month after session's end from the Bill Room. While the Final Legislative Report contains some budget information, additional detail is contained in the **Legislative Budget Notes** available about two months after the biennial budget has been adopted.

For those who plan to write a bill or an amendment or want to know how it is done, the **Bill Drafting Guide,** published by the Statute Law Committee (Code Reviser), is very useful. It is available from the Office of the Code Reviser on the first floor on the Legislative Building.

Early in a regular session, two self-descriptive pamphlets are available: A **Pictorial Guide to the Washington State Legislature,** also called the **Baby Book,** contains pictures and biographical data on every legislator; and the **Telephone Directory and Committee Assignments of the Washington State Legislature,** obtained from the Bill Room.

A few weeks into each 105-day session, the **Legislative Manual** for the two-year Legislature becomes available. This valuable little red book (much the same format and style of presentation since first published in 1889) contains the federal and state Constitutions, the Joint Rules, Rules of the House and of the Senate, committee membership, and personal biographical information for each member.

The **Daily Clips,** sometimes called the **Media Digest,** is a compilation of articles about legislative activities culled from newspapers throughout the state. It is prepared by the communications staff of one or more of the four caucuses and is available from the caucuses.

The Legislature publishes a weekly **Legislative Meeting Schedule** during session, which is usually available on Thursday of the week before. It gives the date, time, place, and agenda for all standing committee meetings of the House and Senate, as well as times of session and meetings of the caucuses. There is also a combination **Bill Status/Daily Meeting Schedule** available early each morning from the Bill Room, which contains the latest meeting schedule and indicates the status of every bill introduced. Both the House and Senate also publish a weekly one-page spreadsheet meeting schedule.

Following regular legislative sessions, each house publishes a **Journal** of the proceedings. This is required by the state Constitution (Article II, Section 11). The Journal contains information such as roll call votes, motions, remarks by members, parliamentary inquiries, and messages from the governor and the other house. It is the official record of the House and Senate.

Other publications which may be useful include Senate and House **Roll Call Transcripts, Media Guide, Session. Calendar,** and assorted other lists, all available in the Bill Room located at the southeast end of the first floor of the Legislative Building.

Some publications are free and some are sold at cost. Mailboxes can be rented in the Bill Room in order to receive copies of all bills introduced and amendments proposed and/or adopted. The Bill Room will also mail Bill Digest Supplements and Status Sheets on a daily basis for a fee. For more information, call the Bill Room at (360) 786-7573.

LEGLink is the electronic link to dial-up computer access to legislative information. LEGLink provides full printed documentation, classes and help-desk support for a fee. **LEGInfo** provides much the same information, updated at the end of every business day, via the Internet. For more information call the Legislative Service Center (LSC) at (360) 786-7001 or contact them via the Internet at http://www.leg.wa.gov. Most subdivisions of the Legislature, including all the standing committees, have their own Internet addresses and publish a good deal of information on the Internet. A list of Internet addresses is available from the Bill Room.

Committee meetings and House and Senate floor action can also be seen and heard live or in a rebroadcast over **TVW**, Washington State's version of C-Span. Check your local area for channel and schedule of broadcasts.

The hearing and conference rooms of the House and Senate plus the two chambers are available via an audio service on a yearly subscription basis. Subscribers must obtain a speaker box, pay an annual charge to the Legislature, and a monthly fee to US West for each circuit. Information about this service can also be obtained from LSC listed above.

5

Management of Legislation
Through Cutoffs

Over 4,700 bills were introduced during the 1995-96 legislative sessions. Nearly half were reported out of the standing committees of the House and Senate. If there were no deadlines for getting bills out of committees, for consideration of own-house bills on the floor, and for passage of bills, it would be a little like trying to bake a cake without using a recipe or maybe like trying to find Chicago merely by driving east. At a minimum it would be inefficient and there would be the possibility of general chaos. Legislative cutoffs form the basis for the entire session schedule. They determine in general terms when bills need to be introduced if they are to be considered in the session, when committees will have the opportunity to meet and what types of bills they will consider, when the Rules Committee will meet to schedule bills for the floor, when there will be floor action, and what will be considered. Methods vary from state to state, but all legislatures use cutoffs of some kind.

Cutoff dates are deadlines within the sixty or 105-day session established by the Constitution or the Legislature itself by which certain actions must be taken. Most are set by concurrent resolution passed in the first few days of a regular session (see 1996 Session Calendar with cutoff dates indicated). Cutoffs set by the Legislature are typically in this order: introduction of bills, passage of own-house bills out of committees, passage of own-house bills in the originating body, passage of opposite-house bills from committees, and passage of opposite-house bills on the floor of the opposite body. The Constitution sets one additional cutoff: that no bill can be considered unless it was introduced prior to the final ten days of the session, unless two-thirds of each body agree (Article II, Section 36). The purpose of cutoffs is to provide a logical outline to the session in order for the Legislature to complete its work in the time allotted. One could argue that in most years members don't get done on time anyway, but without cutoffs it would be much worse.

INTRODUCTION AND FIRST READING

The only requirements for the **introduction** of a bill are that the bill have a **title**, a **sponsor** and a **number**. Only a duly elected member of the House or Senate may introduce or sponsor a bill. The title is determined in the Code Reviser's Office and the number is assigned when the bill is delivered to the Chief Clerk of the House or the Secretary of the Senate. Bills must be filed with the Secretary of the Senate or Chief Clerk by 10:00 A.M. (House) or noon (Senate) of the preceding day (House Rule 9, Senate Rule 56). This is usually done by handing the bill and sign-up sheet to the clerk in the Code Reviser's Office.

Until ten years ago there was a cutoff date for the introduction of new bills. In the 1985 session, for example, members had nineteen days to request bills be drafted by the Code Reviser's Office, and twenty-six days to read in (introduce) bills on the floor. To put that another way, members had nineteen days to request the attorneys in the Code Reviser's Office to take an idea and draft it into a bill and another week to decide whether to sign it and drop it in (according to the Code Reviser, only about half of the bills drafted are actually introduced). After the nineteenth day of the 1985 Regular Session, it would have taken a two-thirds vote of all the members elected to the body to introduce a bill. In the 1986 session, members had only five days after the start of the Regular Session to get bill requests to the Code Reviser's Office and could introduce no new bills after the tenth day of the Regular Session.

The idea behind cutoffs on the introduction of new bills is to put an end to the production of additional work and to bring a measure of predictability to the session. By closing the tap to new bills, committee chairs can determine the time needed to hear and study bills already introduced.

However, the cutoff for introduction of new bills gave rise to the widespread use of title-only bills. Since there was no limit on the number of bills that could be introduced before the cutoff, nor any requirement that they say anything, members figured out that they could introduce any number of bills that contained nothing but a title, a sponsor and a number. These title-only bills could then be amended when needed, effectively taking the place of new bills. Title-only bills are like empty ferry boats waiting to be loaded.

In the 1985 session, Senator Jim McDermott, then chair of the Senate Ways and Means Committee, was the chief sponsor of over one hundred title-only bills which said nothing more than "AN ACT Relating to government," or "AN ACT Relating to the budget," or "AN ACT Relating to fiscal matters," or "AN ACT Relating to education." He had over one hundred broad-titled bills just in case something came up later in session and he needed a new bill. Nor was the practice limited to McDermott. In the absence of being able to introduce a new bill, it was simply a prudent thing for every committee chair to make sure one did not get caught short later in session. Over the years a number of major bills that became law started as empty title-only bills.

Seeing the proliferation of hundreds of title-only bills, legislative leaders in 1987 began to back away from cutoffs on the introduction of bills. In 1987 they limited the cutoff for introduction of new bills to executive and agency request measures only. The hope was to force agencies to get their bills in early in session. But for a variety of reasons that didn't work either, so in 1988 the cutoff for introduction of new bills was dropped altogether (except for the constitutional prohibition against introductions in the last ten days). With the elimination of this cutoff, the number of title-only bills dropped dramatically. As will be seen below, however, their usefulness has not entirely disappeared and a title-only bill played a key role during the 1996 session.

There are other ways of limiting bill introductions. The Legislature could pass a law or a rule limiting the number of bills any member may introduce or could penalize members for introducing more than a certain number. Several attempts along these lines have been tried. The latest was in 1996 when Representative Shirley Hankins (R-Richland) introduced a bill which would have limited members to introducing three bills each during regular sessions at public cost. After that, a legislator would have to personally pay the costs of additional bills, estimated at $1,500. Hankins' bill would have allowed committee chairs to introduce an unlimited number of agency request bills. Members were not taken with

Hankins' idea, though, and her bill died in the House Government Operations Committee.

Once a bill has a title, sponsor and a number, it is now **introduced.** The rules in both chambers require that every bill have three readings. **First reading** is by title only (HR 10(A) and SR 63). New bill introductions along with their committee assignments are printed and distributed to members. As indicated earlier, members have about a day to look over the list and decide whether to add their names as sponsors.

The job of assigning bills to committees generally falls to the majority floor leader in the two bodies. A staff attorney will go through the list first and provide recommendations and flag any questions. In the majority of cases, it is obvious from the title of the bill and the sponsor where it should go. Many of the jurisdictional issues are resolved well before the start of session when the committee structure is set and chairs are named. For example, in 1995 the Senate Democrats split what had been the Health and Human Services Committee into two: the Health and Long-Term Care Committee and the Human Services and Corrections Committee. At the time of the split it was agreed between the chairs that welfare would go to Health and Long-Term Care, even though it might be seen as part of human services. A decade ago, when anti-smoking legislation was still in its infancy, Senate leaders could determine the fate of smoking legislation by whether they referred bills to the anti-smoking chair of the Ecology Committee or the pro-smoking chair of the Commerce and Labor Committee.

When there is a dispute about which committee should hear a bill, leadership can require that the bill be heard by more than one committee or pick a neutral third committee or, as indicated above, seal its fate with a pro or con chair.

On the following page is a copy of the 1996 Session Calendar. Notice the various cutoffs on the right side with the date and day of session in the center.

1996 Session Calendar

Date	Day of Week	Day of Session	
January			
8	M	1	— First day of session.
9	T	2	
10	W	3	
11	Th	4	
12	F	5	
13	S	6	
14	Su	7	
15	M	8	
16	T	9	
17	W	10	
18	Th	11	
19	F	12	
20	S	13	
21	Su	14	
22	M	15	
23	T	16	
24	W	17	
25	Th	18	
26	F	19	
27	S	20	
28	Su	21	
29	M	22	
30	T	23	
31	W	24	
February			
1	Th	25	
2	F	26	— Last day to read in committee reports from original house, except House fiscal committees and Senate Ways & Means and Transportation committees.*
3	S	27	
4	Su	28	
5	M	29	
6	T	30	— Last day to read in original house committee reports from House fiscal committees and Senate Ways & Means and Transportation committees.*
7	W	31	
8	Th	32	
9	F	33	
10	S	34	
11	Su	35	
12	M	36	
13	T	37	— Last day to consider own bills (5 p.m.)*
14	W	38	
15	Th	39	
16	F	40	
17	S	41	
18	Su	42	
19	M	43	
20	T	44	
21	W	45	
22	Th	46	
23	F	47	— Last day to read in committee reports from opposite house, except House fiscal committees and Senate Ways & Means and Transportation committees*
24	S	48	
25	Su	49	
26	M	50	— Last day to read in opposite house committee reports from House fiscal committees and Senate Ways & Means and Transportation committees.*
27	T	51	
28	W	52	
29	Th	53	
March			
1	F	54	— Last day to consider opposite house bills (5 p.m.) *(except amendments, differences, conference reports, the interim, and business related to closing session.)*
2	S	55	
3	Su	56	
4	M	57	
5	T	58	
6	W	59	
7	Th	60	— Last day allowed for regular session under state constitution.

> *Budgets and matters necessary to implement the budgets are exempt from cutoffs until the 54th day.
>
> After the 54th day, only initiatives, alternatives to initiatives, messages pertaining to amendments, differences between the houses, conference reports, and matters relating to the interim or closing the session may be considered.

Prepared by Senate Committee Services

COMMITTEE CONSIDERATION OF OWN-HOUSE BILLS

The deadline for signing own-house bills out of committees is the first true cutoff of a legislative session. It affects all bills that are not exempt from the cutoffs. It occurs at about the midway point in a regular session. Actually, it is a two-step cutoff, one for the policy committees and a second, two or three days later, for the fiscal and transportation committees. In 1996, a sixty-day session, this cutoff came on the thirtieth day. In 1995, a 105-day session, it came on the fifty-seventh day. Own-house bills must be in Rules Committee by then or they are dead. When a bill is referred to as "dead" it means it cannot go further in the process that session. However, the ideas contained in the bill or even the language may be amended onto another bill on second reading or in conference committee. No bill is really dead until the session adjourns sine die.

Roughly one quarter of the bills passed out of policy committees contain a significant fiscal impact (usually defined as $50,000 or more) and must go to Ways and Means in the Senate or to one of the fiscal committees in the House *before* going to the Rules Committee. In a typical 105-day session that might mean about 200 to 300 bills referred to the fiscal committees of the House and Senate from their respective policy committees.

Fiscal committees examine these bills in terms of their impact on the budget rather than their policy implications. However, sometimes the line between policy and fiscal impact is vague and the urge to discuss policy in the fiscal committees hard to resist. It is up the chair to make the distinction and rule appropriately on amendments and discussion. As with their original committees, it takes a majority of the members of the fiscal committees to sign a bill out and move it along.

Policy committees tend to disgorge the bulk of their bills in the week before the first cutoff, leaving the fiscal committees suddenly faced with hundreds of bills and only a few days to deal with them. These final meetings of the fiscal committees are necessarily long and fast-paced. Staff typically give a very quick overview of each bill under consideration, there is brief testimony, if any, a short discussion, then the chair and vice-chair swiftly bounce the appropriate motions back and forth and the bill is "out subject to signatures," in the Senate (SR 45(6)), or a vote is taken in the House (HR 24(D)(5)). If a vote is called for and taken in either body, it is by roll call and recorded.

This two or three-day difference between the deadline for bills out of policy committees and the deadline for fiscal and transportation committees gives rise to an interesting and still unresolved question illustrated during the 1991 session in the Senate. The deadline for Senate bills out of policy committees was March 6 and the deadline for fiscal committees was March 11 that year. On March 8, Majority Floor Leader Irv Newhouse moved to transfer a bill which had died in the Senate Government Operations Committee to the Ways and Means Committee, thereby bringing it back to life, at least for three more days. Democrats raised a point of order, arguing this violated the cutoff resolution. Senate President Joel Pritchard said that under the rules a simple majority of the body could move bills among the committees as it desired but he would not rule on the larger question of whether the move violated the spirit of the cutoff resolution until and unless the bill came to the floor. Democrats appealed the ruling of the chair. His ruling was upheld twenty-five to twenty-four on a straight party-line vote. In hindsight it's still a tough call. On the one hand, there was little doubt that the purpose of the move was to frustrate the cutoff resolution, and this is generally poor policy. On the other hand, cutoffs are not part of Senate rules so a simple majority should be able to do as it wishes.

In 1996, 70 percent of all the bills assigned to committees made it to Rules. In 1995, the figure was 42 percent (see Fig. 5.1 and Fig. 5.2). These numbers need explaining. The bills referred to fiscal committees before going to the Rules Committee are counted twice since they passed two committees. Plus, the 1996 figures include some bills introduced in 1995 but not passed until 1996. That is the reason for the higher percentage of bills that made it through the first cutoff in 1996 as opposed to 1995. Still, the numbers illustrate the existence and success of a deliberate process to gradually reduce the number of bills by use of cutoffs.

Members and staff will often say a committee has amended a bill or adopted a substitute or taken some other action. Two points should be noted about this. First, amendments adopted in committee become **committee amendments.** The same is true for substitute bills. The committee becomes the chief sponsor, although the system will continue to list the original sponsors. Second, one should keep in mind that nothing a committee does is binding on the whole body. A majority of the committee may vote to amend a bill, but it hasn't actually amended the bill. Only the full body can do that. The committee vote is merely an expression of the will of the committee, a kind of recommendation. Once on the floor, the committee chair must ask the full body to adopt the amendments or the substitute bill recommended by the committee.

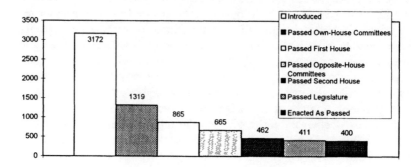

Fig. 5.1. The Winnowing Process: 1995 Regular Session

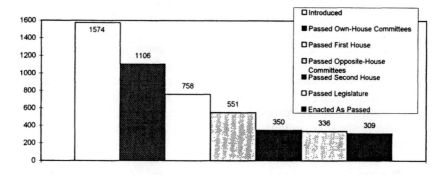

Fig. 5.2. The Winnowing Process: 1996 Regular Session

EXEMPT BILLS

As noted earlier, own-house bills must be out of committees by this first cutoff or they are dead, but there are exceptions to the rule. For example, legislatures have always exempted budgets and matters necessary to implement the budgets from the cutoffs. From time to time they have also designated specific exemptions. In 1986, the Legislature exempted bills dealing with public works projects; in 1987, public employees health coverage; in 1988, tax reform; in 1989, growth strategies; in 1990, access to health care; and in 1992, the Governor's Blue Ribbon Commission on Education and the Juvenile Justice Task Force recommendations. Some of these items might have fallen into the exemption for budgets and matters necessary to implement budgets. Their specific listing is more the political statement of a high priority.

Initiatives, alternatives to initiatives, amendments, bills in conference or dispute, and matters relating to the interim or to closing of the session are also generally exempt from cutoff deadlines.

THE RULES COMMITTEE

After a bill is assigned on first reading, has had a hearing(s), amendments have been considered, is reported out of the committee and has also been considered by the fiscal committee, if appropriate, it must be sent to the **Rules Committee.** Long seen as the most powerful committee, composed of senior legislators, the job of Rules is to determine which bills will be scheduled for second reading on the floor of their respective house. Since there are usually far more bills in Rules than can be considered on the floor of the Legislature, getting a bill selected or "pulled" from the Rules Committee is a critical step in the process. Traditionally, many bills fail this step and die in Rules.

The official function of the Rules Committee is to set the second and third reading floor calendars. **Second reading** is where bills may be amended and **third reading** is the debate and vote on final passage. Technically, bills must be voted out of Rules to get on the second reading calendar, then returned to Rules where they must be voted out again to get to third reading calendar. In practice, bills are rarely returned to the Rules Committee after second reading. The floor manager for a particular bill will ask the body to suspend the rules and advance the bill to third reading without going back to Rules, and the body will almost always agree. This is called **bumping** a bill. Any suspension of the rules takes a two-thirds majority, but the minority rarely blocks a bill at this point since it would only delay the inevitable.

In the Senate, the Rules Committee is presided over by the lieutenant governor, who is also a voting member (SR 50). In the House, the Speaker presides (HR 4(H)). Members are appointed to Rules in the same manner as the other committees, but both bodies have usually had the policy that members cannot simultaneously be committee chairs and serve on the Rules Committee. It's one or the other.

The Rules Committees are located on the first floor of the Legislative

Building, the Senate at the south end of the building, the House at the north end. Members sit at tables arranged in a U-shape or rectangle, facing one another. There is limited seating for the public in chairs facing the tables. There are benches and chairs along the walls for staff.

The two houses use different terminology but follow essentially the same procedure in their Rules Committees. We'll use the Senate terminology here. There are two calendars: a **white sheet** where all bills go when they are first sent to Rules; and a **green sheet** made up of bills "pulled" from the white sheet. In Rules, a **pull** is a method of advancing a bill without a vote. Bills on the green sheet are eligible to go onto the second reading floor calendar. Thus, the process is first to white, then to green, then to the second reading floor calendar.

When a Rules Committee meeting is announced, the leader will usually indicate how many pulls each member will have. Pulls from the green sheet to the floor go first because if a pull fails to get a majority, the bill drops back to the white sheet. Pulls from the white to the green sheet are simply announced by each member in turn. There is no debate and no vote on pulls from the white to the green. When a member names the number of a bill to go from the green sheet to the floor, there is limited debate among the members of the Rules Committee. In the House there may be testimony from the chair of the committee that passed the bill, but this is not done in the Senate. A vote is taken by show of hands. Any member may request an oral roll call. If the bill passes, it goes onto the second reading floor calendar. If not, back to the white sheet. Occasionally, packages of bills may be pulled as a group from one or both Rules calendars or a consent calendar may be formed. The packages are formed by the majority leader and are dealt with as one. More on these later.

The Rules Committee chair may adopt additional procedures. For example, when John A. Cherberg was lieutenant governor and presided over the Senate Rules Committee in 1989, he announced that if a bill is defeated twice in Rules it would be sent back to the committee from whence it came. During the 1970s, the House Rules Committee required the chair of the committee referring the bill to attend meetings and personally present bills from the committee.

The Rules Committees of the House and Senate traditionally served as a fine screen which sifted out many bills. In recent years, however, the mesh of the screen has gotten wider so fewer bills die in Rules. But not all the power is gone. Committee chairs must still go begging to Rules members to pull their bills to the floor. The Rules Committee continues to be a highly regarded appointment.

It is interesting to contrast our Rules Committees with that of the United

States House of Representatives. In Congress, each bill gets its own "rule." The rule determines the number of hours allotted for debate, the scope of amendments, and other vital matters, making the congressional Rules Committee extremely powerful. The Rules Committees in our Legislature are limited to the single question of whether the bill moves on.

FLOOR CONSIDERATION OF OWN-HOUSE BILLS

The timing and schedule of the two legislative bodies suddenly changes at the session midway point, following the cutoff for committee consideration of own-house bills. Instead of going from one committee meeting to another in the Cherberg or the O'Brien buildings, members remain in the Legislative Building, spending long hours on the floor working bills or in caucus going over bills about to be considered on the floor. This phase of session lasts about a week in a short session and ten days in a long session. There are periodic Rules Committee meetings to keep the floor calendars filled.

Second reading on the floor is the first opportunity the full body has to examine a bill and to offer amendments. A bill is called for consideration when the presiding officer announces the bill number and the title. The committee chair, who is generally floor manager for bills signed out of his or her committee, rises to be recognized. The chair then moves the committee amendments or the substitute bill. House rules provide that amendments adopted by the committee and recommended to the full body are considered first (HR 11(D)). This is also the usual Senate practice. Then the bill is fair game for the rest of the body to offer amendments. These are called **floor amendments.** The House requires that they be in writing, and given to the Chief Clerk for distribution to the members, and read to the body, although this latter provision is usually waived (HR 10(B)). Senate rules are a little more general, requiring only that amendments be sent to the Secretary's desk in writing and read by the Secretary (SR 64), but the practice is similar to that of the House.

When a committee has adopted several amendments to a bill, it is the usual practice to "roll the amendments into a substitute bill."

The Rules Committee places the original bill, not the substitute, on the second reading calendar. The substitute is actually a new bill that has its introduction and first reading when the motion to substitute for the original bill is made on the floor (SR 45(9) and HR 10(C)). The wording of the motion is "that Substitute Senate/House Bill No. 0000 be substituted for Senate/House Bill No. 0000 and that Substitute Senate/House Bill No. 0000 be placed on today's second reading calendar." Floor amendments are then offered to the substitute bill. No title amendment is needed on a substitute bill.

When there are no more amendments to a bill, the presiding officer declares that the bill has passed its second reading. Under the rules no vote is taken (SR 64, HR 10(B)) at this point since the purpose of second reading is merely to consider amendments. The bill is returned to the Rules Committee. However, it has become the common practice in both bodies to **"bump"** a bill; that is, suspend the rules and move the bill immediately to third reading without returning it to the Rules Committee. The motion for this is "that the rules be suspended, that Senate/House Bill No. 0000 be advanced to third reading, the second reading considered the third, and that the bill be placed on final passage." The bill is now ready for debate and a vote on final passage.

THE RULES OF DEBATE AND VOTING

The rules of debate in the two bodies are similar, fairly structured, and limited, with the clear overall intent to keep arguments to the specific issues at hand and away from personalities. Here are some of the key points:

- A member is to rise, wait to be recognized by the presiding officer, address the chair, speak to the question, and avoid personalities.
- No member should impeach the motives of another member.
- A member may not speak more than twice on one question in the same day.
- The member who presents the motion may open and close debate.
- The presiding officer decides who may speak and decides points of order, subject to appeal to the full body.
- Members may rise on a point of personal privilege to explain a personal matter unique and peculiar to the member. This is not to be used for a discussion of pending matters or for introducing guests.
- Only the presiding officer introduces and recognizes guests and visitors.

Before a vote is taken, the presiding officer must **"put the question;"** that is, inform the body what it is about to vote on. For example, the Speaker might say, "The question before the House is the adoption of amendment number 45 to House Bill 1001. As many as are in favor say 'Aye' [pause]. As many as are opposed say 'No.'" Just prior to a vote, floor leaders from the two sides will move to excuse absent members by name, so their absences are noted in the Journal as excused. If not excused, a member is listed as "absent." Members who are present are not allowed to abstain or sit silently without permission of the body. All members in the chamber must vote (HR 19(B) and SR 22(1)).

Any member who has a private interest in a measure before the Legislature is required by the state Constitution to disclose the fact to the body and refrain from voting (Article II, Section 30, HR 19(D) and SR 22(1)). Generally, a **private interest** refers to a benefit unique to an individual member as opposed to a benefit to a class of people to which a member may belong. For example, a teacher-member may vote on teachers' salaries because the member is part of the class of teachers, all of whom will benefit. The private interest question came up during the 1996 session regarding a lawyer-legislator who sent a letter to clients of his law firm offering to be helpful in the Legislature. The Legislative Ethics Board reprimanded him because, among other things, the offer could be construed as indicating a willingness to sell his vote or provide assistance to clients for payment, potentially a violation of the private interest provision. The Legislative Ethics Board is likely to be dealing with this again because Washington State has a part-time citizen Legislature made up largely of individuals working at various jobs and professions which on occasion may touch on legislative issues.

Voting in the Senate is usually done first by **voice vote** where members sound off aye or no; then by **division,** where members are asked to stand; then by **roll call,** where each member is called alphabetically and answers aye or no. Senators must be in the chamber to vote. One-sixth of the members present may demand a roll call following a voice or **standing vote.** Once begun, a roll call may not be interrupted except for a call of the Senate (SR 22), explained below, and not at all in the House (HR 19(E)). When there is a **tie vote** in the Senate, the lieutenant governor casts the deciding vote, except on final passage of a measure (SR 1(9)) which takes the approval of a **constitutional majority** of the members; that is, a majority of members elected to the body. In the event of a tie vote on final passage in the Senate or on any matter in the House, the motion or bill fails (HR 19(G), SR 22(5)).

The House has had **electronic voting** since 1961. This allows members to vote by flipping a switch at their desks: green (up) for aye and red (down) for no. The Speaker warns members when the machine is about to be locked, and when the machine has been locked, before the clerk announces the result. House rules still permit voice vote and division. An oral roll call may also be demanded by one-sixth of the members

(HR 19(F)).

The Senate has thus far declined to install an electronic voting mechanism. Votes on final passage or when demanded otherwise still require that at the direction of the President, the clerk reads each member's name once, then the President watches the wings for those members who arrive late and indicates their vote. It is a slow process, repeated hundreds of times each session.

A **call of the Senate**, which essentially compels members to be present unless excused by the body, may be demanded by three members of the Senate or, for a **call of the House**, one-sixth of the members in the House. The body then votes on the demand for the call. If it is sustained, an oral roll call is taken to determine that all members are either present or excused. The sergeant at arms is instructed to lock the doors of the chamber and to "take into custody" any unexcused members. Members are confined to the chamber (including the cafeteria and offices off the wings) while **under the call**. When all the members are either present or excused, a motion is made to **proceed under the call** and members go back to work on bills on the calendar (SR 24, HR 21). Members cannot leave the chambers until the call is removed.

The purpose of a call is to force members' attendance on the floor because they are needed to pass a bill or adopt an amendment. It is considered an extreme measure and used infrequently, sometimes not at all during a session. Prior to the 1980s it was used quite often. At times it has been employed to force reluctant members back who were boycotting a vote on a tough issue, to force members to return who had gone home or off on a trip, or even to embarrass members who had no good excuse for being absent. It is primarily a tool of the majority since it requires a majority to impose it. However, since it requires only a majority of members present to impose a call, it can be a constant worry for the leadership of a one-vote majority that on any given day when two of their members are absent, they can lose control to the minority.

The final votes have been counted and the long battle over a controversial bill is finally over. Or is it? On important measures that pass or fail by a close vote, after the result is announced, a member may rise and give notice of **reconsideration**. The motion can only be made by someone who voted on the prevailing side, must be made on the same day as the vote, and before the body has transmitted the bill to the other house (SR 37, HR 20). Thus, leaders from both sides will be counting carefully in the Senate or watching the electronic board intently in the House on close votes. They must be quick. After the vote is announced but before the presiding officer bangs the gavel and declares the measure passed or failed, a member may rise and change his or her vote in order to have voted on the prevailing side and thus be eligible to give notice of reconsideration. Notice the phraseology: one gives notice of reconsideration to the body. There is no motion and no vote on the notice.

Up to the last ten days of a regular session in the Senate and up to the last five days in the House, reconsideration of a vote on final passage would be taken up on the next day of session. During the last ten (or five) days, reconsideration can take place at any time during the same day. Reconsideration of the vote on an amendment is done immediately.

Reconsideration of a vote is done by motion, a motion so privileged it takes precedence over all but a motion to adjourn. The motion is to "reconsider the vote by which Senate Bill 5000 failed (or passed)" or to "reconsider the vote by which amendment number 293 passed (or failed)." If the motion is adopted by a majority of the members present, another vote is taken. If the motion to reconsider fails, it cannot be made again.

Obviously, reconsideration is employed when the losing side believes it has a chance to persuade a member to change his or her vote. Or it can be used to gain time to negotiate further. Sometimes, after notice of reconsideration is given and talks held, a bill will be bumped back to second reading for purposes of an amendment to accomplish the agreement. And sometimes, the vote is taken again with the same result and the matter is ended.

Here is a snippet from the *Senate Journal* on March 8, 1945 (pp. 872-873), to illustrate some points about reconsideration:

Senator Bargreen stated that the bill had passed the Senate and he inquired as to the effect of a vote to reconsider.

The President announced that if the motion to reconsider carried, the bill would be before the Senate the same as any other bill.

About three-fourths of own-house bills passed by standing committees to Rules before the first cutoff are approved by the full body before the second cutoff, the one for consideration of own-house bills (see Fig. 5.1 and Fig. 5.2). Looking at the numbers another way, about half of all bills introduced before and during a legislative session are passed by one house.

Unlike the other cutoffs which merely specify dates, the second cutoff for floor consideration of own-house bills has a time certain, 5:00 P.M. But the legislative process is nothing if not flexible and so this hard deadline gives rise to the **"special order of business"** in the Senate (SR 18). As the session nears the 5:00 P.M. deadline, the majority floor leader will typically move that a certain bill be made a special order of business at 4:55 P.M. When that time arrives, the body will interrupt the work in progress to take up the special order, then return to the interrupted work. Thus, the 5:00 P.M. deadline is not so hard as it seems. There is no specific provision in House rules for a special order of business, but since the majority party's leader presides, the Speaker could presumably rule in such a way as to accomplish the same result.

COMMITTEE CONSIDERATION OF OPPOSITE-HOUSE BILLS

Following the cutoff for floor consideration of own-house bills, action moves back to committees for consideration of the bills passed by the opposite house. This occurs at about the sixty-seventh day of a 105-day session and the thirty-eighth day of a sixty-day session. Members then spend ten days to two weeks back in committees hearing the bills that passed the opposite house.

Persons trying to follow legislation in the committees need to pay particular attention at this point in the session. Committees are required to submit their agendas for printing in the weekly schedule a week or more ahead of time. But they have limited knowledge of which opposite-house bills will pass, so schedules are tentative at best. The daily schedule is posted each morning and is more current. One can also call directly to a committee to determine when particular bills will be heard.

Less than half of all the bills introduced have made it this far in the process, have passed their house of origin (see again Fig. 5.1 and Fig. 5.2 on p. 58).

One of the first things committees chairs must do is to figure out which opposite-house bills had companion measures or similar bills that have already passed the house of origin. House and Senate chairs may meet to discuss which committee, House or Senate, will handle which bills. Effective committee chairs meet regularly throughout the session with their opposite-house counterparts to discuss mechanics and, in the best of circumstances, substance, in order to avoid duplication.

Committee procedures when hearing opposite-house bills are the same as for hearing own-house bills with one major difference. Since a member or a committee of one body cannot introduce a bill in another body, substitute bills are not possible. Remember that substitute bills are essentially new bills. Amendments, however, are allowed to opposite-house bills. So, instead of rolling amendments into a substitute bill as was done with own-house bills, committees may roll the amendments adopted into one big **"striking amendment."** This device gets its name from its first eight words: "Strike everything after the enacting clause and insert...." The striking amendment serves the same purpose as a substitute bill. And, just as with substitute bills, a member (often at the prodding of the committee chair) will move in committee to adopt the striker immediately upon conclusion of consideration of the amendments.

This period for hearing opposite-house bills provides some of the more entertaining testimony when opposite-house committee chairs come to plead for their bills. Committee chairs have presided over hearings and committee action on their bills, then shepherded them through Rules and second and third reading on the floor. Chairs were always in charge of bills sent to their committees. Not now. Now they must enter an unfamiliar building, sit in a strange hearing room, wait to be called to testify and then humbly plead for their bills. Of course, they are still in a superior position back in their own committee rooms, but this is the first time for many chairs to see how it feels to be testifying before a committee. These pleas even have a familiar ring: that the bill has been carefully crafted and the amendments strike a delicate balance among the various interests so any changes the opposite-house committee might make would probably doom the entire bill. The response is also familiar, which is to be gracious, listen politely, then completely change the bill.

One other significant thing usually happens during this period of session, so significant in fact that all else pales by comparison. The operating budget makes its first appearance. There will be several sections later in this book just on the budgets, but the appearance of the operating budget, even if only in outline form at competing House/Senate press conferences, reduces all other bills to secondary status.

FLOOR CONSIDERATION OF OPPOSITE-HOUSE BILLS

With just ten days left in a short session, twenty in a long, the cutoff for committee consideration of opposite-house bills arrives. Members move back to the floor, aware that time is getting short and there is much left to do, still clinging to the hope of finishing on time. They will use much of the remaining time on the floor considering opposite-house bills passed by committees, some of it in caucus and some in the Rules Committee.

Committees have winnowed the numbers substantially by now, so only about one quarter of the bills originally introduced are still alive. By the end of the period for floor consideration of opposite-house bills, the number will be further reduced to about 20 percent of those introduced. Typically, about 25 percent of opposite-house bills die in opposite-house committees; another 5 to 10 percent die in Rules or on the calendar.

This is often the point in session where anger and frustration on the part of sponsors break out openly as they see their bills wounded or killed by opposite-house chairs and committees. It was described earlier about committee chairs pleading for their bills before the opposite-house committees, often to no avail. There will usually be a story in one of the newspapers of a committee chair accusing an opposite-house chair of duplicity, nefariousness or downright stupidity for not recognizing the worth of the bills delivered. There is no more reason to "be nice" to opposite-house chairs because they have done whatever they intended to do.

As this deadline nears, there is sometimes a last-ditch effort by someone, usually in the minority, to salvage a bill that failed to get out of a standing committee. Under both Senate and House rules, a simple majority of members elected may **relieve a committee of further consideration** of a bill and pull it directly to the floor (SR 48, HR 24(D)(2)). This would be proper during the ninth order of business in the Senate and the eighth order in the House, so a member must play his or her cards close to the vest and pounce at just the right moment. The **order of business** refers to the order in which daily business is conducted in a body. In the House, the first order is the roll call, presentation of colors, prayer, and approval of the journal of the preceding day; second comes the introduction of visiting dignitaries; third is messages from the governor, the other body, and other state officials; fourth is introduction and first reading of bills; fifth is committee reports; sixth is second reading of bills; seventh is third reading; eighth is floor resolutions and motions (here is where a member may attempt to pull a bill from committee); ninth is petitions and memorials addressed to the body; tenth is introduction of visitors; and eleventh is announcements. The presiding officer announces which order the body is on and moves quickly from one to another.

It is difficult to get a majority of members on the floor to pull a bill because it's considered a "procedural" motion, and no matter how popular the bill, members of the majority party don't want to cross their own leadership, a committee chair from their party and their party caucus. Pulling a bill is probably the harshest action a member can take against a committee chair of the same party.

The deadline for floor action is usually a specific time, normally 5:00 P.M. Sounds like a hard deadline, but this is where the special order of business provision is used. In 1996, for example, on the day of this cutoff, Senate Majority Leader Sid Snyder (D-Long Beach) moved at about 4:30 P.M. to make HB 2343 (the transportation budget, second biggest bill of the session) a special order of business for 4:55 P.M. At 4:55 P.M. the Senate had already begun consideration of another bill. Senator Snyder moved to defer further consideration and take up the special order of business, after which the Senate returned to the original bill. Thus, two bills were actually considered after the cutoff.

CALENDARS

Calendars give notice of the status and priority of measures pending before the body. They proliferate in the last couple weeks of session when so many things are going on simultaneously. Following are the types of calendars one is likely to find during the last couple of weeks of a session.

We have already mentioned the **second reading calendar**, which is a list of the bills passed by the Rules Committee to the floor, eligible for amendment; and the **third reading calendar**, which is a list of bills awaiting final debate and vote.

In addition there may be a **consent calendar** in the Senate. To make this calendar, a bill must have passed committee with no known contro- versy, be easily understood, have no amendments pending or expected, and have no known opposition. It is created in the Rules Committee. The 1996 Senate Rules also provided that any member, with the support of three other members, may strike a bill from the consent calendar, in which case it takes its place at the bottom of the regular second reading calendar.

Related to the Senate consent calendar is the House **suspension calendar.** It is created by the majority party in Rules with the consent of at least two members of the minority. Bills on this calendar are not subject to amendment except for a committee amendment or substitution. The only question on second reading of a bill on the suspension calendar is whether to adopt the committee recommendations and advance the bill to third reading. If the question does not receive the support of two-thirds of the members present, the bill is returned to Rules.

Consent and suspension calendars usually make their first appearance about one month into session. They are typically made up when a staff attorney is instructed to put together a list of bills in Rules that were signed out of committees unanimously and have no known opposition. The list is circulated in both caucuses and any member may strike any bill from the list. Bills remaining on the list are moved out of Rules and onto the second reading floor calendar in one motion. If a floor amendment is subsequently offered to any bill on the consent calendar, it may be moved to the regular second reading calendar.

In addition to these calendars, in the final two weeks or so there will be a **concurrence calendar**, which is a list of own-house bills that were amended by the opposite house and returned for possible concurrence in the amendments; a **dispute calendar**, which is a list of bills amended by one body, where the second body refuses to concur in the amendments, and asks the first body to recede (the dispute and concurrence calendars were combined in the House in 1996); a **conference calendar**, which lists bills to which both bodies have appointed conferees to discuss differences and seek a resolution; and a **gubernatorial appointments calendar** in the Senate which lists persons appointed by the governor to positions requiring Senate confirmation, where a committee has acted and made a recommendation. This last calendar is made up by the Rules Committee, but the concurring, dispute, and conference calendars are made up of bills that have long since passed Rules and are in the process of resolution by the entire bodies.

DISPUTES AND CONFERENCES

A bill cannot become a law until it is passed in identical form by a majority of the members elected to each house of the Legislature (Washington Constitution, Article II, Section 22). Since most bills are changed by one or both bodies, it is necessary to have a process to facilitate working out these differences. The procedure for settling disputes may be found in a body's rules, the Joint Rules, or *Reed's Parliamentary Rules* (both bodies defer to Reed's for points not covered in their own rules).

There are five motions relating to disagreements which can be illustrated with a fictional bill. The Senate passes SB 5000 and transmits it to the House. The House adds an amendment to SB 5000 and returns it to the Senate. The highest ranking motion in the Senate is to **concur** in the amendment, pass the bill as amended, and send it to the governor. The contrary motion is to **not concur** in the Senate and return the bill to the House. If both motions are made, the positive motion to concur is put to the body. If the House once again passes SB 5000 with the amendment, the highest ranking motion in the Senate is to **recede** from its opposition to the amendment to SB 5000, or, on the contrary, to **insist** on its position and once again ask the House to pass SB 5000 as passed the Senate. If either body wants to let the other know that it is determined not to back off its position either for or against the amendment, the proper motion is to **adhere** to its position and ask the other body to recede. If both bodies adopt motions to adhere to their positions, the bill is lost unless one of them asks for a conference (Reed's Rules 245-253). At any point in the process either body while in possession of the bill can ask the other for a conference committee on the bill and its amendment.

In the really old days—before Washington State was a gleam in a fur trader's eye—conference committees negotiated by paper only. The purpose of conference committees was to determine a body's thinking behind the differences in a bill, the reasons for coming to different conclusions. So the conferees from the body asking for a conference on a bill (usually the body which passed the original bill) would prepare a written statement explaining its reasons for disagreeing with the proposed changes. This statement would be laid before the second body. If it proved satisfactory, the second body would relent in its proposed changes and agree to the original bill. If not, the conference committee of the second body would prepare a written statement of its reasons for continuing disagreement over the changes. That would end the duties of the conference committee. If the dispute continued further, one of the bodies would ask for a **free conference** committee. Notice that discussion in the conference committee is limited to the specific amendments or changes one body made to the other's bill (Reed's Rule 241 et. seq.). Once the powers of free conference are granted, however, the conferees can literally rewrite the entire bill (provided they stay within the scope and object of the original bill).

During the 1993-1994 sessions of the Legislature, the term "free conference" was eliminated altogether and the definition of conference committees expanded to include what previously was free conference. That was also the practice during the 1995-96 sessions. It is the most efficient method and is likely to be the usual practice in the future.

A copy of a conference committee report from the 1996 legislative session is shown on the next page. Notice that the conferees dumped all previous amendments to the bill and rewrote the entire bill in the form of a striking amendment. Under the old rules they would certainly have needed the powers of free conference to do this.

Whichever house is in possession of a bill in dispute may ask for a conference when there is a disagreement as to amendments. This is done in the form of a message to the other body asking for a conference and naming the conferees appointed. The other body would normally agree to the request and announce its conferees at that time, also in the form of a message. Three conferees are appointed from each body. They are supposed to represent the two sides in the dispute. In practice that almost always means two members from the majority party and one from the minority party (Reed's Rule 240).

```
                                                      SENATE ROSTRUM
        ********************************************************
                *    REPORT OF CONFERENCE COMMITTEE   *
        ********************************************************

HB 2490                                              March 5, 1996

Prepared by:  David Cheal (7576)        Includes "NEW ITEM":   YES

        Providing for credit for reinsurance of trust fund maintained
    that meets national association of insurance commissioners standards.

MR. PRESIDENT:
MR. SPEAKER:

        We of your CONFERENCE COMMITTEE, to whom was referred HOUSE BILL
    NO. 2490, Reimbursement of credit risks, have had the same under
    consideration and we recommend that:

        All previous amendments not be adopted; and

        That the striking amendment(s) by the Conference Committee (see
        attached 2490 AMC CONF S5832.1) be adopted,

    and that the bill do pass as recommended by the Conference Committee.
    ==================================================================


    _____        _____
    Senator Prentice                        Representative L. Thomas


    _____        _____
    Senator Hale                            Representative Smith


    _____        _____
    Senator Fraser                          Representative Wolfe
```

In the past, conference committees would often meet privately behind closed doors. The rationale was that this facilitated deal-making and compromise, which is more difficult with lobbyists and the public watching. There was an agreement, however, that during the 1995-96 sessions all conference committees would take place in public. In addition, many of the conferences on major subjects such as the budget and welfare reform are now televised live by TVW.

A majority of members from each body must sign the conference committee report in order to reach agreement (Reed's Rule 244). This is not always the case. At various times in the past, the Joint Rules have required a total of four or five or even all of the conferees to sign the final report. Here, for example, is a brief ruling from the *Senate Journal,* March 8, 1945, p. 865:

> In a case where a conference committee can agree, there must be a unanimous report, and in a case where they cannot agree, they may come in and a new committee would have to be appointed.

The Conference Committee Report goes first to the opposite-house—that is, House bills to the Senate and Senate bills to the House. No amendments are allowed to the conference report or to the bill reported by the conference committee. The procedure is to first adopt the report of the conference committee, then vote up or down on final passage of the bill as reported out of the conference committee.

Conference committees are tricky, can be difficult to follow even when open to the public, and are fraught with danger for proponents of a bill. Anything that fits within the scope and object of the bill under consideration can be added under the rules for free conference. One former senator used to boast about the number of bills that had died under the cutoffs but that he was able to resurrect by adding to a conference committee report. It is just these efforts that give rise to a plethora of scope and object objections during the last few days of every regular session. Amendments to a bill must be germane to the subject matter of the original bill or else they fall outside the scope and object. When bills die as a result of the various cutoffs, sponsors will often have the bills redrafted in the form of amendments. They will then try to attach these amendments in conference or on second reading to a likely "host" bill; that is, a bill with a title able to embrace the proposed amendment.

Conference committee procedures are usually governed by the joint rules adopted by the two bodies in the first few days of the first session of the biennium. However, no joint rules were adopted by the Legislature during the 1995 or 1996 sessions. Instead the two bodies relied on their own house rules, *Reed's Parliamentary Rules* (HR 29, SR 40), which apply when nothing else does, and a sort of general agreement as to how things have always worked.

THE LAST WEEK

The last few days of session are hectic and is often a time when a procedural problem will arise which threatens to derail legislators' efforts to get their work done. For example, what if there is a need to take up a substantive bill not already in dispute and the final cutoff for consideration of bills from either house has passed? The first suggestion might be to amend the cutoff resolution to exempt the bill. But wait, cutoffs are concurrent resolutions which are filed with the secretary of state after passage and thus not in the possession of either body and thus cannot be amended. Not so easy. These are the type of knots that tie up a body at the end of every session.

With less than four days remaining in the 1996 Regular Session, Senate Democrats thought it might help to break the budget impasse if they could pass a new budget bill, different from the one then in dispute in the conference committee—sort of like sending a new offer to the House by mail. This posed two problems: since the budget document was in the possession of the conference committee and not before the Senate, they couldn't amend it. They would need to find another bill able to carry the new budget offer. Secondly, how could they get around the cutoff since they were in the last ten days of the session and didn't think they could get two-thirds of the body to agree to a new bill. Whatever they did they would need to do with a bare majority.

The solution was to take a title-only bill that was introduced in 1995 and was still in the Ways and Means Committee (bills introduced in the first session of a two-year Legislature are alive for all succeeding sessions). Leaders called a quick Ways and Means Committee meeting to amend the new budget proposal onto the title-only bill and pass it out. Senate Republicans saw no harm in moving negotiations along, so they permitted the bill to go directly to the floor. But there was a second problem in that the cutoff for consideration of own-house bills had passed. So Majority Leader Sid Snyder (a master parliamentarian by virtue of his many years as Secretary of the Senate) moved passage of a new concurrent resolution, SCR 8431, which said simply that SSB 6069, the amended title-only bill, was exempt from the cutoff dates established in the earlier resolution. First the new concurrent resolution was approved, then the amended bill was passed and both were immediately transmitted to the House. It took about half a day.

Normally, members of the House are allowed to speak on any issue for up to ten minutes. During the last five days of session, and during the three days preceding any cutoff, no member may speak more than three minutes without the consent of the body, except for the maker of the motion or chair of the committee who may close debate (HR 16). Senate rules are not as specific on this point, but in the waning days the floor leader will typically move to limit speeches to three minutes, one speech per member on any bill, except the maker of the motion who may open and close debate, and to prohibit any member from yielding time to another (SR 29). The motion is subject to approval by a majority of members present.

6

The Budgets

Passing the state budget is not only the most important action of the Legislature—it is the one thing the state Legislature must do itself.

> No moneys shall ever be paid out of the treasury of this state, or any of its funds, or any of the funds under its management, except in pursuance of an appropriation by law; nor unless such payment be made within one calendar month after the end of the next ensuing fiscal biennium, and every such law making a new appropriation, or continuing or reviving an appropriation, shall distinctly specify the sum appropriated, and the object to which it is to be applied, and it shall not be sufficient for such law to refer to any other law to fix such sum. (Washington Constitution, Article VIII, Section 4)

In 1981 and 1982 the Legislature met in two regular sessions and four special sessions to cope with a severe economic recession. Revenue from the sales tax and the timber tax fell with each new tax collection. The Legislature made deep cuts in programs and increased taxes to comply with the state requirement for a balanced budget (RCW 43.88) but each quarter the picture worsened. Finally, in July 1982, the Legislature passed SB 5033 which essentially told Governor John Spellman that if things continued to worsen he had the authority to make whatever additional cuts were needed to balance the budget.

Senator Phil Talmadge (D-Seattle) sued the Legislature on the ground that this was an unconstitutional delegation of the legislative powers to the executive (see Article VIII, Section 4, quoted above). Talmadge won a clear victory three months later in Thurston County Superior Court with the judge incorporating his brief in the court's opinion. The decision was so one-sided that the attorney general's office, representing the Legislature, did not bother to appeal. Of one thing there is no doubt: the Legislature itself must set state spending and write the budget.

The term "state budget" generally means the biennial state operating budget which, for 1995-97, is a plan for spending about $19.6 billion from the state's general fund. That is more than double the amount spent just a decade earlier. Before discussing the budget process itself, however, here is a brief overview of where the money comes from and where it goes.

WHERE THE MONEY COMES FROM

One of the most difficult but important jobs in state government is that of forecasting the state economy and the amount of revenue the state will receive. This duty falls to the supervisor of the state **Economic and Revenue Forecast Council** (Forecast Council). The forecaster gathers information from various public and private sources as well as his or her own computer forecasting models and reports to the council (representatives from the governor and the four political caucuses) and others. The forecaster is required by statute to give forecasts on November 20, February 20, March 20, and in odd-numbered years, on June 20 and September 20 as well. The forecaster gives an official revenue forecast as well as optimistic and pessimistic ones (RCW 82.33). These forecasts form the basis for the biennial operating budget and for the supplemental budget.

The state economy is inextricably linked to such variables as interest rates set by the Federal Reserve, the value of the dollar against other currencies, federal spending determined by the President and Congress, and a host of regional factors such as the sale of airplanes to China and software to Japan. The forecast as to what the economy will be like in two or four or six years is necessarily an educated guess and bound to be wrong at times. In 1981-82, for example, the state took in almost 20 percent less revenue than was forecast. In the 1989-1991 biennium, the November revenue forecast was nearly 12 percent lower than the final actual collections. However, for the last three bienniums, there has been less than a 2 percent difference between the November forecast and the amount actually collected, accounting for legislative changes (see Fig. 6.1).

The **general fund** is the repository for most of the money the state takes in for operations. The state gets money from the following sources, listed in order of importance.

State Retail Sales Tax. This is the tax added to the retail price of most articles (excluding items of food and medicine) and some services such as construction, repair, telephone, and some recreation and amusement services. The state tax rate is 6.5 percent.

Business and Occupation (B&O) Tax. This tax is a percentage of the gross receipts of business activity conducted in the state. There are 26 separate categories and 13 rates, including manufacturing, wholesaling, and extracting (.506 percent), retailing (.471 percent); business services (2.5 percent); and financial services (1.7 percent).

State Property Tax. This is an annual tax on the market value of real property as determined by county assessors. The total state and local rate is limited to $10 per $1,000 of assessed value unless more is specifically approved by the voters.

Motor Vehicle Excise Tax (MVET). This is an annual tax of 2.2 percent of the value of motor vehicles, based on the Manufacturer's Suggested Retail Price.

Use Tax. This tax is generally applied to purchases of tangible personal property made outside the state. The rate is 6.5 percent of the selling price.

Real Estate Excise Tax (REET). This is a 1.28 percent tax applied to the selling price of real property.

Public Utility Tax. This is a gross receipts tax on public utilities such as electric, water, gas, garbage, and transportation businesses. There are four separate rates but most utilities pay 3.852 percent.

Other taxes are levied on such things as tobacco and liquor. (See Fig. 6.2 for the percentage of each tax.)

These various taxes brought almost $18 billion to the state's general fund during the 1995-97 biennium.

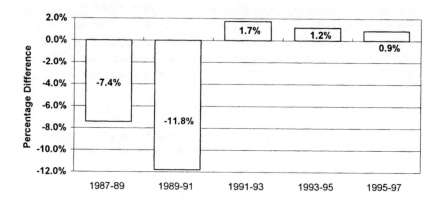

Fig. 6.1. Revenue Forecast History Adjusted
for Legislative Changes: 1987-1997

Initiative 601 (I 601), whose spending limits are discussed below, added Washington to the growing list of states that require a supermajority vote in order to raise taxes. There are now twelve states, mostly in the west and south, that require from three-fifths (Delaware, Florida, Mississippi and Oregon) to three-fourths (Arkansas and Oklahoma) approval by legislators to raise taxes. Six states, including Washington, require two-thirds of the members of both houses to vote for tax increases (Arizona, California, Colorado, Louisiana, and South Dakota). Six of the states, including Washington with the passage of Initiative 601, adopted the supermajority requirements by initiative. A 1996 article in *State Legislatures* magazine expresses the view that the spread of supermajority requirements is probably limited to the states, mostly in the west, with the voter initiative process.

Washington's tax restrictions are even tougher than the other supermajority states. Any tax-raising action by the Legislature which would have the effect of exceeding the overall spending limit established under I 601 not only requires two-thirds approval by the Legislature, but also by a majority of the voters. The only exception to this is if the governor declares an emergency, in which case taxes and expenditures could be approved as before but without a vote by the people.

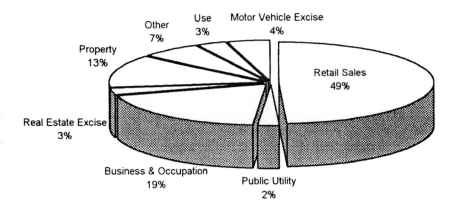

Fig. 6.2. Sources of Revenue in the General Fund: 1995-1997

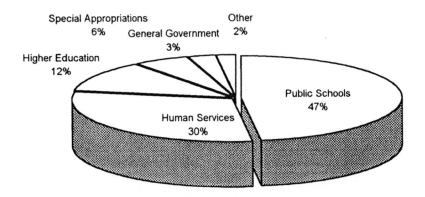

Fig. 6.3. Where the General Funds Go

INITIATIVE 601

Initiative 601 was approved by the voters (51 percent) on November 2, 1993. It limits state expenditures, taxes and fees. A few of the tax provisions went into effect immediately; the rest took effect July 1, 1995.

Initiative 601 establishes a state spending limit and prohibits the state treasurer from issuing or redeeming a check, warrant or voucher that would result in spending over that limit. The annual increase in state spending is limited to the average growth in inflation and population over a three-year period. Any revenue collected in excess of that spending limit goes into an emergency reserve fund which can only be spent with approval of two-thirds of the members of each house of the Legislature. Once the emergency reserve fund exceeds 5 percent of biennial general fund revenues, the excess is transferred to an education construction account. Funds from that account must be spent for school construction, except by a two-thirds vote of the legislators in each house and approval by the people in the next general election.

The ability of state agencies to raise fees comes under the same formula that applies to increases in general fund expenditures. Local governments must be reimbursed by the Legislature for the costs of any new programs imposed on them. And, state and local governments are prohibited from expanding current state taxes to intangible assets that are not now taxed such as stocks, bonds and bank accounts.

Opponents of Initiative 601 went to court shortly after passage and sought a writ of mandamus to prevent the state from implementing it on the grounds that it was unconstitutional. The Supreme Court dismissed the action in August 1994, in a 7-2 decision. The majority said the lawsuit was premature because most of the initiative had not yet taken effect and there were no injured parties. The court left open the door to a challenge, based on the argument that the initiative changes the state Constitution, once there are plaintiffs that can show they have been directly harmed.

Initiative 601 continues to be controversial. In an article for the Tacoma *News Tribune* on May 26, 1996, Peter Callaghan describes the reactions of gubernatorial candidates to the I 601 restrictions. Democratic candidates Jay Inslee, Gary Locke and Nita Rinehart support amendments to I 601 to allow for faster growth. Republican candidates Norm Maleng, Pam Roach, Dale Foreman and Ellen Craswell oppose any changes. For the present, despite its uncertain constitutional and political basis, Initiative 601 is the law in Washington State and legislators must follow its provisions in writing biennial budgets.

WHERE THE MONEY GOES

The chief recipients of money from the state's general fund are public schools, human services, higher education, special appropriations, and general government (see Fig. 6.3).

Funding for the state's public kindergarten through high schools takes nearly half the state budget. The main components of this funding are:

- General Apportionment accounts for more than three-fourths of state funds for K-12. Funds are provided to school districts by a formula based primarily on the ratio of students to staff. The money pays for certificated administrators and instructional staff, classified staff (secretaries, custodians, aides, etc.) and non-employee related costs (books, supplies, equipment, energy costs, etc.)
- Special Education accounts for about 11 percent of the public schools budget. There are fourteen separate disability categories, including physical, medical, and behavioral.
- Pupil Transportation for students who live more than one mile from school or who have hazardous walking conditions takes about 5 percent of the money.
- Other public education funding goes to levy equalization, bilingual education, block grants (money provided to districts on a dollar per student basis without restrictions), and to fund education reform (several programs including planning/resource days, readiness-to-learn grants, improved technology, and mentor/beginning teacher grants).

The second largest recipient of general fund money is human services, accounting for about 30 percent of the total. The state Department of Social and Health Services (DSHS) is the umbrella organization responsible for coordinating a wide range of programs and receives about three-fourths of the nearly $5 billion spent. Over 60 percent of this money is paid to contractors, vendors and local governments for services. DSHS is divided into twelve separate "programs." The largest programs in order of general fund money received are:

- Medical Assistance, which administers the federal Medicaid (low-income) and Medicare (elderly) programs and other state and federal medical programs for low-income persons. These programs disburse more than $3 billion per biennium in Washington State, about a third of which comes from the state general fund.
- Economic Services is the second largest program in DSHS, spending over $2 billion, about half from the state general fund. Services include

Aid to Families with Dependent Children, emergency cash assistance to low-income families or pregnant women, food stamps, general cash grants for low-income women in early stages of pregnancy, cash grants for food, shelter and clothing for indigent adults prevented from working, assistance in job search, training, transportation and child care, and the state and federal cash assistance to indigent people who are permanently disabled, blind or aged.

- Long Term Care is the third largest program. It subsidizes nursing home care for low- and middle-income persons as well as providing help for the aged and disabled in their own homes. About half of the roughly $1.4 billion spent in this state comes from the state general fund.
- Mental Health Division of DSHS provides funds to counties which contract for community services for the mentally ill and runs five state residential treatment facilities. It spends about three-quarters of a billion dollars, half from the general fund.
- Division of Developmental Disabilities of DSHS provides services to children and adults who have mental retardation, cerebral palsy, or related developmental disabilities. It operates five state facilities for 1,300 persons and provides various other services to another 19,000. The budget is about $640 million, half from the general fund.
- Children and Family Services provides in-home services to resolve family conflicts, out-of-home services to protect children from neglect or abuse at home by placing them in foster family or group homes, and day care assistance. It costs about half a billion dollars, about 60 percent from the state general fund.

Other services provided by DSHS include juvenile rehabilitation, alcohol/substance abuse programs, vocational rehabilitation, and child support collections.

Human services, other than DSHS, include the Department of Corrections, which runs thirteen institutions and manages a variety of community-based programs like work release and victim/witness notification; the Department of Veterans Affairs; the Department of Health (public health programs); the Department of Labor and Industries; and the Department of Employment Security.

The third largest recipient of state funding at about 12 percent of the general fund is higher education. This includes twenty-seven community colleges, five technical colleges, one state college, three regional universities, two state universities, and four state-level agencies. There are roughly 200,000 students in the state's higher education facilities and about 20,000 staff, including faculty.

A category called "Special Appropriations" accounts for about 6 percent of the 1995-97 operating budget. It includes contributions to the state retirement system and cost-of-living salary adjustments given to all state employees, and costs of bond retirement and interest.

General Government takes about 3 percent of the state's general fund. It includes the Legislature, the courts, secretary of state, attorney general, Department of General Administration, Department of Personnel, Department of Information Services, and Office of Financial Management.

THE OPERATING BUDGET

The state **operating budget** is a two-year plan for funding all state activities except for construction and transportation. It is adopted in odd-numbered years to begin July 1 and end June 30 two years later. In even-numbered years, the Legislature will typically pass a **supplemental budget** which is a modification of the previous two-year plan, and in odd-numbered years it may pass a **second supplemental budget** with small modifications to the earlier documents.

The biennial operating budget, for all its importance, is still a bill, subject to the same requirements as any other. It needs a sponsor, title and number; is assigned to committee after first reading and introduction where it is given a hearing and must be signed out by a majority of the committee members; goes to the Rules Committee then to the second reading calendar on the floor; needs to be bumped to third reading or returned to Rules Committee; endures third reading and final passage; is then amended in the opposite house; comes back and generally is part of a do not concur motion; then there is often a conference committee at which it is picked apart and finally pieced back together when a majority of the conferees sign the report; is sent back to its house of origin, where it must be passed on third reading again; and repeat the process in the other house—just like any other bill.

Budgeting is a full-time operation for twelve months of the year. There are typically long lead-in times. However, the chronological pattern is similar for each biennium. Below is a month-by-month listing of the probable key events in the budget process beginning with July 1997, looking at it from a legislative perspective:

July, 1997	1997-99 fiscal biennium begins
August, 1997	Agency requests for 1998 supplemental budget submitted to OFM
September, 1997	September 20 revenue forecast
November, 1997	November 20 revenue forecast—serves as basis for governor's supplemental budget proposal
December, 1997	Governor's supplemental budget proposal revealed and introduced as executive request bill
January, 1998	Sixty-day Regular Session begins
February, 1998	February 20 revenue forecast—serves as basis for legislative changes to governor's proposed supplemental budget
March, 1998	Regular Session ends, supplemental budget adopted
June, 1998	June 20 revenue forecast
August, 1998	Agencies submit budget requests to OFM for 1999-2001 biennial budget
November, 1998	November 20 revenue forecast—serves as basis for governor's 1999-2001 biennial budget
December, 1998	Governor submits 1999-2001 proposed biennial budget to the Legislature
January, 1999	Legislature convenes for 105-day Regular Session
March, 1999	March revenue forecast—serves as basis for legislative changes to governor's budget
April, 1999	Regular Session ends, biennial budget for 1999-2001 adopted by Legislature
May, 1999	Governor vetoes portions of biennial budget
June, 1999	June revenue forecast, end of 1997-99 biennium

Revenue projections are crucial to the budget process but were even more important before passage of I 601. In 1991, for example, the Legislature waited until the end of June to pass a budget in order to get the latest forecast. That is unlikely to happen again because under I 601 it is no longer essential to know the latest revenue forecast. One only needs to know the amount that can be spent. As indicated earlier, this is based on a formula that uses the spending from the previous biennium and factors in inflation and population growth. The amount of revenue available can be determined with reasonable accuracy by the end of the year before the long session and will not be changed by a swing one way or the other in the revenue forecast. It just means more or less money for the reserve account.

Below is a chart showing when the biennial operating budget passed the first house, when it passed the second house, when an agreement was publicly announced, and the length of the session(s) from 1989 through 1996. The days indicated are the number of days into the regular and special session(s) for the year when the event occurred.

Biennial Operating Budget

Year	Passed 1st Body	Passed 2nd Body	Agreement	Session Days
1995	76th day	82nd day	130th day	137 days
1993	82nd day	96th day	113th day	116 days
1991	83rd day	92nd day	121st day	126 days
1989	80th day	96th day	122nd day	126 days

Supplemental Operating Budget

Year	Passed 1st Body	Passed 2nd Body	Agreement	Session Days
1996	40th day	44th day	59th day	60 days
1994	40th day	47th day	59th day	64 days
1992	17th day	35th day	57th day	60 days
1990	45th day	51st day	77th day	84 days

There is almost always more than one budget bill and various versions of budget bills may be passed by the two bodies before the real one finally emerges. This is illustrated more fully in the description of the 1991-1992 sessions in chapter 12. However, in terms of the dates listed above, "passed 1st body" and "passed 2nd body" refers to the *first* time each body passed a biennial operating or supplemental operating budget. "Agreement" refers to a formal announcement made to the press that the sides have agreed on a budget (and didn't subsequently change their minds). "Session Days" refers to the total number of days the Legislature remained in session to wrap up after the budget agreement was reached, not to the total days in session that year. In some years the Legislature had additional special sessions on other matters which are not counted for the purposes of this chart. To determine the number of days it took to reach agreement, one could subtract the date when the budget passed the second body from the date of agreement.

It was pointed out earlier that the budget bill is subject to the same procedural requirements as other bills. While that is true, there are some differences around the edges, including the following.

While the first budget proposal is developed and written in OFM and the governor's office, it must be introduced and considered as any other legislation. It has been the tradition for more than a decade for the House and the Senate to take turns acting first on the operating budget. The turn lasts for two years. Thus, in 1995 and 1996 it was the House's turn to pass the operating budget first. The Senate acted first on the transportation budget. In 1997 and 1998, the Senate should pass the operating budget (including the supplemental) first and the House should pass the transportation budget first. There is no written rule requiring that this happen or a penalty for noncompliance, but it is a tradition that seems to make sense and is likely to endure.

It has also become an annual rite for the fiscal chairs from the House and Senate to introduce their budget proposals at a press conference a day or two before beginning committee hearings on the bill. The fiscal chair of the originating chamber will go first, then the fiscal chair of the other chamber may counter within a day or two or wait until after the first body actually passes a bill. These press conferences are more in the nature of policy statements by the majority caucuses from each body rather than a detailed itemization of the numbers. It is an attempt to let the public understand the priorities used in putting the numbers together. It is also evidence of a consensus by the majority party that it thinks it has the votes to pass the proposal described.

The majority party gets to write the budget (actually, rewrite the governor's budget). In the process, members of the majority party find they need to make some very difficult funding choices, something members of the minority party don't have to worry about. Consequently, in committee meetings and on the floor, members of the majority find themselves in the uncomfortable position of defending cuts in some popular programs or refusing to fund increases in others. As the majority they are responsible for writing and balancing a budget. The minority members, on the other hand, have no such duty. They are free to offer amendments to fund almost anything, regardless of cost. These are sometimes called **hero amendments.** They can be used in subsequent campaigns against "responsible" majority members.

In an effort to protect itself against hero amendments, as well as avoiding what might otherwise be hundreds of amendments and to expedite the process, the majority has often put in the rules a requirement for a supermajority to pass floor amendments to the operating budget bill. For example, the Rules of the House for 1963 state:

> No amendment to the general appropriation bill, commonly known as the budget, adding any new item, or items, thereto not incorporated in the bill as reported by the committee of the whole, shall be adopted except by the affirmative vote of two-thirds of the representatives elected. (HR 81)

The 1996 Senate rules have a slightly softer version which reads:

> No amendment to the budget, capital budget or supplemental budget, not incorporated in the bill as reported by the ways and means committee, shall be adopted except by the affirmative vote of sixty percent of the senators elected. (SR 53)

The **60 percent rule** makes most floor amendments tough to pass and thus reduces their number. It also permits a few members of the majority to peel off and vote for a particularly attractive amendment without giving the amendment enough support to be adopted by the body at large. Coupled with the ability to set the membership of the fiscal committees and the Rules Committees, the 60 percent rule gives the majority party more clout than their numbers might actually warrant.

In *Pannell v. Thompson*, 91 Wn 2d 591 (1979), the Supreme Court ruled on the question of whether the Legislature must fund programs that it sets up. This case involves a class action to prevent the Secretary of the Department of Social and Health Services (DSHS) from reducing payments under the general assistance-unemployed program from $200 to $50 per month, once special funding was used up. State law provides that general assistance is to be a "minimum necessary for decent and healthful subsistence." (RCW 74.08.040) Claimants argue that this creates a "statutory entitlement" and that $50 per month didn't meet it. The Supreme Court held that statutory expectations are "subject to the specific limitations of the appropriation." The case seems to say that legislative intent can be determined as much from the money it appropriates as from what it says in other statutory language. This court case gave rise to the **null and void clause.**

The null and void clause is like a nicely wrapped Christmas gift with an IOU inside. It has become commonplace to put it in most bills that have a fiscal impact. It says that unless funding for the measure is provided in the budget, then it doesn't count. The technical language is: "If specific funding for the purposes of this act, referencing this act by bill or chapter number, is not provided by June 30, in the omnibus appropriations act, this act is null and void." At its worst, the null and void clause allows legislators to claim credit for passing measures they know are not funded. The argument for the clause is that it allows the Legislature to make budget decisions as a whole rather than piecemeal.

A last and major difference between the budget and other bills is the power granted to the governor by the Constitution to veto "items" in the budget bill as opposed to "sections" in other bills. In 1996, for example, Governor Lowry vetoed fourteen items in the supplemental budget. We'll discuss this power at some length in a subsequent chapter on the Governor and the Legislature.

THE CAPITAL BUDGET

The **capital budget** provides funding for construction and repair of state buildings and facilities such as public schools, colleges, prisons, parks and other long-term investments. It covers the same two-year period from July 1 to June 30 as the biennial operating budget. However, since many of the items in the capital budget represent a long-term investment, bond funding (debt) is often used to amortize the costs over the term of a project's useful life. Debt service (principal and interest) comes from the general fund and currently represents almost 5 percent of the operating budget. The sale of bonds and taking on debt is limited both by the state Constitution and by statute. Article VIII, Section 1(b) of the state Constitution says:

> The aggregate debt contracted by the state shall not exceed that amount for which payments of principal and interest in any fiscal year would require the state to expend more than nine percent of the arithmetic mean of its general state revenues for the three immediately preceding fiscal years as certified by the treasurer.

The effect of the somewhat convoluted language is to establish a 9 percent debt limit in the state Constitution. This limit does not include bonds approved by a vote of the people. In addition to the 9 percent constitutional limit, there is a 7 percent debt limit in statute (RCW 39.42.060) which includes bonds approved by the people. This was approved by the people in 1972 as House Joint Resolution No. 52. The statutory limitation says the total amount spent for principal and interest on debt in any given year may not exceed 7 percent of state revenues. There have been proposals to raise the statutory limit up to the constitutional 9 percent limit but thus far they have failed.

The 1995-97 state capital budget (see Fig. 6.4) provided $1.640 billion in new funding, which is a reduction of 3 percent from the amount spent in the 1993-95 biennium and is 14 percent below the capital budget for 1991-93. The reduction is largely due to a direct appropriation of $110 million from the state general fund for capital projects at the close of the 1993-95 biennium.

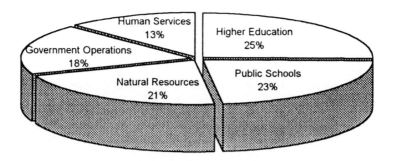

Fig. 6.4. Capital Spending: 1995-1997

Of the $1.640 billion appropriated for 1995-97, $811 million is supported by state bonds. The remainder of the capital budget comes from thirty separate dedicated funds, the largest being the common school construction fund. This fund receives revenues from the sale of timber on common school trust lands.

The capital budget and its accompanying bond bill(s) rarely arouse the level of controversy of the operating or transportation budgets. That's because every agency has a six-year construction plan which is updated every two years. OFM identifies each project by fund source and comes up with a prioritized list. The governor reviews it and it becomes the capital budget request bill. Legislators and legislative staff are involved throughout. The bill goes through the same legislative process as any other bill and is subject to amendment.

One former member has described the state capital budget as "the largest source of pork west of Iowa," a view shared by many. The problem, however, is in the definition of pork. A branch campus of the University of Washington in Tacoma would probably be described as pork by many citizens of Yakima, just as the Yakima River Greenway would be called pork by many citizens of Tacoma.

One final thing should be noted about capital expenditures and that is that they can have a large effect on the operating budget. For instance, the state may allocate $100 million in the capital budget to build a prison, but once it is built the cost of operating the prison comes from the general fund. The cost of debt also comes from the general fund. Legislators need to think well beyond their terms of office when making capital budget decisions. They must build both wisely and well. The state capitol is an example of a construction project that looked wildly extravagant to many citizens in 1911 when it was being planned, but it has held up well and has proved to be a wise investment. At the other extreme is the Kingdome (which was not a state project) as an example of a project built with little thought of the future, constructed as inexpensively as possible and poorly maintained.

THE TRANSPORTATION BUDGET

The transportation budget is different from the operating and capital budgets in that it is largely user funded. A person who does not obtain a driver's license, own a car, truck, motorcycle, airplane, boat or camper or ride a ferry can escape most of the taxes and fees that fund the transportation budget.

The three largest sources of transportation funding are the gas tax (currently at 23 cents); licenses, permits and fees for using the transportation system; and the motor vehicle excise tax which is based on the value of the vehicle owned. The 18th Amendment to the state Constitution requires that money from the first two of these sources (vehicle fuel and licenses) be "placed in a special fund to be used exclusively for highway purposes." The third source of funding, the motor vehicle excise tax, is divided among the general fund, transportation fund, transit districts, ferries, HOV/transit projects, cities and counties.

There are more than twenty separate accounts and dedicated funds that hold money collected from a number of fees and taxes such as the aircraft excise tax, camper excise fee, vanity license plate fee, commercial driver's license fee, ferry fares, monthly tonnage fee, motorcycle examination fee, and vessel pilot license fee. The funds include such things as recreational vehicle, highway safety, search and rescue, aeronautics, pilotage, grade crossing, rail development, etc. Some of the transportation budget is simply a matter of allocating specific money to the proper dedicated fund or from the proper fund to the appropriate purpose. For example, money collected from the annual pilot license fee goes into the Puget Sound pilotage account to be used for related purposes.

The largest source of funding for the transportation budget is the motor vehicle fund which derives its money from the fuel tax, licenses, permits, fees, grants, bonds and motor vehicle excise tax. The money is used to fund programs in the Department of Transportation, Department of Licensing, State Patrol, county and city roads, and the ferry system.

Washington State didn't start transportation planning until 1936. A Planning Division was created in 1948. In 1977 the Washington State Department of Transportation (WSDOT) was created (replacing the Highways Department) and was required to develop a "coordinated and integrated transportation policy and plan" by 1980. (See Ziegler article cited in bibliography for this chapter.)

Passage of the Growth Management Act in 1990 had a big impact on transportation funding and spending because it requires local governments to develop twenty-year comprehensive land use plans that include transportation. In 1990 the Legislature also passed a statute requiring WSDOT to adopt a statewide, intermodal transportation plan for all areas of the state. Part of the planning process includes "service objectives," which are the "desirable" services to be provided by transportation systems over a twenty-year period. WSDOT released its latest twenty-year plan on April 25, 1996, for highways, rail, ferries and mass transit, and the cost exceeded the anticipated revenue by $28 billion (*The Olympian,* April 25, 1996).

In effect, WSDOT prepares and continually updates twenty-year and six-year plans. It examines "all needs," "service objective needs," and "financially constrained needs." WSDOT began preparing a six-year plan in January 1996, by identifying the highest priorities from the twenty-year plan. The 1997 two-year budget will include the highest priorities from the six-year plan (Ziegler article). Thus, planning has taken on a central role. In addition, WSDOT has increased its ability to monitor the performance of the state transportation system.

Agencies in the transportation area submit their budgets to OFM, the same as other agencies. OFM may revise according to the priorities of the governor and submit an executive-request bill to the Legislature. That bill goes through the same process as any other. There is a tradition of rotating responsibility for originating the transportation budget every two years, opposite to the operating budget. Since the Senate will originate the operating budget in 1997, the House will originate the transportation budget.

There are several major differences in the way the transportation budget is handled that serve to highlight the process.

The Department of Transportation has its own commission, seven persons appointed by the governor to six-year terms and subject to Senate confirmation. This commission sets transportation policy and hires the secretary of Transportation to run the department. Thus, the Department of Transportation is different from a department such as Social and Health Services because it is removed from direct control of the governor. The governor may appoint some of the commissioners during his or her four-year term but it would probably take more than one term to appoint a majority. Even if the governor did appoint a majority of the commission, once confirmed by the Senate there would be no way to force the commissioners to follow the governor's policies.

Transportation funding resembles the capital budget more than the operating budget. It involves construction and repair of infrastructure. It requires longer term planning than a biennium. As indicated, the Department of Transportation continually updates twenty-year and six-year transportation plans. The biennial budget comes out of that long-range planning process.

Another difference between the transportation budget and the operating budget is the existence of the Legislative Transportation Committee (LTC), composed of twelve House members and eleven senators. It serves a continuing oversight function for all elements of the transportation budget. Major transportation agencies submit monthly reports to the LTC and the committee closely monitors spending. The LTC also tends to narrow the gap that exists between the House and Senate Transportation Committees through joint meetings and the interchangeable use of House and Senate transportation staff. The result is that there are usually fewer changes to and less controversy about the transportation budget as it moves through the two bodies. Some members would say that the reason for less controversy about the transportation budget is because there is less scrutiny by the general membership of the Legislature. Some members have urged melding the transportation budget into the process with the operating and capital budgets by having one committee look at all three. They argue that all the state's programs should be on the table so members can prioritize and spend the limited resources where needed most.

7

The Governor and the Legislature

This book is about the legislative process, so the discussion here will focus primarily on the governor's responsibilities within that process. It needs to be noted, however, that unlike legislators whose job is lawmaking, the governor has other responsibilities as well. While the governor is central to the legislative process, he or she has many other functions which are not directly related to lawmaking.

The governor's powers come from Article III of the state Constitution and from a body of statutes that has grown up over more than one hundred years. It is instructive, though, that in Washington's Constitution the first article deals with the rights reserved to the people, the second article deals with the Legislature, and the third article covers the eight state-elected officers including the governor.

The general powers of the governor are stated in one sentence: "The governor may require information in writing from the officers of the state upon any subject relating to the duties of their respective offices, and shall see that the laws are faithfully executed." (Article III, Section 5) Thus, the paramount duty of the governor is to enforce the laws of the state. The

Constitution also gives the governor power to call extraordinary sessions of the Legislature, for which he or she must state specific reasons, makes the governor the commander-in-chief of the state military, and delegates on him or her the power to pardon prisoners, veto bills, and make designated appointments.

Additional powers are given to the governor by statute. These include the supervision of executive and ministerial offices, making additional appointments and filling vacancies, acting as the "sole official organ" of communication between the government of this state and that of other governments, including that of the United States, the power to direct the attorney general regarding legal proceedings on behalf of the state or to assist local prosecuting attorneys, the right to offer rewards in criminal cases, the power to issue election proclamations, the power to require boards of state officers to submit written reports, the right to declare public disasters or states of emergency or imminent danger of pest infestation, and the power to enter into compacts with recognized Indian tribes on behalf of the state (see generally RCW 43.06).

POLICYMAKER

Governors are popularly viewed as the chief policymakers of their states, even though some authors have suggested this power is shifting to the state legislatures. Some even claim that governors have little or no influence on policy decisions set by states (see selected bibliography for this chapter). A recent study of the role of the governor of Florida in policymaking, reported in *Spectrum* magazine, concludes that governors are important in setting policy. However, the authors point out that there are many variables. The success of a governor in passing laws or setting policy depends on 1) gubernatorial priorities, 2) gubernatorial skills, 3) political control of the two legislative bodies, 4) the timing of the proposals, 5) national forces and events, and 6) the nature of the state economy.

Governors of this state are central to setting the policy of this state. The Constitution and statutes would seem to require this even if the governor were inclined otherwise. The governor is required to submit the first operating budget proposal for the biennium and no document determines policy more than that. The governor is required to report annually on the state of the state. The governor appoints hundreds of managers including all the trustees of the state's institutions of higher learning and the heads of state agencies such as the departments of Social and Health Services, Licensing, Health, Labor and Industries, Corrections, Agriculture, and Ecology. The people the governor appoints and how they enforce laws and rules in their areas has a great impact on policy, often lasting beyond a governor's term. We will focus in this chapter on the areas where there is a direct connection between the governor and the Legislature. The final chapter about the 1991-1992 legislative sessions offers a more complete picture of the various roles the governor plays in setting policy.

In Washington State, the governor must submit his or her proposals to the Legislature. Article III, Section 6 of the Constitution requires the governor to communicate with each Legislature on "the condition of the affairs of the state, and recommend such measures as he shall deem expedient for their action." This has evolved into a practice of delivering a "state of the state" message within the first week of each regular session. In 1977 the Legislature added a statutory requirement that the governor submit a biennial budget by December 20 of each even-numbered year and within twenty days of any session in which a budget is to be considered (RCW 43.88.060).

VETOES

Only two of the fifty states, North Carolina and Nebraska, do not give their governor any **veto** power; that is, the power to kill measures passed by the Legislature. All but seven states give their governors a **line-item veto**, meaning the right to veto parts of bills. All but thirteen give their governors a **pocket veto** which means a bill is dead unless the governor signs it within a certain period of time. The opposite of the pocket veto is true in our state, where bills become laws if the governor does not act. The President of the United States has had only the power to veto entire bills. However, in 1996 Congress gave the President a limited item veto power beginning in 1997 for the first time in our history.

The Washington State Constitution (Article III, Section 12) requires that every bill not only must pass the two houses of the Legislature in identical form but must be presented to and signed by the governor before it can become law. If the Legislature is in session, the governor has five days (not counting Sundays) to either sign a bill, do nothing in which case it becomes law automatically, or return the bill to the house of origin with his objections, which is a **veto**. If the Legislature is not in session, the governor has twenty days (not counting Sundays) once again to sign a bill, do nothing in which case it becomes law, or to return the bill with his or her objections to the secretary of state for safekeeping until the next session of the Legislature.

The same Amendment 62, approved by the voters in 1974, which sets out veto powers of the governor also provides that the Legislature may call itself into a five-day **special session** within 45 days of adjournment of the regular session for the sole purpose of reconsidering vetoed bills. It takes a petition by two-thirds of all members elected in each body to call this kind of special session and it has never happened. The 68th Amendment adopted in 1979 allows members to call themselves into special session by two-thirds vote of each body and, since it allows for thirty-day sessions, makes the use of the earlier amendment unlikely, although it, too, has never been used.

Our Constitution gives the governor the power to veto not only entire bills but **sections** of bills and appropriation **items** in the budget. The question of what constitutes a section or an item has been a matter of much dispute for many years. In 1974, the people approved an amendment to the Constitution to clarify that the veto could only be used on whole sections of bills except for "items" in appropriation bills (Amendment 62). But the "section" issue wasn't settled for another fourteen years.

In 1988 the Washington State Supreme Court, in *Washington State Motorcycle Dealers Association v. State of Washington*, 111 Wn. 2d 667 (1988), finally settled the question of whether the governor could veto less than a section in a non-budget bill. That case involved a 1985 bill passed by the Legislature which contained fifteen numbered sections and many unnumbered subsections. Governor Booth Gardner vetoed all of some sections and parts of other sections.

The Motorcycle Dealers Association, joined by the Legislature, agreed that the governor had the authority to veto whole sections but challenged his vetoes of parts of sections. The issue on appeal was simply whether the governor could veto parts of sections of bills under Article III, Section 12 (Amendment 62). The Supreme Court said no, the governor did not have authority to veto less than an entire section of a bill, except in budgets. Justice James Andersen, speaking for six of the nine Justices, said that Amendment 62 of the state Constitution was passed in 1972 in response to a greatly expanded use of vetoes of partial sections of bills by the governor during and after the 1971-72 legislative sessions. He said the 1972 amendment accomplished three things: it limited use of the "item" veto to appropriation bills; it specifically prohibited vetoing anything less than an entire section; and, it gave the Legislature authority to call itself into session within forty-five days after adjournment to override vetoes (this became moot after the 1980 annual session amendment which allows the Legislature to call itself into session at any time).

The *Motorcycle* case appears to have resolved the dispute over vetoes of sections of bills, but other arguments continue. In September 1994, the Legislature filed suit challenging the constitutionality of several vetoes by Governor Lowry in order to get answers to three questions: First, can the governor veto less than a section of substantive language in a non-budget bill? Second, can the governor repeal less than a section in the repealers part of a bill (**repealers** are the list of statutes that are abrogated by a new law)? Third, what happens to the money when the governor vetoes an item or specific proviso in a budget bill? An example of the last question: The budget allocates $5 million to the Department of Transportation for improving highways near a new race track. The governor vetoes the language about the race track. What happens to the $5 million? Can the Department of Transportation or the governor spend it elsewhere without further authorization by the Legislature?

In May 1995, Thurston County Superior Court Judge Tom McPhee ruled the governor cannot veto less than a section in a non-budget bill or less than a section of repealers. Two wins for the Legislature. However, the judge ruled for the governor on the third question saying the money left unspent may be spent elsewhere when a specific proviso in a budget is vetoed. The Legislature has appealed this last part and the matter was pending before the Supreme Court at the time this book went to press.

Vetoes and the threat of vetoes are probably the strongest weapon the governor has in his capacity as a legislator. And Washington governors have not been reluctant to use them, even on bills sponsored by members of their own political party.

The last five governors of this state have been Mike Lowry, Booth Gardner, John Spellman, Dixy Lee Ray and Dan Evans. In terms of popular image, Booth Gardner is remembered as least combative and most congenial. It is surprising, then, to note that Gardner used his veto more than any of the other governors mentioned (we are counting partial vetoes the same as full vetoes for purposes of this discussion). He vetoed 14 percent of all the bills sent to him during his eight years as governor. In 1989 alone, he used his veto a record 83 times, on almost 18 percent of the bills passed by the Legislature. He vetoed more bills both in 1987 and in 1989 than Dixy Lee Ray did in her entire four years in office (see Fig 7.1).

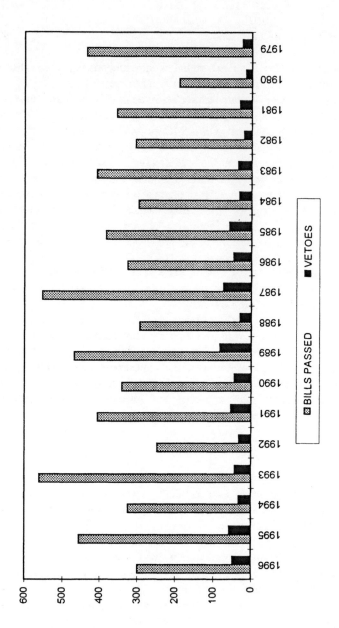

Fig. 7.1. Bills Passed and Vetoes: 1979–1996

By contrast, in 1975, Dan Evans' last year as governor, when he was facing a heavily Democratic Legislature, he vetoed only fifty-one bills, 12 percent of the total sent to him. John Spellman vetoed a mere 9 percent during his four years. Combative, outspoken Dixy Lee Ray used her veto only seventy times in four years, for 6.4 percent. And Mike Lowry, for all his public disagreements with both Republicans and Democrats, vetoed only about 10 percent of the bills sent to him.

Washington's governors appear tame by contrast to some other states' governors. In 1995, Governor Gary Johnson of New Mexico exercised full vetoes of 48 percent of the 424 bills sent to him by his state's Legislature and used his line item or section veto on most of the others.

Vetoes are serious stuff to members of the Washington Legislature. It is not easy to shepherd a bill through the process. In 1995, for example, there were 3,198 bills introduced. Only 455, a mere 14 percent, passed both houses, and almost all of these had been amended or rewritten. When a legislator finally gets a bill over that last hurdle and it is on the way to the governor's office, there is a feeling of relief. Members and staff work with the governor's office and eagerly await the notice of bill signing when they can stand proudly next to the governor for the official photo. But instead, on fifty-eight occasions in 1995, the sweetness of victory turns to vinegar when the governor instead signs a dreaded veto message. When that happens, legislators' thoughts turn to revenge and their ultimate weapon, the veto override.

VETO OVERRIDES

The basic requirement for the override of a governor's veto is approval of the override motion by two-thirds of the elected members of each body of the Legislature. An override may be of a full veto of a bill or of sections of a bill or items in an appropriation bill. Overrides must be taken up at the current session or at the "next session" but there is some dispute about what this means. The dispute, which is illustrated below in our discussion of the 1995 special session, boils down to whether next session means the next legislative session of any kind, including special, the next regular session, the next session in the following biennium, or all of the above. The issue has not been finally resolved by the courts, but the attorney general has declared that next session means the next regular session.

Over the past ten years, governors have used their power of veto an average of fifty times per year, counting both full and partial vetoes. This is true even when the governor and both houses of the Legislature were of the same party. Considering the frequency of vetoes (about 14 percent of all bills passed in 1996 were either fully or partially vetoed), it is surprising that there have been only two veto overrides by the Legislature in the past decade, one in 1989 and one in 1996. The explanation lies only partly in the difficulty of achieving the necessary two-thirds of the members of each house needed to vote for an override. Other factors include the part-time nature of the Legislature, the turnover of legislators and governors, and the fact that it is often easier to just pass a new bill, perhaps disguised a bit, thus avoiding the two-thirds requirement and a direct confrontation with the governor.

The stories of the veto overrides in 1989 and in 1996 illustrate some of these considerations.

During the 1989 Regular Session, the Legislature passed SB 5233 which created the new crime of residential burglary. The intent of the bill is to distinguish between the burglary of a home as opposed to the burglary of a nonresidence, such as a warehouse, and to increase the penalty for residential burglary. The general theory is that burglary of a residence poses more of a threat to human life. The idea makes sense and had wide support. The bill sailed through the Senate 46-1 and the House by 97-0.

To the surprise of many legislators, Governor Gardner vetoed the heart of the residential burglary bill which prescribed increased jail time. He said that while he supported the intent of the bill, he thought that there was insufficient funding in the budget to carry out the longer sentences. Ordinarily, legislators would try again next year or work out a solution with the governor. But in 1989 legislators were called back into two special sessions, had become increasingly unhappy with the governor and wanted a way to show it.

In 1989, Democrats controlled the House and the governor's office while Republicans controlled the Senate. The main area of contention during the legislative session involved Gardner's efforts at "tax reform" (viz., an income tax). A majority of legislators were willing at one point to raise the gas tax, but few wanted to go near the political tar pit known as the income tax. Governor Gardner decided on a strategy of linking a substantial gas tax increase to an income tax along with reductions in the sales and B&O taxes.

The Senate took politically tough votes to pass one gas tax increase at seven cents and another at five cents. Gardner let it be known he would veto both efforts without overall tax reform, so much-relieved House Democrats let the proposals die. To make up for their earlier tax increase votes, senators passed a transportation budget with no gas tax increase at all and the House concurred. Neither body had passed "tax reform."

That's where things stood at the end of the First Special Session on May 15.

The residential burglary bill had passed in April. Governor Gardner returned it to the Senate, its originator, "without my approval as to section 3" in the form of a veto message on May 13, 1989, just before the end of the First Special Session. Section 3 was the increased penalty provision.

Governor Gardner called legislators back into a second special session on May 17, despite the fact there was still no agreement on taxes. Members had been in session for more than four months. They were tired, wanted to go home, and were in no mood to take more unpopular and unnecessary tax-increase votes only to have the governor back away. Many members, including Democrats, felt the governor shouldn't have called a second special session until he had a firm deal in hand. They wanted a way to vent their frustration and SB 5233, the residential burglary bill veto, was just the ticket.

House Democrats were in such a hurry to send the governor a message about their unhappiness that they voted to override his veto of SB 5233 on the first day of the Second Special Session only to discover to their embarrassment that they didn't actually have possession of the bill. Under the rules, vetoed bills are returned to their house of origin so the veto message was in the Senate.

On May 19, Gardner publicly announced that he would accept a four cent increase in the gas tax but by then few legislators cared. Legislators were no longer willing to vote for any increase. With little to do, the Senate took up SB 5233 on a motion to override. Governor Gardner and grim-faced Senate Democratic leaders pleaded with fellow Democrats to "stand fast," to no avail. Only nine of the twenty-four Senate Democrats voted with their governor against the override. The final vote in the Senate was 38-9 to override the governor's veto of section 3 of SB 5233. The bill was immediately transmitted to the House, where it was gleefully approved 71-9 the next day. The moment for a gas tax increase had passed as well and both houses moved quickly to adjourn sine die. Leaders made it known they were prepared to vote to override six more Gardner vetoes if he called another special session. The governor got the message and called no more special sessions that year.

The veto override in 1996 was quite different but had its own set of interesting complications.

Conservative Republicans controlled the House, Democrats had a one-vote majority in the Senate, and liberal Mike Lowry was the governor. The state was awash in a $700 million surplus in the 1995 session, most of which could not be spent under the limitations of Initiative 601. Legislators from both parties thought it would be a prudent thing to return some of the budget surplus to the people in the form of tax cuts. The governor disagreed.

Following the legislative sessions in 1995, Governor Mike Lowry vetoed two tax cut bills, one reducing the B&O tax and the other reducing the state's portion of the property tax. House Republicans, as well as many Democrats, vowed to override the two vetoes on the first day of the 1996 Regular Session, January 8, thinking that would be their first opportunity. However, a "crisis" arose in September 1995, when King County voters turned down a proposition to raise the county portion of the sales tax to pay for a new outdoor baseball stadium. The Seattle Mariners baseball club issued an ultimatum that it would leave town unless the Legislature acted within one month.

Governor Lowry was mindful of Republican override threats and said he would not call a special session without an agreement on the part of legislative leaders not to bring up the vetoes. House Republican leaders suggested to Senate Democratic leaders that the Legislature go around the governor and call itself into session, but the Democrats said no deal.

Complicating matters for Republicans was language in the state Constitution saying that veto overrides must be taken up by the Legislature at its next session. Their dilemma was how to deal with the stadium in a special session without forfeiting the right to override Lowry's vetoes in January. Senate Minority Leader Dan McDonald submitted the "next session" question to Attorney General Christine Gregoire for a formal opinion. Attorney General Opinions have no force of law but are usually accepted by the courts and have the virtue of speed.

The Attorney General delivered her opinion on October 4, 1995, and solved the problem (AGO 1995 No. 12). Gregoire opined that the original framers of the Constitution expected there would be few special sessions and those only for extraordinary purposes (like baseball stadiums?). She reasoned that unless the Legislature specifically made a veto override a purpose of a special session, the override could wait until the next regular session. In short, "next session" meant next regular session, not next session of any kind.

And so that hurdle was cleared. A special session was called in October 1995, solely to provide legislation for funding the construction of an outdoor baseball stadium. Nothing else was considered. The final formula imposed the bulk of the costs on King County. In three days the bill was passed and the Legislature adjourned sine die. The veto override was not brought up.

On January 8, 1996, the first day of the 1996 Regular Session, as promised by Republican leaders, the House voted to override Governor Lowry's veto of the B&O tax cut by 70-28 and of the property tax cut by 73-25.

Senate Democrats saw things a little differently. They believed the vetoed bills were dated because of their effective dates and decided instead to pass new bills. They were prevented from doing so on the first day of the session when Senate Republican leaders refused to permit a suspension of the rules. However, two days later, on January 10, the Senate passed new tax-cut measures similar to the ones Lowry vetoed and sent them to the House.

House Republicans swallowed their pride of authorship and passed the Senate's B&O tax cut, SB 6117, on January 12. It took a couple days for the bill to be signed by the two presiding officers and delivered to the governor, then he had five days, not counting Sundays, to decide what to do. As expected, Governor Lowry vetoed SB 6117, and returned it with his message to the Senate on January 22.

On January 24, 1996, only seventeen days into the Regular Session, the Democrat-controlled Senate voted to override SB 6117 by 41-7. The bill was immediately transmitted to the House where, in less than two hours, the override motion was passed 76-21. The state Constitution says that every bill passed must be signed by the presiding officers of the two houses. An old Washington case (*State ex rel. Dunbar v. State Board*, 140 W 446, 1926), held that there was no such requirement upon repassage after a veto. Thus, the 1996 veto override became law immediately upon passage of the override by both bodies.

GUBERNATORIAL APPOINTMENTS

To a greater extent than most people realize (and to the chagrin of some governors), the success or failure of a governor lies not on the shoulders of the individual governor but on the quality of the people he or she brings to Olympia. It is probably better to elect as governor a person of modest personal abilities who appoints excellent people to run agencies and departments than a brilliant individual whose appointments are mediocre.

The governor derives the authority for making appointments partly from the Constitution and partly from statutes passed since 1889. (1) The state Constitution requires that the governor's appointments to educational, reformatory, and penal institutions be subject to Senate confirmation (Article 13, Section 1). This includes 206 trustees and regents at the state's institutions of higher education. (2) Some offices such as heads of agencies like Licensing or Corrections are coterminous with the governor. (3) Others, such as the Pollution Control Hearings Board (six years), may go beyond a governor's term and are made whenever there is a vacancy. (4) And still others, such as judges, are made only if a vacancy occurs during the term of office.

Of course, the number of appointments a governor makes depends on how long he or she is in office and the health of other officeholders. However, during a four-year term a governor normally appoints well over a thousand individuals to various agencies, boards, commissions and other offices, and indirectly hires thousands more.

The governor not only has a lot of jobs to fill but has great discretion in filling them. Statutes rarely require any special training, education or experience even for the most difficult positions. As an example, take the largest agency, the Department of Social and Health Services, with over 15,000 employees and billions of dollars in expenditures and hundreds of programs: the law simply says the director (secretary) "shall be appointed by the governor with the consent of the senate, and shall serve at the pleasure of the governor." (RCW 43.20A.040)

An argument could be made that this job-giving power of the governor is potentially the strongest weapon in dealing with the Legislature. Consider that legislators are paid the low wages of part-time employees but that they accrue the pension benefits of full-time employees. The result is that some legislators accumulate a substantial number of years of service but, under the pension formula, have a low salary to multiply against. A legislator with years of longevity needs just two years at a higher salary to greatly increase his or her pension. Even without the years, an appointment to something like the Liquor Control Board or the Tax Appeals Board can look pretty good to a harried underpaid House member facing reelection every two years and term limits in the future.

At any given time there are confidential letters from more than a few members of the Legislature on the governor's desk seeking an appointment of some kind for themselves or others. The surprise is that few modern governors have tapped this potentially rich vein as a means of garnering support on tough votes. Governors Lowry and Gardner both adopted unofficial policies against appointing sitting members of the Legislature and they made few exceptions. They both suffered the ultimate ignominy of a veto override by at least one house with a majority from their party. Would the outcome have been different if they had been more skillful (or more ruthless) in the use of appointments? This is not to say either governor should have acted unethically. It assumes legislator-candidates are qualified for positions sought.

The possibility of a future appointment can be used as a carrot for friendly legislators or their friends, but can also be used as part of a longer range strategy. For example, suppose there is an opening on the five-member Pollution Control Hearings Board. And suppose there is a senator from the other party who represents a swing district that includes a House member from the governor's party. The appointment of the opposition senator clears the way for his or her possible replacement by a House member from the governor's party in the next election.

This job-giving power is a sword that can also be used against a governor. A politician scorned can be like a wounded elephant: it has a mighty hurt and a long memory. This is especially true if the legislator comes from the same political party, shares a similar philosophy, and supported the governor in the last election. There is the expectation of a pay-back. If it is not forthcoming, that friend can turn into a bitter foe.

SENATE CONFIRMATIONS

There are well over 200 gubernatorial appointments subject to Senate confirmation. The list includes major appointments such as to the Board of Regents of the University of Washington, as well as relatively anonymous positions on the Board of Pilotage Commissioners. Legislation passed the Senate in 1996 to pare the list to just below one hundred but it died in the House.

The confirmation of a gubernatorial appointment is the only legislative function that is unique to one body. Only the Senate has the power of confirmation. But the House has no cause for jealousy because in Washington the power of confirmation is rather weak. Unlike the United States Senate and most other state senates, where an appointee must be confirmed prior to taking office, in Washington State an appointee serves unless **not** confirmed.

When the governor makes an appointment requiring Senate confirmation he or she sends a letter to the Senate. It is done in a highly stylistic format containing the words: "Ladies and Gentlemen: I have the honor to submit the following appointment, subject to your confirmation." The appointment is then recorded in the *Senate Journal* and referred to whichever committee has jurisdiction over the board or commission to which the individual is being appointed. Along with the letter, the governor is required by Senate rules to send a completed copy of a six-page standard questionnaire (SR 69) filled out by the appointee. If the office is one that comes under public disclosure laws, as most are, a copy of the individual's financial disclosure form is also attached.

Senate rules permit committees to require appointees to submit additional written information related to the appointment. For example, a few years ago the chair of the Higher Education Committee, Senator Jerry Saling (R-Spokane), required all appointees to college boards of regents or boards of trustees to answer a series of hypothetical questions designed to elicit their philosophies. It made the usually boring confirmation hearings quite lively. Senate rules require committees to hold public hearings on appointments but make personal appearance by the appointee optional on the part of the committee chair. If the committee chair does require the appointee to appear, as is usually the case, testimony must be taken under oath.

While the Senate confirmation process itself is weak compared to the federal government and most other states, some committee chairs have used it as a weapon in policy battles with the governor. A good example of this occurred during the 1989 Regular Session.

Senator Jack Metcalf (R-Langley) was chair of the Senate Environment and Natural Resources Committee. Governor Booth Gardner appointed Curt Smitch, a long-time fish and game professional, to be the first director of the new Wildlife Department. The nomination was sent to Senator Metcalf's committee. Senator Metcalf strongly disagreed with Governor Gardner's policies favoring set-asides for spotted owl habitat and the terms of settlements with Indian tribes over hunting rights. Mr. Smitch, as Governor Gardner's appointee, naturally defended the governor's policies.

Senator Metcalf set the Smitch confirmation hearing for an extraordinary evening meeting of his Environment and Natural Resources Committee on February 21, 1989. He sent letters to 1,700 sportsmen's clubs encouraging attendance for the specific purpose of opposing the Smitch confirmation and asked for and got permission from the Senate to hold the committee hearing in the Senate chambers. The game was on but the deck was stacked.

By 7:00 P.M. an overflow crowd of angry lumbermen and hunters had filled the galleries on both sides above the Senate chamber and spilled over into the rotunda. A few Senate security staff (mostly retired law enforcement officers) eyed the crowd warily knowing there was little they could do if trouble broke out. The audience looked down at a desk in the center of the floor of the Senate chamber where the appointee, Curt Smitch, sat with maybe half a dozen wildlife commissioners and staff. It looked like a basketball arena filled to capacity with the star player from the visiting team and a couple of out-of-town friends sitting alone in the middle of the court. Remarkably, the governor did not appear to support his appointee nor did he send anyone to speak on his behalf.

The hearing lasted about three hours and, to his credit, Senator Metcalf kept it civil. Smitch was allowed to speak first about his background and qualifications, followed by brief statements of support from three wildlife commissioners. That was followed by about two hours of testimony from persons hostile to the governor's policies. Through it all, Smitch remained calm, held his ground, and in the end gained grudging respect if not for his policies certainly for his courage in facing down an antagonistic crowd.

Smitch's confirmation got out of committee with no recommendation and sat on the floor calendar for the remainder of the 1989 session without ever coming up. Republican leaders regularly counted votes and remained one or two shy of a majority to not confirm. Meanwhile, Curt Smitch continued to be director of the wildlife agency. He was finally confirmed on February 13, 1991, after two-and-a-half years on the job. He served for the balance of Gardner's term and briefly into that of Governor Lowry. He now works for the federal Fish and Wildlife Agency.

Once into the system, confirmations are treated much like bills. They are moved out of committee by a majority of signatures on a "do confirm" report; with no recommendation, as was the case with Mr. Smitch; or a "do not confirm" report. Like bills, confirmations go to the Rules Committee. If voted out of Rules, they are placed on a confirmation calendar. They must be approved by a majority of elected senators on a recorded vote, the same as third reading and final passage of bills. Unlike bills, however, appointees take office from the date of appointment. Inaction on the part of the Senate in terms of confirmation is no impediment to service. Some appointees are never confirmed but continue in office for as long as the governor who appointed them. In principle, it is the same as if a bill became a law unless the Legislature voted against it.

Efforts by legislators over many years to change the system to reduce the number of appointments subject to confirmation, to require that appointees must be confirmed before service, or to prohibit appointees from serving beyond a certain period of time without confirmation have all failed. Special select committees on gubernatorial appointments and Senate confirmations were appointed in 1981 and in 1989. They held hearings, wrote reports, and drafted legislation, but to no avail. A strong effort was made in 1996 merely to reduce the number of confirmations with the Secretary of the Senate personally testifying, but again, the efforts failed. The governor is either unconcerned or does not want to diminish his or her power and the House has little interest.

Confirmations can get a little tricky in gubernatorial election years. An example from 1996 will illustrate some of the complexities. There were three openings on the Fish and Wildlife Commission. Under an initiative passed the previous year, the commission was given the power to hire the Department of Fish and Wildlife director itself, a power previously held by the governor. The commission (and its predecessors) has a long history of controversy because it deals with diminishing resources and habitat for hunting, fishing, and with relations with Indian tribes.

Governor Lowry had three Wildlife Commission appointments pending Senate confirmation in the 1996 session: a former official with the National Forest Service, an ex-congresswoman, and an ex-tribal leader. Senate Democratic leaders thought the votes were there for confirmation of the first two, but not the third. A hearing was held and a bare majority, all the Democrats on the committee, signed a do confirm report for confirmation of the ex-Forest Service official. One Democrat on the committee refused to vote for the ex-congresswoman and several refused to vote for the ex-tribal leader. This rift among the Democrats allowed minority Senate Republicans to block two of the three nominations from confirmation, which they were delighted to do in the hope that one of their party would be elected governor, withdraw the remaining two of Lowry's appointees, and submit ones more to the Republicans' liking in 1997.

That brings us to the last point about confirmations, which concerns their withdrawal. Probably the main reason the Senate so rarely votes to not confirm a gubernatorial appointment is that if such a prospect appeared imminent, Senate leaders would scuttle the vote and the governor would request that the nomination be returned. Notice that this is a request, something quite different from action by the governor alone. It requires a majority vote of the members of the Senate to agree to a governor's request to withdraw a nomination (SR 69). The Senate could refuse to return a nomination, although that hasn't happened yet. However, if there is a Republican governor in 1997 replacing Democrat Governor Lowry, and simultaneously there is a Democratic majority in the Senate, there is a possibility that the Senate Democrats would refuse to return at least some of Governor Lowry's appointees.

There have been only two gubernatorial appointments that failed on the floor of the Senate in modern, post World War II times. The last one to be voted down by the Senate was a druggist named Robert L. Hagist, appointed by Governor Dan Evans to be chair of the state Liquor Control Board in 1967. On March 3, 1967, the forty-fifth day of the regular session, the Senate voted 31-14 with four excused to not confirm Mr. Hagist. According to former Senator William A. Gissberg, who voted with the majority, it was felt by many members of both parties that the candidate did not have the appropriate background. One has to go back another twenty years to 1947 for the next appointment to lose, John M. Fox, appointed by Governor Mon C. Wallgren to the Board of Regents of the University of Washington. The Senate Committee on Higher Education and Libraries had recommended eight to four that Mr. Fox not be confirmed. Nevertheless, the governor persisted and Mr. Fox was rejected by the full Senate 24-20, with two absent. The author has been unable to determine the reasons for the negative vote. This description is in no way meant to denigrate the character or qualifications of Mr. Hagist or Mr. Fox. It's just politics.

8

Legislators

Number of Legislators

Since 1973 Washington has had ninety-eight members in the state House of Representatives and forty-nine senators. But those figures are not enshrined in our Constitution and, in fact, have changed fairly regularly since statehood in 1889 (see Table 1). The Constitution provides that the House be composed of not less than sixty-three nor more than ninety-nine members. It says of the Senate that there are to be not less than one-third nor more than half as many as House members, thus anywhere from twenty-one to forty-nine. The Senate is currently at its maximum and the House is one below at ninety-eight.

The first state Legislature in 1889 had seventy state representatives and thirty-five senators, the fewest in our history. In the early years the number of members changed almost every session. That was because the Legislature was still in the process of drawing new lines and of creating new counties. For example, when the Legislature created Ferry County in 1899 it included the county in the already-existing second senatorial district but gave Ferry County its own state representative.

It was common during the first several decades of statehood for House and Senate districts to be entirely different. For example, in the 1901 redistricting the Legislature created forty-two single-member senatorial districts and fifty-six representative districts which contained anywhere from one to three representatives each.

But the historical trend has been to keep enlarging the number of legislators to the maximum. The current number of 147, with two representatives and one senator from each of forty-nine districts, has been in effect for about a quarter century now, the longest period without a change. Given the stability of the current system, the complexity of redistricting, and the adoption of a redistricting commission as part of the state Constitution, the Legislature itself is unlikely to change its numbers. However, as will be seen shortly, redistricting has been a popular subject of initiative. It wouldn't be surprising someday to see a diminution in the number of legislators as part of a general "government reform" initiative.

TABLE 1.   Number of Members of the Washington State Legislature, 1889 to 1997

	House	*Senate*	*Total*
1889	70	35	105
1891-1899	78	34	112
1901	80	34	114
1903	94	42	136
1905	86	42	128
1907	94	42	136
1909	95	42	137
1911	87	42	129
1913-1919	97	42	139
1921-1923	96	42	138
1925-1931	97	42	139
1933-1957	99	46	145
1959-1971	99	49	148
1973-1997	98	49	147

LEGISLATIVE DISTRICTS AND REDISTRICTING

Since 1973 the state has been divided into forty-nine legislative districts, each district electing one senator and two representatives (sometimes subdivided so the representatives come from separate halves of the senatorial district). Every ten years, following the national census, the state is required by our Constitution to redraw the districts to keep them equal in population (Article II, Section 3). This adjustment in districts is called **redistricting** and historically has been the single most wrenching, agonizing and sometimes comical legislative action of each decade. Finally tiring of the task themselves, in 1983 legislators passed, then submitted to the voters the creation of an independent, bipartisan redistricting commission.

What caused the change in 1983 was ninety years of sometimes ugly but more often petty warfare between and within the political parties over district lines. A few examples will make the point.

The very first redistricting effort by the state Legislature was a portent of things to come. It was vetoed by the governor on March 4, 1901. On the same day, the House overrode his veto and the Senate did the same two days later.

From 1901 until 1930, the Legislature was unable to redistrict the state. Instead, it had standing committees in both the House and the Senate which made minor adjustments.

1930 was the first genuine redistricting in the state. It was not done by the Legislature but by initiative. In 1956 the state was again redistricted by initiative.

In 1962 the voters turned down a redistricting initiative. The following session legislators were unable to reach agreement and adjourned without redistricting. The matter went to court and in 1964 the United States District Court instructed the 1965 Legislature that it was forbidden from passing any bills until it first passed a redistricting plan. It took the 1965 Legislature forty-seven days before they finally reached agreement. But the history of redistricting gets even more ridiculous.

In 1971 the Legislature adjourned again without coming to agreement on a redistricting plan. This time the United States District Court gave them a deadline: unless the Legislature came up with a plan by February 25, 1972, it would redistrict the state itself. The threat didn't work. The Legislature failed so the court hired a University of Washington cartographer to establish the district boundaries and set them out in *Prince v. Kramer, et.al.*, Civil Order No. 9668.

The problem most years was that neither party had firm enough control of both houses of the Legislature and the governor to get its way. In 1981, though, the Republicans had a fifty-six to forty-two lead in the House, a twenty-five to twenty-four edge in the Senate after the mid-session switch by Senator Peter von Reichbauer (R-Vashon Island), and Republican John Spellman in the governor's chair. Finally one party was able to draw the lines to suit itself. It still wasn't easy to accommodate everyone. For example, the plan included what came to be known as the "Kiskaddon pimple." This was a little blip on the straight line separating King and Snohomish counties to include incumbent Senator Bill Kiskaddon's (R-Mountlake Terrace) residence. Kiskaddon was reelected for one more term in 1984, then defeated in 1988 by Patty Murray. But the Republicans' 1981 plan was a failure if judged by the fact that the Democrats swept to victory in the first elections from the new districts, in November 1982, and kept control in the state House for the entire decade.

After 1981, the two parties had enough and looked for a better way. The Legislature passed and the people approved constitutional Amendment 74, creating a **redistricting commission.** The leader of each of the four legislative caucuses appoints one commissioner by January 15 of every year ending in one. By January 31, three of these commissioners must agree on selection of a chair who presides but cannot vote. If any of the deadlines cannot be met, the state Supreme Court has five days to make the appointment or selection.

The Redistricting Commission has until January 1 of the year ending in two to agree on a plan. The districts must be equal in population, and as nearly as possible contiguous, compact, convenient, and honor natural and political barriers. The plan must be approved by three of the four commissioners, thus ensuring a measure of bipartisanship. If the commission cannot meet its January 1 deadline, the Supreme Court has until the following April 30 to draw a plan.

The Legislature can amend the commission's redistricting plan by a two-thirds majority in each house but must do so by the end of the thirtieth day of the first session following the day of submission. The plan takes effect at that time with or without legislative amendment or approval.

Washington's Redistricting Commission was given power not only over state legislative districts but congressional districts as well. Washington joined Hawaii and Montana as the only states to redraw congressional districts by commission (New Jersey became the fourth state in 1991).

The first Washington State redistricting commissioners were appointed and began deliberations in early 1991 as prescribed. The Legislature appropriated funding for sophisticated (for their time) computer programs to help in analyzing data and drawing lines. Federal census results were received and entered. The ideal size for each legislative district was determined to be 99,320, and for congressional districts to be 540,743. Since there is no registration by political party in Washington State, commissioners used the 1988 presidential election results to determine the demographic and political makeup of areas and potential districts.

It became clear very early that the city of Seattle and eastern Washington would each lose one district, both going to the fast-growing suburbs of King and Snohomish counties. By the end of May, the commission began to take public testimony, consisting mostly of pleas from individuals and groups asking the commission not to divide cities or counties. It was all new but it appeared that the system was working.

Problems surfaced in mid-December. Commissioners were rumored to be close to agreement for legislative redistricting but far apart on congressional districts. Staffers were told to research whether the commission could submit just the legislative plan by the January 1 deadline and leave the congressional district boundaries for the court. The answer is not clear. The commission broke up in anger several times. Many observers said the commission would fail. And it nearly did.

At 11:16 P.M. on December 31, 1991, just 44 minutes before the deadline, the four political appointees on the commission reached agreement on both legislative and congressional redistricting. Commissioners clearly did their best to protect incumbents but were unable to do so in every case. As expected, the city of Seattle and the Spokane area lost seats to suburban King and Snohomish counties, so incumbents from those two districts had the choice of moving across the state or being forced to leave office at the end of their terms (no one moved for the 1992 elections but this has happened in previous years).

Most political pundits thought the 1991 redistricting would help the Republicans because they were thought to be stronger in the suburbs which gained seats, while Democrats were forced to make choices between incumbents in their dwindling urban base. If judged by the Democratic sweep in 1992, the experts were wrong, but if judged by the 1994 Republican landslide, they were correct.

The essential lesson about redistricting is that the Legislature has great difficulty doing the job itself. It is just too close to the question, too tied up in speculation about politics and protection of incumbents. The 1991 Redistricting Commission worked hard and was ultimately successful, freeing up the Legislature to do what it does best, set policy for the state.

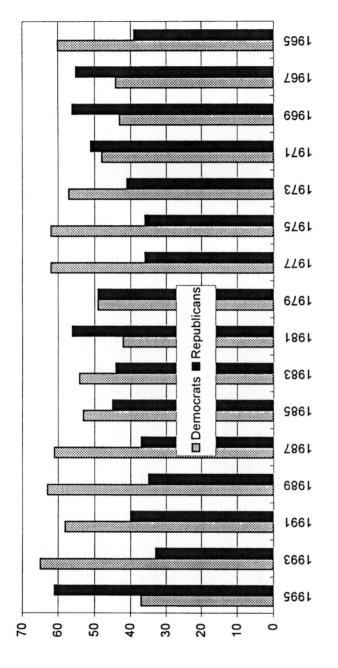

Fig 8.1. Partisan Membership of the Washington State
House of Representatives: 1965-1995

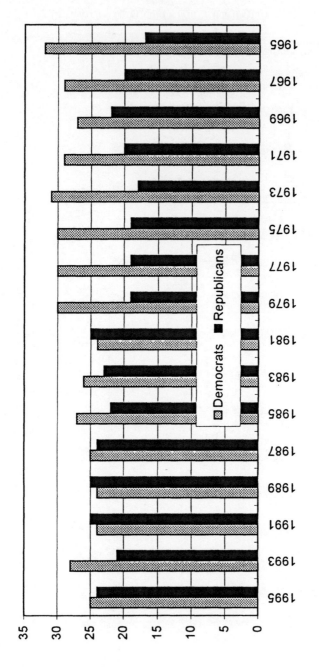

Fig 8.2. Partisan Membership of the Washington
State Senate: 1965-1995

POLITICAL PARTIES

Washington is a genuine two-party state but in the period since the end of World War II, Democrats have had the upper hand more often than not in the Legislature. There have been twenty-seven biennial elections from 1947 through 1995. Democrats lead Republicans twenty to six in terms of a majority in the House over that period. There was one tie. In the Senate, Democrats won nineteen times to Republicans' seven, with one tie in 1947 (see Fig. 8.1 and Fig. 8.2).

This is a complete reversal over the period before the Great Depression. Republicans had a lock on the state Senate from 1889 until 1933. The same is true of the House, except in 1897, when the Populists gained a majority. There was even one year, 1899, when not a single Democrat was elected to the House: Republicans had sixty-eight seats, the People's Party had nine, and the Citizen's Party had one.

The Depression and the New Deal flipped politics over like a pancake. In 1931 there were forty-one Republicans and only one Democrat in the state Senate. Four years later that had reversed itself to thirty-seven Democrats and only nine Senate Republicans. In the same four-year period, the House went from eighty-nine to eight in favor of the Republicans to ninety-one to eight in favor of the Democrats. The Democrats took control of both houses in 1933 and kept the Republicans at bay until 1947 in the House and 1953 in the Senate. In reality, however, during the 1940s the Legislature was generally ruled by a coalition of conservative Democrats and Republicans. In fact in 1947 in the Senate, this coalition actually met together as a caucus rather than just voting in unison on the floor.

Only once in our history has a party other than the Republicans or Democrats had a majority in either the House or Senate. In 1897 there were forty-four Populists elected to the House, Republicans had thirteen, Silver Republicans had eleven, and Democrats ten. During most of the 1890s, the People's Party provided the main opposition to the Republicans. The last person elected to the Legislature who did not run as a Democrat or a Republican was Knute Hill who was elected as a Progressive in 1927 from the 58th House district in Benton County. Representative Hill switched to the Democrats in 1929. It would be a fair generalization to say that the current two-party system did not emerge in the Washington State Legislature until 1945. Republicans usually had a lopsided majority from statehood until the 1930s when Democrats ruled for about a decade prior to the emergence of the current two-party system.

In more recent history, voters made a huge switch in 1994 when the House went from sixty-five to thirty-three in favor of the Democrats to sixty to thirty-eight in favor of the Republicans. Defections added two more House members to the Republican majority after the election. In the Senate, Democrats lost three seats but clung to a one-vote majority. The combined results of the 1992 and 1994 elections on the 1995-1996 Legislature is that the House reflected strongly conservative voter attitudes from 1994 while the governor and half the Senate reflected more liberal voter attitudes from the 1992 election.

Washington State voters are generally not political party-oriented and clearly delight in creating divided government. In the past nine years they have entrusted control of both houses of the Legislature and the governor to a single party only once, the Democrats, in 1993-1994. Republicans have to go back to 1981-1982 for their last time of controlling all three centers of power. Readers should keep this in mind the next time they see a news report criticizing the "do nothing Legislature" or gridlock. The system of staggered terms for the House and the Senate was specifically designed by our founding fathers to temper actions and slow things down.

TERMS, TERM LIMITS AND TURNOVER

Members of the House of Representatives are elected to two-year terms and state senators to four-year terms. Put another way, all the House seats and half the Senate seats are up every November of even-numbered years. Terms of legislators normally begin on the opening day of the odd-numbered year's legislative session (second Monday in January).

A proposed constitutional amendment to increase the length of the terms of Washington State legislators passed the Legislature and was placed on the ballot in 1987. It would have lengthened House members' terms to four years and senators' terms to six years. Voters rejected it.

Washington voters rejected term limits the first time it was proposed, too. Voters turned down Initiative 553 in November 1991. It would have imposed term limits retroactively on the governor, lieutenant governor, Washington members of the United States Congress, and state legislators. Term limits proponents came right back the next year with Initiative 573, this time without the retroactive provision, and it passed. It limits the right of persons to appear on the ballot or to file a declaration of candidacy for certain offices, but presumably someone could still run as a write-in candidate. Its effective date was November 3, 1992.

Washington State's Term Limitations

Office	Limitation
Governor	8 of last 14 years
Lieutenant Governor	8 of last 14 years
U.S. Senate	12 of last 18 years
U.S. House	6 of last 12 years
State Senate	8 of last 14 years
State House	6 of last 12 years

In addition to these limits, no person can serve as a member of either legislative body for more than fourteen of the previous twenty years.

United States Congressman Tom Foley (D-Spokane) challenged the congressional provisions of the term limits initiative shortly after adoption. In 1994 a federal district court agreed with Foley that congressional term limits are a qualification for office and states cannot impose additional qualifications beyond those already in the United States Constitution, eliminating that part of the initiative which applied to Congress. The United States Supreme Court followed suit in 1995, declaring unconstitutional the term limits for congressmen in 22 states. Foley won the court case but he was defeated for reelection in 1994.

The state term limit provisions of Initiative 573 have not yet been challenged in our courts. There was a decision in February 1996 by the Nebraska Supreme Court that threw out state term limits there, but it was based on drafting errors rather than on the merits of term limits themselves. At some point the Washington Supreme Court will probably rule on the two most basic issues involved in Initiative 573: whether the initiative amends the state Constitution; and whether term limits constitutionally violate the freedom of choice of voters.

As Washington law stands today, House members who were elected or reelected in November 1992 cannot appear on the ballot for reelection in 1998. Over half the members of the House serving during the 1996 session come under this restriction.

In the Senate it means that persons who were elected or reelected in November 1992 cannot serve after the year 2000. That includes almost two-thirds of the senators serving during the 1996 session. Eliminated by term limits will be all the 1996 elected leadership and most of the committee chairs of both the House and the Senate.

Washington is just one of twenty states to impose term limits on state legislators. California, Oklahoma and Colorado adopted them in 1990. In 1992, our state was joined by Arkansas, Michigan, Oregon, Wyoming,

Florida, Missouri, Ohio, South Dakota, Montana and Arizona in passing term limits. Maine signed up in 1993. Nevada and Utah joined the crowd in 1994. Only seven states west of the Mississippi did not have term limits at the end of 1996, and five of those do not have the initiative process. That is the key. Term limits have rarely been imposed by legislators on themselves. Most of the states which have the initiative process have term limits; those without the initiative do not.

It will be interesting to watch how Washington legislators react as the deadline for actual imposition of term limits in the House in 1998 and the Senate in 2000 nears. The initiative creates only a state law, and it takes a simple majority of the two houses and the signature of the governor to change the law.

During the 1996 session, House Minority Leader Marlin Appelwick (D-Seattle) proposed extending the limits to twelve years total, House or Senate. That is the limit most common in other states and is similar to a bill that failed in the state Senate in 1991. In return he would enshrine term limitations in the state Constitution so future changes would have to be approved by the people. His suggestions were quickly dismissed by the backers of Initiative 573 and went nowhere in the session. Appelwick said he would try again in 1997 and, if unsuccessful, would challenge the limits in court in 1998 once an incumbent is refused access to the ballot.

In the past two or three decades, state legislatures have generally become more professional by improving staffing, adopting new technology, increasing salaries, and modernizing procedures. States have become more important in the administration of federal programs and spending federal funds. There has been a devolution of power from the federal government to the states that is now part of the program of both political parties. How will term limits for state legislators affect all this?

George Peery, writing in *State Legislatures* in June 1996 (see bibliography for this chapter), suggests several changes ahead for states with term limits for state legislators. (1) He says that term limits "strike at one of the central tenets of what it means to be a modern legislative institution—stable membership." (2) Peery argues that term limits will shift power to the executive. As an example, he cites the fact that in 1994 for the first time the governor of Maine was given the line-item veto. (3) Term limits usually give senators more time than House members (as is the case in Washington) and could thus make Senates more powerful. (4) Rural legislators have tended to stay longer in office than urban, and term limits could further reduce the influence of farming and rural counties in legislatures. (5) There is preliminary evidence to suggest that new lawmakers under term limits bring a different set of values and priorities.

Apprenticeships and deferential learning curves are discarded in favor of early specialization and a strong desire to hit the ground running. There is more urgency and risk-taking in order to get things done quickly.

There are many unanswered questions about term limits. How will it change the type of candidates who choose to run for part-time legislative jobs? How will special interests and lobbyists, who tended to form long-term relationships with senior members, adapt? What will the effect be on the selection and operation of legislative leadership and committee chairs? It seems likely that the traditional seniority system will be scrapped. What will be the effect on handling perennial problems, such as another recession? There will be no legislators around who remember the last severe recession of 1981.

Adaptation to term limits is already occurring in several states. For the first time, freshmen like Representative Tom Huff (R-Gig Harbor) are being appointed chairs of fiscal committees. Freshman orientation programs are being expanded. Longer and more intense sessions are being held.

A decade from now political scientists will be able to compare the thirty states with no term limits to the twenty that have them and form some conclusions. For now, we can only watch with interest and hope that our state made the right decision.

. Whether because of impending term limits or low pay or stress of the job, turnover among legislators is increasing. According to a 1994 study by Miriam Barcellona for *WESTRENDS*, the upper houses of state legislatures experienced a 14.85 percent turnover between 1979 and 1993. Statistically that means a 100 percent turnover in seven elections. During the same period, the lower houses experienced an average turnover rate of 15.74 percent which means a statistical 100 percent turnover after six elections. The turnover rate is naturally higher right after redistricting because of the changes in boundaries. In 1972 and 1982, state legislatures experienced a 38 percent and 32 percent turnover.

Most state legislators serve for a relatively short period of time anyway so term limits would have little impact on them. The main effect is on those few legislators who become "entrenched incumbents," meaning those from safe districts who stay ten, twenty, thirty or more years. Representative John L. O'Brien (D-Seattle) served in the Washington House from 1939 to 1993, missing four years from 1946-1950, for a total of fifty years.

The 1994 elections produced a higher-than-usual turnover in state legislatures, mostly at the expense of Democrats. Nationwide, the turnover in upper houses was 19.5 percent and in lower houses it was 24.4 percent in 1994. In Washington State, there was an 18.4 percent turnover in the Senate and an amazing 40.8 percent in the state House. A staggering 65 percent of the sixty-one Republicans serving in the Washington House of Representatives in 1995 were freshmen. Only a dozen House Republicans had served more than one term. The average length of service for all sixty-one House Republicans was about two years. Only two House Republicans had ever served in a majority. And all of this happened before term limits took effect in this state.

QUALIFICATIONS AND PRIOR EXPERIENCE

It's pretty easy to qualify as a candidate for the Legislature: All that is required is to be an American citizen and be qualified to vote in the district (Washington Constitution, Article II, Section 7). In order to qualify to vote, one needs to be eighteen years old and a resident.

Citizenship and age are easily determined. Residence is a little less certain, as former Senator Ray Moore (D-Seattle) can attest. It seems that Moore, who was over seventy years of age at the time, had started planning for retirement in 1988 by buying a piece of property; then, over several years, building a house on it—in Kona, Hawaii. At some point in the early 1990s Senator Moore and his wife, Virginia, began dividing their time between Olympia when the Legislature was in session, an apartment in his Queen Anne legislative district, and their new place in Hawaii. There was little doubt that Senator Moore resided in his district when reelected in 1990 or that he served his constituents faithfully and well.

In 1994 first one newspaper then others began a relentless campaign "exposing" the senator who lived in Hawaii but served in the Washington Legislature. Whenever there was a slow news day, there was certain to be another article about Senator Moore. Moore was the butt of many clever political cartoons (which he thoroughly enjoyed). Moore, however, turned out to be a lot "Moore than just a pretty face" (his 1990 campaign slogan). He survived all attempts to force him out of office before the end of the 1994 session, even though his Seattle voter registration was revoked. He retired later in the year, and, as of the publication of this book, is happily retired with Virginia and seven cats on a small coffee plantation in Kona, Hawaii.

Residency is defined as "a person's permanent address where he physically resides and maintains his abode" (RCW 29.01.140). Questions about residency are usually raised as a challenge to filing for office rather than during an official's term, as in Senator Moore's case. More typical is the case involving state Representative Tom Campbell.

Representative Campbell announced in early summer of 1996 that he intended to run for the Senate seat in the 2nd District of southeast Pierce County. In July, several voters in the 2nd District filed a registration challenge with the Pierce County auditor claiming that Campbell actually lived in another district where he owns a home rather than the 2nd District where he owns a rental property. They claim the rental property is uninhabited. The county auditor makes the initial determination as to whether a person is a qualified registered voter in the district, subject to appeal to Pierce County Superior Court. It is strictly a matter of determining the facts: where does Campbell physically reside? If Campbell is found not to be a resident of the 2nd District, he would be prevented from filing for election to the Senate or for reelection to his House seat in that district. In August 1996, the Pierce County auditor ruled in favor of Campbell.

One of the marvelous things about the state Legislature is that it brings together such a diverse group of people. Not only must they legally come from forty-nine different parts of the state, but they have a wide variety of backgrounds and professions. The National Conference of State Legislatures did a study of the professions of all the state legislators in the country in 1994. Here is the breakdown of what legislators said they did for a living:

Attorney	16.5%	Consultant	3.5
Full-time legislator	14.9	Real estate	3.2
Business owner	10.0	Insurance	3.2
Agriculture	7.9	Gov't. employee	2.5
Retired	7.2	Communications/arts	2.4
Business exec./mgr.	6.2	Medical	2.4
K-12 educator	6.2	College educator	2.0
Business	5.1	Other or unknown	6.8

A study by the *Seattle Times,* published October 15, 1990, of Washington State legislators found somewhat different results:

Bus./consulting	24.0%	Medicine	4.1
Full-time legislator	13.7	Trade labor	3.4
Retired	13.0	Accounting	2.1
Attorney	11.6	Engineering	2.1
Agriculture	9.6	Government	2.1
Education	6.2	Union official	1.4
Administrator	4.8	Other or unknown	3.0

According to the Legislative Manual, the leading occupations listed by legislators themselves in the first Legislature in 1889 were Agriculture (28 percent), Businessman (12 percent) and Attorney (11 percent). Just after the second world war, the top three were still Agriculture (19 percent), Attorney (17 percent), and Businessman (10 percent). In the latest Red Book (1995-96), the three top occupations were Businessman (20 percent), Legislator (12 percent) and Agriculture, Attorney, and Retired (all with about 8 percent). However, if one adds all those who list legislator, retired, homemaker, consultant, and none, it comes to about 36 percent who are probably spending their full time at being legislators and this is really the single largest group.

Looking through the Red Book for many sessions, it appears that fewer legislators today come from the agricultural and labor sectors and more from the professions such as doctors, engineers, chiropractors, professors, and teachers. Businessmen have generally constituted the largest group (albeit a very diverse one) and, if anything, their numbers have increased. Lawyers' numbers have remained fairly constant between 10 and 15 percent.

Prior experience will become increasingly relevant in the Twenty-first Century Washington Legislature when the most senior House members will have served only two terms. Gone will be members like John L. O'Brien who in his fifty years in the Legislature became a living encyclopedia of knowledge about the rules and the traditions of the House. Hopefully, they will be replaced by members like Representative Tom Huff, a retired Sears executive, whose prior knowledge and experience enabled him to be chair of the House Appropriations Committee in only his second year in the Legislature, and Sid Snyder, who was elected to the Senate after a distinguished career as Secretary of the Senate, and was elected caucus chair in his first term and majority leader in his second.

AGE

The average age of the first Washington State legislators in 1889 was just over forty-three. In 1995 the average had risen more than seven years to over fifty. It appeared in 1987 in the first edition of this book that there was a strong upward trend since the seventies (see Fig. 8.3). The 1992 and 1994 elections, however, produced a younger average each time so the trend is broken. The averages may mean little in any case since they can be skewed by one or two members at the extreme end. In addition, the author could find no study showing a correlation between age and public policy over a long period of time. In the 1960s a liberal philosophy was generally equated with youth and a conservative one with age. In the 1990s it appears to be the opposite. So, readers can draw their own conclusions as to what meaning, if any, to give to Fig. 8.3 below.

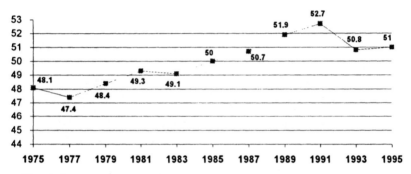

Fig. 8.3. Average Age of Washington State Legislators: 1975-1995

RACIAL DIVERSITY

According to the state Office of Financial Management, in 1995 Asian or Pacific Islanders accounted for 5.9 percent of the total population of Washington State, African Americans for 3.4 percent, and American Indians, Eskimos and Aleuts for 2 percent (Mindy Chambers' article in *The Olympian* of May 14, 1996). In the 1995-96 Legislature, there were two Asian American members and two African American members, meaning 1.34 percent each of the total membership of the Legislature. That was down from 1993-94 when Asian Americans made up almost 3 percent of legislators and African Americans were at 2 percent.

Following is a list of Asian Americans and African Americans who have served or are serving in the Washington State Legislature. The author regrets that he was unable to obtain similar information for Native Americans, Hispanics and other minority groups.

Asian Americans
Eng, John, D-37th District (Seattle), 1973-1983, House
Locke, Gary, D-37th District (Seattle), 1983-1994, House
Shin, Paull, D-21st District (Snohomish), 1993-1995, House
Shinoda, Paul, R-39th District (Snohomish), 1977-1979, House
Tokuda, Kip, D-37th District (Seattle), 1995-present, House
Veloria, Velma, D-11th District (Seattle), 1993-present, House
Wang, Art, D-27th District (Tacoma), 1981-1995, House

African Americans
Bush, W.O., R-20th District (Thurston Co.), 1889-1891, House
Fleming, George, D-37th District (Seattle), 1969-1991, Senate
Flemming, Stan, D-28th District (Tacoma), 1993-1994, House
Franklin, Rosa, D-29th District (Tacoma), 1991-present, Senate
Mason, Dawn, D-37th District (Seattle), 1995-present, House
Maxie, Peggy, D-37th District (Seattle), 1971-1983, House
Ryan, John H., Farmer-Labor-38th District (Tacoma), 1921-1925, House; R-38th District (Tacoma), 1931-1933, House; D-28th District (Tacoma), 1933-1937, Senate
Smith, Sam, D-37th District (Seattle), 1959-1969, House
Smitherman, Bill, D-26th District (Gig Harbor), 1983-1991, Senate
Stokes, Charles, R-37th District (Seattle), 1951-1959, House
Wineberry, Jesse, D-43rd District (Seattle), 1985-1995, House

All minority legislators in Washington State were elected from districts in which they were a racial minority. There has never been a legislative district in this state in which a minority group was the majority. Most were pioneers in one sense or another.

Two minority members achieved particular prominence in the Legislature and should be recognized as such. George Fleming was Senate Democratic Caucus Chair from 1980 to 1990 and finished a close second to Joel Pritchard in the election for lieutenant governor in 1988; and Gary Locke was House Appropriations Chair from 1991 to 1995, then elected King County Executive, and a candidate for governor in 1996.

LEADERSHIP

There are two major differences in the procedures of the House and the Senate. The Senate has exclusive power of confirmation, discussed elsewhere in this book. The second major difference has to do with leadership. The House elects its leader and presiding officer, the **Speaker**, by a vote of the whole body. Most Senate leaders are elected within party caucuses and are not even mentioned in the rules of the Senate. More importantly, the Senate's presiding officer, the President, is chosen in the statewide election for **lieutenant governor.**

This difference in the selection of a presiding officer is worth further examination because it explains the different tone and behavior of the two bodies. The Speaker is actually first elected by the caucus of the party which gains a majority, then there is a *pro forma* election on the floor. The Speaker is the leader of the majority party in the House, the presiding officer of the House, and the chair of the Rules Committee. Thus, the presiding officer of the House is always partisan and tends to make rulings and decisions that will benefit the majority. It's a little like having the coach of the home basketball team also be the referee of the game.

The presiding officer of the Senate is the lieutenant governor, who may or may not be of the same political party as the majority of the Senate. In fact, it has been more common than not in recent history for the Senate President to come from the minority party. From 1987 to 1988 the Republicans had a majority, but Democrat John Cherberg presided. And from 1993 to 1997, Democrats had a majority but Republican Joel Pritchard presided. Both men were fair and consistent in their rulings and would side with their "home teams" only when all other things were equal. Unlike the Speaker, the Senate President cannot vote on final passage of bills but is permitted to cast the deciding vote when there is a tie on amendments to bills or motions which require a majority of the members present.

Since the Senate President is elected statewide and independently of members of the Senate, he can be above the day-to-day schemes and maneuvers that are part of lawmaking. Both John Cherberg and Joel Pritchard would attend their party caucuses on occasion, but more often would spend that time in their own offices. They kept a kind of separation between themselves and the daily partisan wrangling, not wanting "their side" to view them as an easy mark or the "other side" to see them as inherently unfair.

The Speaker, on the other hand, is the key person planning strategy behind the caucus doors and then gets to make all the decisions from the chair. There is no doubt about his partisanship or loyalty. This gives the majority party in the House a tremendous advantage. In the Senate, the majority leader operates from the floor and is forced to abide by the rulings of the chair. That means that in the Senate the two sides are forced to work more closely together, to be less partisan, more restrained.

Although rare, there are times when having the presiding officer elected by the whole body can be a disadvantage. This was demonstrated in 1976. The Democrats enjoyed a whopping advantage of sixty-two to thirty-six in the House but were split philosophically, so they fell to fighting among themselves. Early in the 1976 Regular Session, they voted thirty-two to thirty inside their caucus to oust Speaker Leonard Sawyer. Technically it would take a vote of the majority of the whole House to remove him, but Sawyer acceded to the wishes of the majority of his fellow Democrats and resigned as Speaker. That left thirty-six Republicans, thirty-two anti-Sawyerites, and thirty pro-Sawyerites in the House with no group able to reach the fifty votes necessary for a majority. The Republicans enjoyed this intraparty squabble immensely and said they would support their minority leader for Speaker in any vote on the floor. Since the anti-Sawyerites couldn't get beyond their thirty-two votes and the thirty pro-Sawyerites wouldn't budge, no one could get a majority and there was no Speaker. The remainder of the session was presided over by Speaker Pro Tem John L. O'Brien.

Every two years shortly after the November elections, the four caucuses meet separately to choose their leaders. A **caucus** is all the members of a political party elected to a body. The side with the most votes in the House elects a Speaker, Speaker Pro Tempore (Tem), majority leader, majority caucus chair, majority whip, and various deputy leaders, assistant leaders, whips and deputy whips. In real terms, the top three in the pecking order in the House are usually the Speaker, majority leader, and caucus chair. Both the Speaker and the Speaker Pro Tem are elected by a vote of the whole body. Incidentally, until the Speaker is elected, the Chief Clerk from the previous term presides (HR 2).

The side that loses the election in the House elects, in order of power, a minority leader, minority floor leader, and a minority caucus chair, as well as assistants to the above. All of these positions are elected by vote in the minority caucus.

The winning caucus in the Senate elects, in order of power, a majority leader, majority caucus chair, majority floor leader, President Pro Tem, majority whip and assistants and deputies to the above. Notice two differences. In the Senate, the top leader is the majority leader—there is no Speaker. Notice also that the second most powerful position is caucus chair. This is because the majority caucus chair traditionally presides over the **Facilities and Operations Committee** which has power over almost everything involved in running the Senate from staffing to parking to postage. This is another perk that goes to the Speaker in the House (you begin to see why the Speaker is often referred to as the second most powerful person in the state). In effect, the Speaker has almost total power in the House while power is shared in the Senate between the majority leader, the majority caucus chair and the lieutenant governor.

Historically, the role of **Senate majority leader** is fairly new. Prior to 1941, the leader of the majority in the Senate was the **President Pro Tem.** This makes sense because the President Pro Tem is the highest officer elected by the whole body—like the Speaker in the House. And, the President Pro Tem chairs the body in the absence of the lieutenant governor. However, with the emergence of a two-party system, the majority leader became dominant. Of course, there is nothing to prevent a person from holding both positions.

The losing caucus in the Senate elects, in order of power, a minority leader, a minority caucus chair, a minority floor leader, whips, deputies and assistants. It's the same as above—just substitute the word "minority."

There is no hard and fast rule about names or numbers of titles or positions of leadership (except for Speaker). While the top positions have been constant for several decades, the power given to or shared with positions such as whips and deputy leaders can change from session to session.

VACANCIES

A vacancy in the office of senator or state representative can occur by death, resignation, expulsion, or recall. The first two are obvious. Expulsion and recall are highly contentious and unusual and require closer examination.

The Washington State Constitution provides that either legislative body may expel a member with the concurrence of two-thirds of the members elected (Article II, Section 9). No particular cause or reason is required, so that is left to the discretion of the members. **Expulsion** is specifically mentioned in the rules of the Senate (SR 7 (5)), repeating the constitutional language. The 1996 House rules do not mention expulsion but the power is there anyway because the Constitution says so.

Along the same lines, House rules provide that any member convicted of a felony punishable by death or imprisonment in a state penal institution is to lose salary, per diem, office and office expenses. Interestingly, though, the person could continue to hold office although expulsion would seem likely. The House expelled Nelson Robinson in 1931 when he was convicted of statutory rape. That was easy compared to the problem the Senate faced a decade later.

On January 13, 1941, the first day of the Regular Session, President Victor Meyers called the Senate to order and received the list of senators elected November 5, 1940, from Secretary of State Belle Reeves. The list included Lenus Westman from the 39th District (Island and Snohomish counties) and Agnes M. Gehrman from the 19th District (Pacific and Grays Harbor counties). After taking the roll and finding all members present, Senator Joseph Drumheller (D-Spokane) moved that members whose elections were contested or were to be investigated be escorted from the chamber and that the remaining members step forward to be sworn in. Gehrman's election was contested and Westman was about to be investigated on the charge of being a communist, so both were removed from the Senate chamber.

After a few more formalities, the Senate created two committees of five members each to investigate the eligibility of the newly-elected but not-yet-sworn-in senators-elect Gehrman and Westman. The issue in the Gehrman election was over an allegation of voting irregularities in a dozen South Bend and Raymond precincts. One week later, the Gehrman Committee found there were many errors in tabulating ballots, but the recount showed a net gain of five votes for Agnes Gehrman, so they recommended that she be seated as a member of the Senate from the 19th District with pay dating back to January 13. The Senate agreed and it was done (*Senate Journal*, 1941, pp. 5-60).

On the twelfth day of the session, the Westman Investigative Committee was ready to report. The Senate was called to order by President Meyers at 2:35 P.M. and immediately put under the call. Senator Shirley Marsh then presented the report of the committee, which she chaired. The committee found, among other things, that Lenus Westman became a U.S. citizen by naturalization in 1936 and lived in Snohomish County; that he admitted being a member of the Communist Party from May 1938 until September 1939; that his membership was verified by one Arthur L. Johnson of Everett who had been the organizer for the Communist Party in Snohomish County since 1937; that Westman said he left the Communist Party because he thought his social and economic beliefs could be better furthered outside; and that Westman was a delegate from the teachers' union to the Central Labor Council without disclosing to them that he was a communist, a fact which would have made him ineligible.

The committee further found that Westman said he did not believe in force and violence and that no witnesses came forward to say they ever heard Westman advocate such; that two witnesses denied that the Communist Party stands for force and violence; and that during the campaign Westman was charged with being a communist and denied it publicly. Based on its findings, three members on the committee recommended that Senator-elect Westman be seated and two members filed a minority report that he not be seated.

There was a variety of procedural moves to table motions or to delay action but all were turned back. The final question before the Senate that afternoon was whether to accept the minority report that Westman not be seated. It passed 27-17. The Senate seat from the 39th District was declared vacant and notice was sent to the county commissioners of Island and Snohomish counties to take appropriate action to find a replacement.

Twelve of the seventeen members who voted against denying Westman a seat submitted for the Journal an explanation of their vote. They affirmed their belief that communism was evil but said there was insufficient evidence that Westman "is now a communist." A thirteenth senator, N. P. Atkinson from King County, who also voted no, said in part: "I voted no on the proposition to refuse Senator Westman his seat because I believe that the people are entitled to the representative of their own choice." (*Senate Journal,* 1941, pp. 78-81)

The Washington State Constitution specifically makes every elective public office except judges subject to **recall** and **discharge** by the voters of the area from which the person was elected (Article I, Section 33). But it's not easy.

In order to recall a legislator, one must first prepare a written petition charging the legislator with an act of malfeasance or misfeasance while in office. That would be any conduct which interferes with the performance of an official duty, or performance in an improper manner, or the commission of an unlawful act. The charge is filed with the same official who received the declaration of candidacy, the county elections officer, or the secretary of state if more than one county is involved. This person prepares a ballot synopsis. The charge and synopsis are then given to the superior court of the county in which the legislator resides. The court has fifteen days to rule on the sufficiency (not the truth) of the charge and synopsis.   If found sufficient, sponsors have 180 days to obtain the signatures of registered voters equal to 35 percent of those who voted when the legislator was last elected to office.

If sufficient signatures are obtained and certified, a special recall election is held forty-five to sixty days later.   The recall ballot is simple: FOR or AGAINST.   If the majority is for the recall, the legislator is discharged and the office is declared vacant.   If not, nothing changes.

No legislator in this state has ever been recalled.   The only serious effort to do so was in 1981 when Senator Peter von Reichbauer switched from Democrat to Republican.   Democrats were somewhat miffed at his rebuff and mounted a recall campaign.   They actually got through the petition and synopsis and gathered enough signatures to get it to the ballot, but it was all for nothing.   The voters decided they still liked von Reichbauer, even as a Republican.

Vacancies occur fairly regularly in the Legislature, which is not surprising since there are 147 members.   If a vacancy occurs more than four weeks prior to the September primary election, the county (or counties) central committee of the party involved submits a list of three names to the county commissioners who can **appoint** any of the three.   If the county commissioners cannot make a decision within sixty days, the governor does it, also from the list of three.   In most cases, the party central committee polls the precinct committeepersons prior to submitting its list of three candidates.   Usually the county commissioners choose the top candidate from among the three, but they are not bound to do so.

The appointee must then run at the next general election for the balance of the unexpired term (Article II, Section 15 of the Constitution, and RCW 42.12).

If the vacancy occurs less than four weeks prior to the primary election, the successor is appointed as above but runs at the general election a year away, again for the unexpired term.

The process of appointment takes on more meaning when one considers that of the forty-nine senators serving in 1996, thirteen were first appointed to seats in the Legislature.   Seven of the 1996 House members were first appointed to the office.

PAY, PERKS AND THE GOOD LIFE

Would you apply for a job that requires working ten to twelve-hour days and many weekends, where you give up your privacy and anonymity, which requires you to spend from two to five months a year away from home and make tough decisions on almost every imaginable topic where you are bound to offend large blocks of constituents regardless of what you do, which pays only $28,300 per year, and for which about three-fourths of the public will hold you in low esteem if not contempt?

If you are still interested, the application process is even worse. It requires that you shamelessly ask everyone you know for money and help; that you fill out detailed questionnaires; have interviews with, and, if you want their support, make commitments to organizations you only partially agree with at best; that you knock on the doors to people's homes uninvited and accost strangers in malls begging for support; that you take positions which you are expected to never change on a multitude of issues you really don't know much about; and where you must deal with at least one opponent who wants the job as much as you and will say and do almost anything to keep you from getting it.

If successful, you assume the job of state legislator. An article by Lynda Mapes that appears in the *Spokesman Review* on February 11, 1996, paints a bleak but realistic picture of legislative life. A typical day begins with early breakfast meetings and goes through the evening. Personal lives suffer. She writes that of eleven legislators representing the Spokane area, five had divorced while in office. When in Olympia, home may be a rented trailer, a converted garage, a small room in someone else's house. It can be lonely and depressing in the dark and wet winter months in Olympia. A lucky few may bring family with them but that is difficult or impossible when the spouse is working or the children are in school.

Despite it all, good citizens continue to run for the office. David Ammons, in an article for *The Olympian* on May 26, 1996, writes that top-notch candidates are preparing to file for various state offices. He quotes Secretary of State Ralph Munro as saying, "I really think this is the best contingent of candidates we've ever had—outstanding people on both sides of the aisle, all up and down the ticket." He continues, "These people are terrific."

In 1986 voters approved constitutional Amendment 78 establishing an independent Salary Commission. The commission consists of sixteen members. Seven of the members are selected jointly by the President of the Senate and the Speaker of the House from prescribed sectors, such as higher education, business, etc. The other nine are selected by lot from the list of registered voters, one from each congressional district. Commissioners are appointed to four-year terms and may not serve more

than two terms.   No state official or family member or employee of an
official or lobbyist may serve on the commission.

The Salary Commission has jurisdiction over the salaries of all state
elected officials and judges as well as members of the Legislature.   The
Salary Commission studies pay levels, holds at least four public hearings,
then files its recommendations with the secretary of state.   The recommendations are subject to referendum but if nothing happens, after ninety days
the recommendations become law (they are placed in RCW 43.03).   (See
Fig. 8.4.)

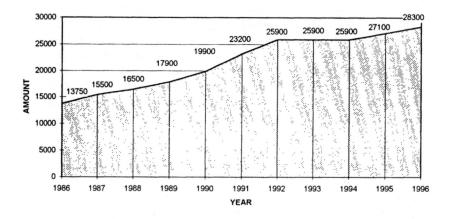

Fig. 8.4.   Washington State Legislators' Salaries: 1986-1996

In addition to their annual salary, legislators receive $66 per diem for
each day in session and for days spent attending meetings during the
interim, up to $5,400 per year for office expenses, a postage allowance,
and mileage reimbursement for travel.   In an *Olympian* article on January
25, 1996, Bob Partlow calculates that the average senator in 1995 received
$26,750 in expenses.   House members received about $2,000 more.

Everything to do with legislators' pay is controversial.   For example, in
1965 legislators raised their per diem (in lieu of subsistence and lodging)
from $25 to $40 per day.   Harley Hoppe, a taxpayer, challenged the

increase as a violation of Article 28, Section 1 of the state Constitution, which states that "The compensation of any state officer shall not be increased or diminished during his term of office." The court points out that the original Constitution provided for payment of $5 per attendance day and ten cents per mile travelled. That was changed in 1948 (Amendment 20) to allow the Legislature to set its own salary subject to the provision above but that per diem was different from salary. The court held that there is no constitutional limit against reimbursement for lodging and subsistence, whether paid as a flat sum or on vouchered expenses.

Legislative leaders receive a little extra salary because they are required to attend more meetings and have greater responsibilities. The Speaker receives $36,300 per year, and the Senate majority and minority leaders and House minority leader receive $32,300 per year.

State legislators' salaries and allowances vary widely across the nation. States with full-time legislatures obviously pay more. California legislators receive $76,600 per year plus $109 per diem. In Michigan legislators receive an annual salary of $50,629 plus an annual per diem of $8,925. Comparing some states similar in size to Washington: Wisconsin legislators receive $38,056 a year plus $75 per diem; Colorado pays $17,500 per year to state legislators and up to $99 per diem; North Carolina legislators receive $13,951 per year, plus $6,708 expense allowance, plus $104 per diem.

In past years some big companies like Boeing and US West would continue to pay the salaries of their employees who were legislators and the legislators would turn their annual salaries over to the company. This kind of subsidization appears to be a thing of the past, however, and may not be allowed under the current rules of ethics.

Salaries of all public officials but especially state legislators are a source of resentment with much of the public. Some people feel salaries should reflect the perceived part-time nature of the Legislature, that it is a matter of public service, and that higher salaries breed a class of professional lawmakers who would not understand the problems of real people. Some wish that we could go back to the days before the end of World War II when legislators received $5 for every day in session. That meant $300 every two years, nothing for special sessions, except for 1909 and 1925 when legislators approved $5 per day extra for those special sessions.

On the other hand, some would argue that term limits changes the equation. It takes care of the problem of the professional legislator. Low pay is not needed as an inducement to move on. In fact, higher salaries—much higher salaries—are needed to attract the best and the brightest people from around the state to take a few years off from their businesses or professions or jobs or families, to serve as legislators, then return. In addition, the higher pay advocates argue that it is necessary to insulate legislators from being a beggar-class which is dependent on the "charity" of special interests.

9

The Gender Revolution

The second half of the Twentieth Century may someday be best remembered as the time when America swept away artificial hindrances based on gender, race, religion and disabilities and freed all its people to develop the full extent of their talents, skills and energies. America has been a world leader in these efforts and Washington State has been and remains a leader within the United States. The Washington State story of the gaining of women's suffrage, the election of women to public office, the steady assumption of power by women within the Legislature, and, finally, the changes resulting from this gender gain should be seen in this context and should offer hope to those who believe progress in this and other areas has not been fast enough.

WOMEN'S SUFFRAGE

The 19th Amendment to the United States Constitution declares that the right "to vote shall not be denied or abridged by the United States or by any state on account of sex." It was ratified on August 26, 1920. In

Washington, however, that battle had been joined much earlier; in fact, as early as when Washington became a territory.

During the first session of the Territorial Legislature in 1853, Seattleite Arthur Denny introduced a bill that would have given white women the right to vote (see G. Thomas Edwards' book in the bibliography for this chapter). It failed by one vote, reportedly because a legislator who was married to a native American objected to her exclusion.

The territorial election law of 1866 extended suffrage "to all white citizens." Some Washingtonians insisted that meant both male and female (*Washington Standard*, June 4, 1870). They were encouraged in this belief by the visit of fifty-year-old Susan B. Anthony to Olympia in October 1870, and by her address to the state Legislature on October 19, 1870, but the courts did not agree.

Women's suffrage was approved in 1883 in Washington State. It was but a brief opportunity, however, because the Washington Territorial Court ruled five years later that the United States Constitution did not intend to include women's suffrage and that it took precedence. The ruling did not preclude Washington State from approving women's suffrage in non-federal elections, however.

In 1889, the question of women's suffrage was placed before Washington voters along with the questions of the location of the state capital and the prohibition of alcohol. These were the three issues left unresolved by the constitutional convention. The suffrage issue may have become entangled with the prohibition question in people's minds in what some describe as a battle between churches and saloons. Prohibition and women's suffrage were both defeated by about 60 percent to 40 percent (and Olympia received more votes than North Yakima or Ellensburg for state capital). Still, the women's suffrage issue wouldn't go away and just one year later, in 1890, women in Washington State were granted the right to vote in school elections.

The battle over women's suffrage was being waged nationwide and women had some successes, especially in the west. In 1894 the first women were elected to any state legislature when three Republican women were elected to the Colorado House of Representatives. In 1896, Dr. Martha Hughes Cannon of Salt Lake City became the first woman elected to a state Senate, as a Democrat in Utah. By the end of the Nineteenth Century, sixteen women had served or were serving in state legislatures in the states of Colorado, Utah and Idaho.

In 1910, Washington voters approved the Fifth Amendment to the state Constitution which struck the word "male" from the description of qualifications of voters in the Second Amendment. Women could now vote in Washington State elections, a decade ahead of the national government, albeit slightly behind some of our neighbors. By 1920, when women's suffrage was adopted nationally, at least sixty-nine women had served in the state legislatures of a dozen states, including two from Washington.

GETTING ELECTED

At the general election in 1912, the first when Washington State women could vote or run for office, two women were elected to the Legislature. Frances C. Axtell was a forty-seven-year-old Republican from Whatcom County who served just one term in the state House then ran unsuccessfully for Congress. She had M.A. and Ph.D. degrees from DePaul University. She was a reformist who was primarily concerned with public safety. She was later appointed by President Woodrow Wilson to the U.S. Employees Compensation Commission where she advocated for improved federal safety standards.

Nena Jolidon Croake, a forty-year-old Doctor of Osteopathy from Pierce County, was elected as a Progressive to the state House also in 1912. She distinguished herself at the beginning of the thirteenth session of the Washington State Legislature when she introduced the first bill, a proposal to improve standards for women's working conditions. Representative Croake also served only one term.

> The pioneering women legislators were considered a novelty and were closely scrutinized by the press and the public. In her first session, Representative Axtell became confused during the election of the Speaker of the House and voted for the opponent of the person she supported. The press reported her confusion was "just like a woman." This unsupportive and at times hostile atmosphere forced many women to cut their political careers short, making it nearly impossible for them to have any real influence. *(Political Pioneers,* p. 2)

Ten years later, Reba J. Hurn, a forty-one-year-old Republican lawyer, became the first female Washington State Senator. She represented a district of Spokane County in the state Senate from 1922 until 1930. She is reported to have said, "I decided to run for the Senate rather than the House because there have been five women elected to the House and none of them have been reelected." At another time she said, "I am qualified for this position, have a right to run for it, and am in the race." Reba

Hurn attended Cornell University, Northwestern University and received her law degree from the University of Washington, with honors, and continued her studies at Heidelberg University. Ms. Hurn was the first woman admitted to the Washington State Bar. She was a quiet person, a "dry" on prohibition, and a devout Methodist. She said, "I have no causes. I am in favor of no reforms, unless it is the enactment of fewer laws and more concentration on codifying the mass of legislation that has been piling up in this state for years." In addition to her many other firsts, Senator Hurn was the first female Senate committee chair when she took over the Public Morals and State Libraries Committee in her first term.

Women continued to be elected to both houses of the Washington State Legislature in small numbers for the next sixty years. They typically made up 3 to 5 percent of the total membership from 1912 through 1973. They were mostly good-government reformers who advocated changing the existing political system. This reformer orientation put them at odds with the entrenched system once elected. According to Kathryn Hinsch, "Part of the problem was the women legislators accepted discrimination outside the Legislature as normal and did not always recognize it in the Legislature." *(Political Pioneers, p.5)*

A major obstacle women politicians had to overcome was the issue of children. Senator Margaret Hurley (D-Spokane) describes how she dealt with the problem while campaigning in the 1950s:

> "There were people who asked me, 'What are you going to do with your children?' And I said, 'Well, the session is only two months long and I have this friend who has been my babysitter and has agreed to come with me and my four small children if I win.' They would say, 'I don't see any reason why you shouldn't run.' They were very accepting."

Starting with the 1974 election, things began to change. The number of women in the Legislature began to rise in a steady and unrelenting upward curve for the next twenty years. In just two decades, women in the Washington Legislature would go from 5 percent to 40 percent of the total membership (see Fig. 9.1). In nine of the eleven biennial elections, the percentage of women rose.

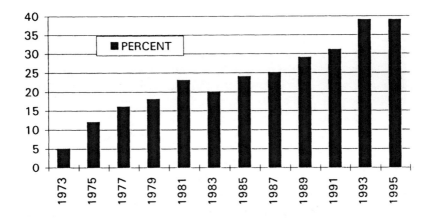

Fig. 9.1. Women in the Washington State Legislature: 1973-1995

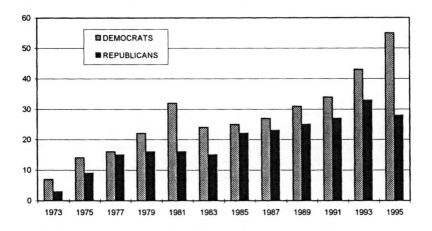

Fig. 9.2. Washington Women Legislators by Party (Percent):
1973-1995

The increase in women legislators took place in both political parties. In little more than twenty years, women rose from 3 percent of Washington Republican legislators to 28 percent. Even more remarkably, women went from 5 percent of Democratic state legislators in 1973 to a solid majority of 55 percent in 1995 (see Fig. 9.2) and became a majority in the majority party in the state Senate and in the minority party in the state House. Washington State's 40 percent led the nation in women legislators in 1995 where the average was 21 percent. Counting appointments to vacant seats, the number of women legislators grew to 41 percent by the end of 1996.

In recent years, Washington women legislators have tended to be Democrats by about 56 percent to 44 percent Republican, roughly the same ratio as Washington women voters at large. Since the 1930s there is some correlation between successful years for Democrats and increases in the number of women legislators. This makes it all the more surprising that following the huge Republican gains in 1994, the number of women legislators did not decrease (although the percentage did drop). In fact, twenty-four Republican women were elected to the Washington State Legislature in 1994, the most ever for that party. That same year, women became the majority in both the House and Senate Democratic caucuses.

TAKING POWER

To a very large extent, committee chairs and leadership positions in the Legislature are determined by seniority. Thus, it is not surprising that the number of women elected tends to be ahead of the number of women in leadership positions or serving as committee chairs. After two decades, though, there are an increasing number of women with longevity claims and there are few positions left in the Washington Legislature that women have not held.

The first women legislators were assigned to committees dealing with subjects such as education, libraries, health, and morals. This was true when it came to assigning committee chairs as well. It is telling that the first two women who held chairs in the Washington Legislature, Anna Colwell (R-Snohomish) in 1921 in the House, and Reba Hurn (R-Spokane) in 1923 in the Senate, were both given the Public Morals Committees in their respective chambers. The third was the House Parks and Playgrounds Committee chaired by Mrs. Harry J. Miller (R-Snohomish) in 1925. Then came the Printing and State Library Committee, Reba Hurn, 1927, and Educational Institutions and Charitable Institutions Committees, Reba Hurn and Maude Sweetman (R-Seattle), 1929.

Belle Reeves and her attorney husband moved to Washington State in 1889, the year of statehood. They eventually settled in Wenatchee and launched that city's first newspaper. After retiring, Ms. Reeves devoted herself to civic and cultural affairs. A group of women convinced her to run for the House in 1922 as a write-in candidate just a few days before the primary. She won by 100 votes and went on to be elected, then reelected seven times. She was one of only four Democrats during her first term and for several terms was the only woman serving in the Legislature. She was a "low-key" member who studied the system carefully and allied herself with more powerful members in order to accomplish passage of desired social legislation such as workmen's compensation and fair compensation for working mothers. In 1938 Representative Reeves was appointed secretary of state, the first woman to hold that position.

Pearl Wanamaker was born in Washington State in 1899. She received her B.A. degree from the University of Washington, worked as a teacher, raised a family, and rose to be superintendent of Island County schools. Her neighbors urged her to run for the Legislature because they thought she could fight effectively for a bridge connecting Whidbey Island to the mainland. She agreed and was elected to the House in 1928 as a Democrat. At her urging, a bridge over Deception Pass was authorized in 1933 but her primary interest remained education. She was appointed to the Senate in 1937, then elected to the position in 1938, and in 1940 was elected as the state superintendent of public instruction. Among her accomplishments are the addition of 875 buildings to the school system, an increase in teachers' minimum salaries, and the provision of basic state support for students.

Mary Ellen McCaffree graduated from Kansas State University as a dietitian. She married and raised five children in Seattle. Having children in school sparked her interest in the education system and its financial underpinnings. She lobbied the Legislature for education funding, then in 1962, successfully ran for the House as a Republican. She became an expert in taxation and was the first woman to chair a tax or revenue committee in the Legislature. In 1970, Governor Dan Evans appointed her director of the Department of Revenue.

Getting into leadership was even more difficult than becoming committee chairs. The first woman to break that barrier was Julia Butler Hansen (D-Cathlamet), who became House Speaker Pro Tem in 1956.

Ms. Hansen was first elected to the House in 1938 as a Democrat from a district including Cowlitz and Wahkiakum counties. She served eleven terms in the state House before being elected to Congress in 1960. Ms.

Hansen was born in Portland, was a lifelong resident of Cathlamet and graduated from the University of Washington. She first worked for the Legislature in a secretarial position, then as a bill clerk, and then was a city council member before she ran for the Legislature in 1938. In 1949 she ran for chair of the powerful House Highways Committee. She said, "I had problems when I wanted to be chairman of Highways. They didn't want a woman because it was the first time. And I said 'Can I do the job?' 'Oh, yes,' they'd say. 'Do you think I'd make a good committee chairman?' The man who wanted the position said, 'Yes, but I'm a man.' I replied, 'To hell with that. It doesn't mean one thing to me. You and I are both elected representatives and I've got more experience in the road and highway field than you do.'" *(Political Pioneers*, p. 8) She battled for the position and won. She was also nominated for House Speaker several times but failed to win that spot. She was elected and served as Speaker Pro Tem from 1956 to 1960, the first woman in a major leadership position. When she was later elected to Congress, she served on the Appropriations Committee.

In the 1995-96 Legislature, women were chairs of seven of the Senate's thirteen standing committees, including Ways and Means (Nita Rinehart, D-Seattle), and chairs of five of the House's seventeen standing committees, including Transportation (Karen Schmidt, R-Bainbridge Island). In terms of leadership, Senator Lorraine Wojahn (D-Tacoma) was President Pro Tem, Senator Valoria Loveland (D-Pasco) was Majority Caucus Chair, Senator Harriet Spanel (D-Bellingham) was Majority Floor Leader, and Senator Ann Anderson (R-Acme) was Minority Whip. In the House, Representative Gigi Talcott (R-Tacoma) was Majority Whip and Representative Lisa Brown (D-Spokane) was Minority Whip.

Nationally, in 1993 twenty-eight women were chosen for formal leadership positions in state legislatures across the country, including all three top spots in the Alaska House. In 1995 the number fell to twenty-one but included the President of the Senate and Speaker of the House in Alaska and the majority leaders in Hawaii and Vermont.

SENATOR JEANNETTE HAYNER

There have been many outstanding women in the Washington State Legislature but only one so far has reached the top rung of power. Her achievements are so remarkable (and little known) that she deserves more than just a reference. Her story bridges the eras of women getting the right to vote, getting elected, taking power, and making a difference.

Jeannette Hayner was born in 1919 in Portland, Oregon, one year before women were given the right to vote nationally. She received her B.A. from the University of Oregon and was one of only two women to graduate from the University of Oregon Law School in 1942. She met her husband there and they moved to Walla Walla in 1947. She raised three children, was active in a variety of civic and charitable organizations and served as chair of the Walla Walla School Board.

In 1972, with her children grown, Hayner decided to run for an open seat in the state Legislature. In a close election, Hayner defeated three primary opponents and a Democrat in the general election. When she took her seat in the state House in 1973, there was one other woman in her Republican caucus and six women in the House Democratic caucus. There were no women in the Senate. After four years, party officials asked Representative Hayner to run for the Senate seat vacated by Democrat Dan Jolly. She agreed, was successful again, and would be reelected every four years until her retirement in 1992.

Republicans were outnumbered thirty to nineteen when Hayner arrived in the state Senate in 1977. They hadn't held a majority in the Senate since 1957. Some thought that Republican leaders had adopted the mentality of a permanent minority, had given up on gaining a majority. Shortly after joining the Senate, Hayner was cautiously sounded out about making a change in leadership in order to seek power by a Republican majority rather than through coalitions with conservative Democrats. For the next year she was part of a growing group of Senate Republicans who secretly met off campus. They gradually became a majority within their minority caucus and decided to make their move at the end of the 1979 session. None of the originators of the coup could garner a majority in their caucus so they turned to Hayner. She emerged as Senate Republican Leader in 1979 and would hold that position until her retirement in 1992.

On February 13, 1981, Senator Peter von Reichbauer from Vashon Island switched from the Democratic to the Republican party giving Republicans control of the Senate for the first time in twenty-six years. Jeannette Hayner was suddenly the Senate Majority Leader. It had been so long since Republicans had held power in the Senate that they sought help from legislative leaders from other states to advise them as to procedures to accomplish a smooth transition in the middle of a session. Hayner learned well and she continued to lead the Senate Republicans for the next thirteen years.

A small, slender woman with a sly sense of humor, Hayner never tried to be "one of the boys." She eschewed the feminist movement. Rather like the first woman senator, Reba Hurn, Hayner let her qualifications and abilities speak for themselves. In the somewhat gentrified Senate where it is easy to succumb to the flattery of staff and lobbyists, and where a few of her fellow legislators adopted morals of convenience, Hayner kept her small-town values and her sense of proportion. She led by displaying the traits of leadership: decisive, consistent, rational, confident. She tried to keep abreast of the political and personal needs of the other twenty-four members of her caucus. She listened to their needs, their differing visions of what the party must do. She never belittled or personally criticized opponents in either party. She stressed cooperation and conversation with House members, something unusual for many senators.

Republicans lost their Senate majority in the 1982 elections but regained a one-vote majority when Linda Smith (R-Vancouver) won an off-year election in 1987. From late 1987 through 1992, Hayner led her slim Republican majority in the Senate against a heavily Democratic House and a popular Democrat governor. Hayner instilled a strong sense of unity in her Republican members. Their only hope for success depended on presenting a common front. She insisted that differences among Republican senators be hashed out internally behind the closed caucus doors. She established what was called "the rule of thirteen." Republicans would vote on bills and issues in caucus and a simple majority of thirteen would be binding on all twenty-five. Senator Hayner turned her small, sometimes fractious and very diverse Republican Senate majority into a powerful, united and effective force that was able to deal on a par with the Democratic House and the governor.

USING POWER

It would mean very little for women to get the right to vote, be elected, and take power if nothing changed as a result. The traditional view is that women legislators have their greatest impact in matters affecting health, education and the family. That may still be true, but it misses the first and, so far, the biggest impact from the gender revolution in this state. In hindsight, it seems obvious that violent crime by men against women and children should be the first priority and the strongest evidence of the presence of women.

Here are just a few examples of the many changes attributable to the increase in numbers and power of women in Washington State's Legislature. Keep in mind that there are really two ways women affect policy: the direct one from their ability to write and introduce laws, a few of which are listed below. Perhaps even greater, though, are changes brought about indirectly on their male counterparts by their presence and leadership.

• Crimes by men against women, such as rape and domestic violence, have received much more attention and the penalties have been dramatically increased as women's numbers and power in the Legislature have grown. There are many examples. A recent one is the battle that occurred about midway through the 1996 session when House Republicans passed a bill which would have had the secondary effect of allowing men convicted of domestic violence to own guns (HB 2420). Seven female Republican House members rebelled against their leadership and sided with Democrats in a vote that was mostly along gender lines. The bill was changed in the Senate, where women held a majority in the majority party, to remove this provision.

• Representative Ida Ballasiotes (R-Mercer Island) got into politics in part because of a personal tragedy in her family caused by a sex offender on work release. She chairs the House Corrections Committee. In the 1996 session she was the chief sponsor of legislation requiring life imprisonment without possibility of parole for persons convicted of two violent sexually-motivated offenses (SHB 2320). She was also the chief sponsor of a bill to shorten prison sentences for nonviolent first-time drug offenders who agree to treatment (SHB 1549). The purpose was to make room for the more violent offenders convicted under her "two strikes" legislation. In a climate of ever-tougher sentences, it took someone with the credibility and respect of Representative Ballasiotes to get this bill passed.

• There has been an increase in efforts to identify and force fathers to pay child support. There was legislation in 1996 to make fathers in arrears on child support, so-called "deadbeat dads," lose any and all state licenses they may have, including drivers' licenses. It passed the Senate but failed when no agreement could be reached on welfare reform.

• Led by women legislators, in 1996 the Senate unanimously passed a bill requiring insurance companies to pay for up to two days of hospitalization for vaginal births and four days for Caesarean sections. It was dubbed the "drive-through baby bill" referring to the practice of sending new mothers home next day after delivery. It was opposed by the insurance companies. The House Health Care chair at first said it was "a solution in search of a problem" and vowed to kill the bill when it came over from the Senate. After one hearing, though, he said "I'm not sure I can stop it," referring to strong support in his own Republican caucus. The bill was eventually rewritten to substitute "medically necessary" for specific time limits, after which it easily passed and is now the law in this state.

• Affirmative action has been enshrined in state law and regulation. It is everywhere in state government from the personnel policies of the House and Senate to the handbook that guides state managers. The policy is simple and well understood: recruit, hire and promote qualified women and minorities. In this state, with a small number of minorities, women have been the major beneficiaries of affirmative action.

• The budget negotiations in 1996 were different in many ways from any that preceded them but none more striking than that there were three women on one side of the table and three men on the other. Little was said or written about it but there could be no more visible evidence that women had achieved real power.

• Sexual harassment, even if only verbal, is no longer tolerated at any level of state government. The Legislature itself has a less than perfect history in this area. For example, there is a story told of twenty years ago when a high ranking married male caucus staffer went to a conference in San Francisco with his girlfriend, a legislative secretary. His wife learned of the trip and called the Senate leader to complain. In what seemed like an obvious solution at the time, the Senate reportedly fired the girlfriend. The male caucus staffer stayed on until he voluntarily retired several years later.

• A senator was forced to resign in 1992 for sexual harassment of his Senate office aide. As part of the settlement of her suit against the Senate, all Senate staff and members were required to take part in anti-harassment training. In 1995, the governor agreed to pay a former deputy press secretary $97,500 out of his own pocket to settle a case involving allegations of sexual harassment that an independent counsel said would not prevail in court. Strict safeguards and grievance procedures have been instituted by the House, Senate and the governor's office. Perhaps even more intimidating to would-be male harassers, though, is the presence of so many women legislators.

• There has been an increase in support for programs which allow women to both have children and work, including state-supported child care. It is not unusual during an evening legislative session to find women staff working at their desks with their children next to them sleeping or playing in cribs or on blankets.

• Much of the debate over welfare can be seen in the context of the politics of gender. Granted that there are lots of exceptions, but female legislators tend to be more supportive of benefits, such as job training and child care for women on welfare, and oppose hard time limits and caps on the number of children.

• In 1995, at the insistence of women legislators, the Legislature passed a law saying health insurance providers must provide direct access to an obstetrician/gynecologist (OBGYN) for female subscribers. It is now a law in this state that women do not have to go through a primary care "gatekeeper" to get to an OBGYN.

10

Legislative Staff

According to a recent article in *State Government News*, there are about 33,000 staff working for state legislatures in the United States, of which 24,000 are full-time and 9,000 are part-time, sometimes referred to as session employees. The range is great, from states with fewer than 100 staff to those with over 2,000, with 200 being the mean. Some states have joint service agencies responding to both houses; others have completely separate staffs for the upper and lower chambers.

In 1957 the only permanent employee in the Legislature who worked full-time was the assistant to the Chief Clerk of the House. The Chief Clerk, the Secretary of the Senate and the secretary to the Secretary of the Senate were part-time during the interim. It is said by former Secretary of the Senate Sid Snyder that at the end of session, "they turned off the lights, locked the doors and went home."

From 1947 until 1963, the Legislature operated in the interim through the **Legislative Council.** This was a joint committee of senior legislators from both bodies that dealt with legislative matters during the interim. It withstood a legal challenge in its first year in *State ex rel. Hamblen v.*

Yelle, 29 Wn. 2d 68 (1947) when the Supreme Court said the Legislative Council "does no more than make available new machinery and new methods by which the members of the committee may keep themselves informed upon specific problems" (at p. 129).

In 1963 Governor Albert Rosellini vetoed funding for the Legislative Council. He did so after the Legislature had adjourned. Under the law at that time, legislators would not meet again until 1965, unless the governor called a special session. Following the veto, State Treasurer Tom Martin refused to issue a warrant to cover the expenses of the Legislative Council, and Senator R. R. (Bob) Greive sued (actually, the case was represented on both sides by attorneys from the office of the state attorney general). Greive and other legislators contended that since the veto came after adjournment of the 1963 special session, they had no opportunity to override and were thereby prevented from performing their legislative function. It was a valid argument but the court said too bad, that is the way the state Constitution set things up.

The veto and the Supreme Court case dealt a blow to the Legislative Council. Although it returned for a few years in the late 1960s, the idea that a handful of members could make decisions for the standing committees was fundamentally flawed. In the early 1970s the Legislature passed a "continuing session" bill which provided for a full-time staff, committee meetings throughout the interim, and a substantial increase in legislators' salaries. A referendum knocked out the salary increase for legislators, but the staff and the use of standing committees during the interim thrived and today are a vital part of legislative oversight of the executive branch, and in developing issues and legislation for sessions.

Today the Washington State Legislature has a wide mix of staff, some serving one body only, others serving both houses. There were about 600 total staff working for the House and Senate during the 1996 legislative session with perhaps half that many staying on during the interim. To a large extent, the legislative staff has grown in response to the even larger growth of the governor's staff, particularly in the Office of Financial Management and the Department of Revenue. The legislative staff provides research, analysis and data to legislators on the many complex issues facing government. In essence, staff keep the legislative vehicle tuned and in good running condition so legislators need only get behind the wheel and drive it in the direction they, and the voters, determine. Staff are also the eyes and ears of the Legislature on government between legislative sessions.

The overall staff directors for the two bodies are the **Secretary of the Senate** and the **Chief Clerk of the House.** Both are elected to their positions by their respective chambers. The Secretary of the Senate reports to the **Facilities and Operations Committee** in the Senate, and the Chief Clerk reports to the Speaker and the **Executive Rules Committee** in the House.

In 1973 Washington voters turned down a "continuing session" proposal to make the Washington State Legislature full time. However, they left intact another part of the same proposal which provided for a full-time staff. That staff today is generally acknowledged to be among the finest in the nation and attracts great numbers of highly qualified and motivated candidates for the prized positions. "Graduates" of the legislative staff include directors of the Department of Social and Health Services, the Insurance Commissioner, the Utilities and Transportation Commission, the Department of Personnel, a King County Executive, many members of the House and the Senate, one governor, a host of deputy directors, and many lobbyists both public and private.

DIRECT LEGISLATIVE STAFF

All legislative staff groups that work directly for the Legislature report to the Secretary of the Senate or the Chief Clerk of the House. They include:

• **Senate Committee Services** (SCS) and House **Office of Program Research** (OPR) are made up of the nonpartisan, nonpatronage, professional committee staff for the two bodies. They study issues, do research, write reports, draft bills and amendments, make presentations, set up and staff meetings, and do many of the technical things required to make a session happen, particularly in the committees. There are about fifty full-time staff in SCS and fifty-six in OPR, made up of lawyers, analysts and legislative assistants. Each group hires additional lawyers, analysts and committee clerks during legislative sessions. Washington State has a higher percentage of its staff in the nonpartisan category than the federal government or almost any other state. As proof of this, the staff in SCS and OPR have remained in place through several changes in the majority in the Senate and House.

• All four political caucuses have permanent staffs of about twenty to thirty persons each to provide partisan policy development and to assist members in communications.

• Security for the House and Senate is under the direction of the sergeant at arms. There is a minimal staff during the interim with perhaps twenty-five in each house during session, mostly ex-law enforcement officers. When additional security is needed, the State Patrol sends help.

State Patrol officers are nearby since it is their responsibility to provide security for the governor and the lieutenant governor.

• There are a variety of smaller specialized staff groups such as Word Processing, Accounting, Work Room, Bill Room, Graphics, Mail Room, Hot Line, Office of Senate Counsel, Journal Clerk, Maintenance, and Supply to perform the many specialized functions that go into making the Legislature work.

• Every member of the Legislature may hire one full-time staff, and senators have an additional staff during session to handle the various office chores such as responding to constituents and following legislation of committees on which the member does not sit. Administratively, the members' staff come under the Secretary of the Senate or Chief Clerk of the House, but they are generally hired and directed by the members themselves.

Senate and House staff are prohibited by the rules of each body from seeking to influence the passage or failure of proposed legislation (HR 6, SR 6). Professional staff are also subject to ethics laws and rules and many must file financial statements with the Public Disclosure Commission.

Specific restrictions on legislative staff are laid out in the Joint Rules. While there were no Joint Rules adopted in 1995-1996, there was an understanding that these would still apply. The key points are:

- A legislative employee may not accept a gratuity or compensation for things done as part of legislative employment except for the legislative salary and benefits; may not accept outside employment which might impair independence of judgment; and may not provide a service to a lobbyist except within the scope of employment.
- A legislative employee can't take an honorarium if it would not have been given except for the employee's status.
- A legislative employee can't use or attempt to use his or her position to obtain anything of value for self or others.
- A legislative employee can't disclose confidential information acquired by reason of employment to anyone not entitled to it, or use such information for personal gain.
- A legislative employee can't enter into any contract with a state agency involving services or property except in an open competitive bid and with approval by the appropriate board of ethics.
- A legislative employee can't solicit or accept contributions for any candidate or cause during business hours or coerce another

employee into doing so or have that as a condition of employment.

To show how far the Legislature has come in restricting the activities and use of its own staff by legislators, here is an excerpt from a memo by Marty Brown, Secretary of the Senate, dated June 24, 1996:

Beginning on July 1st, staff time in the following areas ... must be approved:

Press releases
Press conferences
Editorials
Letters to the editor
Other press outreach activities
Speeches
Large-scale constituent meetings ...
Use of photographic, video or voice recording equipment.

SHARED LEGISLATIVE STAFF

The **Code Reviser's Office** was mentioned earlier in sections dealing with bills and initiatives. This office comes under the **Statute Law Committee** and provides bill drafting services to all state agencies, including the Legislature.

The **Joint Legislative Audit and Review Committee** (called the **Legislative Budget Committee** until June 1996) is made up of equal numbers of members from the House and Senate with rotating chairs. It performs policy studies, management audits, and sunset reviews to assist in the oversight of state agencies by the Legislature. The **Legislative Transportation Committee** is made up of twelve House members and eleven senators and does the same for transportation issues.

The **Legislative Evaluation and Accountability Program** (LEAP) provides legislators with in-depth analysis and monitoring of state agency spending.

The Office of the **State Actuary** provides actuarial services to the Department of Personnel and advises the governor and the Legislature on pension issues.

The **Joint Legislative Systems Committee** oversees direction of the computer and communications needs of the Legislature through the **Legislative Service Center (LSC).** The Legislature has become highly computerized and its members and staff have some of the newest and most sophisticated equipment available to assist in word processing, bill drafting, research, preparing budget spreadsheets, and several levels and types of communications. The computer support and maintenance arm of the Legislature is probably the fastest growing staff section.

INTERNS

There are two intern programs available in the Legislature.

Session interns are college juniors and seniors (usually political science majors) who spend a quarter or semester in Olympia working directly for representatives (as assigned from the Office of Program Research) or senators during a legislative session. The program was founded by and is named after revered Professor Hugh Bone from the University of Washington. About thirty students are selected to work in each house. They receive a small stipend from the Legislature and may receive course credit from their college or university. Interested students should contact their university or college placement office.

Summer interns are students who will have completed their second year of law school or the first year toward a graduate degree in public policy by the beginning of the summer they start the internship. Students work directly with committee staff doing research, as well as participating in a variety of seminars with top state officials. House and Senate programs differ slightly, with the House requiring students to commit to work the following session, while that is a desired option but not a requirement for the Senate. This summer intern program not only provides graduate and law students with valuable experience but provides the Legislature with a recruitment program for future professional staff. Particularly in the Senate, many former summer interns have joined the ranks of the committee analysts and attorneys. The placement offices of universities with a public affairs program and all the state's law schools have information on these internships.

In addition, some legislators will separately hire interns, generally from their districts, to work in their offices during sessions.

PAGES

The Washington Legislature has had a Page program since 1891. It is a wonderful opportunity for youths aged fourteen to sixteen to witness first-hand how state government works and, for many, to get their first taste of a full day's work themselves. Pages, easily identified in colorful standard-issue sports coats, do a variety of jobs for the Legislature from ceremonial presentation of the flags at the beginning of each day's session to distributing amendments and delivering documents. Pages also spend time each day in classes. Pages are limited to one week per year, House or Senate.

To serve as a Page a student needs parent/caretaker permission, school permission, sponsorship by a member of the House or Senate, and a grade average of C+ or better. Pages are paid $32 per day (as of 1996). More information may be obtained from your state representative or state senator.

STAFF PAST AND FUTURE

Starting in May 1992, first Bob Partlow and Mike Oakland from *The Olympian*, then other reporters from major newspapers around the state began reporting on the use of legislative caucus staff for political campaigning on state time. Several former legislative employees admitted to wrongdoing, and there was an investigation by the Public Disclosure Commission and the attorney general's office.

What Partlow and others uncovered was a way of doing business that had gone on for many years by both political parties in the Legislature, was commonly known and was widely accepted. Caucus staff were used to monitor members of the other party for possible vulnerabilities (unpopular votes, absences, ill-considered bills, etc.), pass that information on to potential opponents, write campaign literature, and, in some cases, even recruit candidates, raise money, and actively campaign during regular working hours. Staff from each party did it, possibly because the other was doing it and neither wanted to disarm unilaterally. It had become so commonplace that few stopped to consider the legality or the morality of it. Staff thought, rightly or wrongly, that either they helped on campaigns or they would not gain promotions or might even be fired. Members were accustomed to asking for staff help on legislative matters, so it was a natural extension to seek political help as well. The lines separating the two are not always clear. All of this went on despite that fact that state law clearly prohibits state employees from campaigning on state time.

The newspaper disclosures and several lawsuits forced the Legislature to examine itself and take steps to end the practice. Today, staff know they can and must say no to campaigning on state time. Managers are even more sensitive to the problem, as they can be held accountable for what their workers do. And members understand that there must be a wall of separation between the politics of getting elected or reelected and the state work of serving in the Legislature.

Former Senator Jeannette Hayner said that her greatest fear about term limits was that it would result in too much power for staff. Others have expressed similar views. The argument is that legislators will come to Olympia knowing little or nothing about the process. They will be reliant on staff to tell them how to do things. With that power will come control. Issues like the pension system and aspects of the budgets which may take years to learn will be exclusively the expertise of staff. Missing will be the senior legislators who developed expertise on certain complicated issues but who will have been forced out by term limits. Missing also will be long-serving legislators who have an "institutional memory" about what they were promised by agencies when they first set up a program or what was said when it began to fail and they gave it another chance. In essence, power comes from knowledge and the knowledge will reside exclusively in the staff.

On the other hand, with term limitations, a strong legislative staff is needed more than ever to objectively inform legislators of the background of issues and all the options and their consequences so they can make wise decisions. It is ultimately up to the elected members to know where to draw the line between the job of providing information by staff and lobbyists, and the job of making policy which rightfully belongs only to elected officials.

11

Ethics, Disclosure and Campaigns

Several state legislatures have been rocked by scandals in recent years. In Kentucky in 1992 the former House Speaker, two sitting and five former legislators were convicted of extortion and racketeering; in New Mexico a lawmaker was convicted of taking a bribe; in 1993 in Arizona seven lawmakers were convicted of bribery and money laundering, and most went to prison and were fined; in our own state in 1993 both party caucuses were fined $100,000 by the Public Disclosure Commission following a series of disclosures about campaigning on state time; and in Michigan the director of the House Fiscal Agency was convicted in 1994 of embezzlement, conspiracy, racketeering and tax evasion, sentenced to ten years in prison and ordered to repay the state $834,000.

The executive branch has fared no better. The governor of Arkansas resigned following his conviction in late May of 1996 in the "Whitewater" case. The former governor of Alabama, and many in his administration, and the current governor of Arizona are currently under indictment. Governor Mike Lowry of Washington underwent a lengthy sexual harassment investigation in 1995 and settled the case by paying a large sum from his own funds to his accuser.

Most of these states and others have responded with increased disclosure requirements, ethics rules and restrictions on what legislators and staff may take from lobbyists, sometimes called "no cup of coffee" rules. In Kentucky, for example, following the enactment of perhaps the toughest ethics laws in the nation, in the first month of the 1996 session, lobbyist spending for food and drink dropped to a minuscule total of $26 (see articles referenced in bibliography for this chapter).

According to a study in 1995 by Alan Rosenthal for the Council of State Governments, only fifteen states have ethics regulation of the state legislature by a board or commission comprised in the majority of nonlegislators. Within that fifteen only five have statewide commissions with broad enforcement powers. The other ten, including Washington, have mixed commissions with more limited jurisdiction.

One of the arguments invariably used against independent ethics commissions is that no one but legislators themselves can understand the legislative institution and process and what it requires. Of course, the same argument is used by doctors and lawyers regarding their oversight boards. These arguments can be addressed by appointment of former members. Nevertheless, exclusively nonlegislator legislative ethics boards and commissions are rare, existing in only Alabama, Minnesota, Nebraska and Wisconsin.

The most powerful ethics commission in is Rhode Island. Since 1986 it has had the power to adopt ethics laws for officeholders on its own motion. Rhode Island is the only state—so far—where the legislature does not have the principal say in the promulgation of ethics laws. In 1991, the Rhode Island Ethics Commission amended the ethics code to remove the confidentiality of complaints, to bar legislators from taking state jobs while in office or within one year of leaving office, and expanded the definition of nepotism. Governor Bruce Sundlum and legislative leaders in Rhode Island challenged the commission's authority, but the Rhode Island Supreme Court ruled in 1992 that the commission had acted within its legal powers.

There is a certain nostalgia among senior elected officials for simpler times when a person threw his hat (the use of the masculine tense is deliberate) in the ring, held a few cozy coffee hours and rode in some summer parades, was elected and served without a lot of fuss and paperwork. It was probably never quite that easy, but it certainly has become a lot more complicated to run for and serve in public office than it was before Initiative 276, Initiative 134, and related laws, rules and regulations. What follows is not intended as a comprehensive explanation, but rather an overview to give the reader a sense of what is involved.

1994 STATE ETHICS IN PUBLIC SERVICE LAW

On the heels of our own scandals over the use or misuse of legislative caucus staff, in 1993 the governor and the attorney general set up a special commission to establish clear ethical standards for state officers and employees. Following its recommendations, the Legislature passed Senate Bill 6111 which, for the first time, established standards of conduct for all 100,000 of the state's elected officials and employees. The standards are codified in RCW 42.52. They replace a plethora of confusing statutes, rules and executive orders. The new legislation took effect January 1, 1995.

The overriding principle of the new ethics statute is that a state officer or employee may not use his or her public position for private financial gain or special privileges for self or others. The law is quite specific about what is allowed, such as flowers, promotional pens, and informational material, and what is disallowed, which essentially is anything of commercial value.

A separate provision of the ethics legislation concerns the use of public resources for political campaigns, undoubtedly added as a reaction to the abuses mentioned earlier. To some extent it restates what has long been the law, that no state officer or employee may use state facilities for political campaigns of any kind. For supervisors, just the knowledge of such activity by employees is a violation. The illegal use of facilities for campaigning includes publicly-supplied stationery, postage machines, office equipment, staff during working hours, vehicles, publications, and clientele lists obtained from a public agency.

If a complaint is made that a legislator or a statewide elected official has violated the provisions mentioned above, the attorney general takes over the investigation. If the complaint is against the attorney general, the state auditor investigates.

LEGISLATIVE ETHICS BOARD

The 1994 legislation created three ethics boards, one for each branch of government. This discussion will be limited to the Legislative Ethics Board.

The **Legislative Ethics Board** is composed of nine members: two senators and two representatives representing the four caucuses and appointed by the President and the Speaker, and five citizen members. Four citizen members are chosen by the governor from a list of three individuals submitted by each of the four caucuses, and the fifth is selected by vote of three of the four citizen members. Except for initial members and appointees to partial terms, the regular term for nonlegislative members is five years. Legislative members serve for two years. The chair is selected annually by the citizen members from among themselves.

The basic duties of the Legislative Ethics Board are:

- Develop instructional and training material on ethics.
- Issue advisory opinions.
- Investigate, hear, and determine complaints by any person or on its own motion.
- Impose sanctions including reprimands and monetary penalties.
- Recommend suspension or removal or prosecution of individuals.

The board has the power to subpoena and examine witnesses and documents, administer oaths and affirmations, and receive testimony. After an appropriate hearing and finding, the board may require an individual to pay any damages sustained by the state as a result of a violation; to exact a civil penalty of up to $5,000 per violation or three times the economic value of the thing received or sought, whichever is greater; and to assess reasonable costs of an investigation, not to exceed the penalty imposed. Assessed damages are enforced in the same manner as judgments in civil cases.

In its first eighteen months, the Legislative Ethics Board has adopted rules, heard about a dozen **complaints,** and issued more than thirty **advisory opinions.** The complaints and the board's judgment include:

(1) The circulation of a letter by a senator to his law firm implying that he could be of assistance in Olympia. He was reprimanded by the board.

(2) That a senator who chaired a committee had accepted campaign contributions from lobbyists with interests before the committee. The board found there was no evidence of a violation and the complaint was dismissed.

(3) That two House members had reprinted a partisan legislative agenda in their joint legislative newsletter. The complaint was dismissed.

(4) That a House member who was an insurance agent had solicited support from other agents with the promise to use his legislative powers to work on their behalf. The board dismissed, citing the citizen-legislator status and saying there was nothing improper in citing common interests.

(5) That the chair of the Indeterminate Sentence Review Board lacked legal authority to make decisions because he had not been confirmed by the Senate at the time. The board dismissed for lack of jurisdiction.

(6) That a House employee used her legislative computer to create documents related to campaign activities. The board determined the employee had violated RCW 42.52.160 but imposed no penalty because she was no longer a legislative employee, the documents were never distributed, and the employee had not been formally trained regarding rules of ethics until after the incident occurred.

(7) That a representative violated the state ethics act by including campaign material in a document she mailed at public expense. The document was the Directory of Elected Officials, which included the legislator's picture and name on the front. The complaint was dismissed because it was determined there was no violation.

(8) A complaint from a prisoner at Clallam Bay Correctional Center making various allegations against the director of the Department of Corrections and others. The complaint was dismissed because the Legislative Ethics Board lacks jurisdiction.

As indicated, there have been far more advisory opinions issued by the Legislative Ethics Board than complaints heard. One of the more interesting was Advisory Opinion No. 17, issued November 21, 1995. It is illustrative of the complicated nature of issues presented. It was requested by Tim Martin, House Chief Clerk. It posed the question of whether it would be a violation of the state ethics act for a legislative employee to prepare, at a legislator's request, on official stationery and mailed at state expense, letters which:

- Contain a recommendation to a state agency for a grant (board said okay).
- Solicit contributions to a fund for payment of travel and registration fees to enable legislators to attend an educational conference (board said no).
- Congratulate constituents on achievements such as Eagle Scout or scholastic honor roll (board said okay).
- Contain a recommendation to a congressman in favor of a candidate's admission to a service academy (board said okay).
- Endorse an organization to a nonprofit organization (board said okay).

Alan Rosenthal wonders in his 1995 article for *Spectrum* (see bibliography for this chapter) whether legislators will place too much reliance on ethics boards. In effect, these commissions can become a "security blanket" which allows legislators to delegate or even abrogate their own responsibility for ethical judgments. In a real sense, these boards and commissions are making law when they interpret statutes and rules. In Kentucky, for example, the ethics law prohibits campaign contributions by lobbyists. Its commission interpreted this to mean that lobbyists could not be involved in political action committees (PACs), which was not what the legislature intended. This gives rise to a basic question concerning ethics boards such as the ones in Kentucky and Rhode Island, which is whether an unelected group should dictate how elected officials actually represent their constituents.

Taking ethics legislation a step further, in 1995 Colorado became the first state to adopt a code of ethics specifically for legislative staff. The Colorado Office of Legislative Legal Services is a nonpartisan staff agency that provides bill drafting and research services for Colorado legislators. Legislators have adopted eleven rules or guidelines, mostly relating to bill and amendment procedures. For example, staff may not take requests directly from lobbyists to draft bills or do research. Such requests must come from legislators. Staff may accept no gifts from lobbyists worth more than $5 and may attend lobbyist-sponsored social activities only if other legislative staff are also invited. Staff must file a written disclosure statement for out-of-state conferences where any costs are paid by lobbyists. And, staff are strongly discouraged from dating lobbyists.

PUBLIC DISCLOSURE COMMISSION

Washington State's public disclosure laws date back to the passage of Initiative 276 in 1972. It is important to underscore that the basic purpose of Initiative 276 is public disclosure. The **Public Disclosure Commission** (PDC) is directed to gather information and make it available to the public. It has no power itself to enforce honesty or truthfulness of candidates or campaigns except as they relate to disclosure of finances, although the commission can refer cases to law enforcement agencies.

The PDC consists of five part-time commissioners appointed by the governor for five-year terms, subject to Senate confirmation. It operates with a staff of twenty. The original initiative only covered elected officials, but four years later state-level appointed officials were added to the list. Since 1973, over 100,000 financial disclosure statements have been filed by Washingtonians who were candidates or elected officials or serving in key appointive positions, including local government.

The requirement for disclosure of assets applies not only to candidates for the Legislature but to most legislative staff and lobbyists, public and private. Disclosure of campaign contributions and expenditures applies to all candidates and lobbyists, who must make periodic reports. All persons covered must personally disclose income, real estate interests, investments, interest, dividends, and creditors not only for self but for spouse and dependents as well. The personal financial disclosure reports must be submitted annually, with a shorter form permitted when there are no substantial changes. Reports are made in dollar codes, such as Code A for $1 to $1,999, and Code B for $2,000 to $9,999.

Anyone who attempts to influence state legislation or the legislative action of a state agency is a **lobbyist** and must register with the PDC and submit periodic reports. Exceptions are made for persons who limit their activities to appearing before legislative committee meetings or public hearings of agencies; working members of the press; persons who receive no compensation for lobbying; persons who restrict their lobbying activities to no more than four days during a three-month period; and for the governor, lieutenant governor, legislators, and elected officials (RCW 42.17.160).

Lobbyists are required to file with the PDC and make monthly reports disclosing the total amount spent on behalf of the employer, segregated by categories for compensation, food and refreshments, living accommodations, advertising, travel, contributions, and other (RCW 42.17.170). Employers of lobbyists (individuals and entities who employ, hire or pay the compensation or other consideration of a lobbyist) are required to sign their lobbyists' registration forms and file annual comprehensive expense reports.

Anyone involved in a political campaign or lobbying should contact the PDC to obtain information as to their disclosure requirements. The reporting and disclosure requirements are very detailed. PDC forms are not quite as intimidating as those of the IRS but neither are they simple.

CAMPAIGN FINANCE REFORM: INITIATIVE 134

In 1992 the voters approved **Initiative 134**, a proposal aimed at limiting campaign contributions. Competing contribution and/or spending bills had been introduced in the 1992 Regular Session of the Legislature but neither passed. There followed an attempt by the two political parties to gather the necessary signatures to qualify their competing proposals for the ballot.

Democrats wanted to limit contributions and spending, Republicans favored limiting contributions only. The Republicans won. Only Initiative 134, the Republican proposal, qualified for the ballot and was passed by the voters in November 1992.

Currently the law prohibits any person, except a bona fide political party, from contributing more than $550 to a legislative candidate or $1,100 to a candidate for statewide office in a recall, primary or general election. A caucus or political party may not contribute more than $.50 per registered voter in the candidate's jurisdiction and no county central committee or legislative district committee may contribute more than $.25 per registered voter.

Individual contributions by political action committees to a legislative caucus are limited to $500 and $2,500 to a bona fide political party. These dollar limits are adjusted at the beginning of each even-numbered year by the PDC to reflect any changes caused by inflation. Contributions by family members and controlled entities are attributed to the controlling person or parent. Employers and labor unions are prohibited from increasing a person's salary with the intention that the raise be given to a candidate, party or political committee. No portion of an individual's pay (automatic payroll deductions) may be withheld or diverted for political contributions without the annual written consent of the employee.

Contributions received by a candidate or committee may not be used to further the candidacy of another campaign without written approval from the contributor. Laws permitting candidates or committees to use surplus funds to run for different offices or to reimburse office expenses or to give to other candidates are repealed. However, surplus funds may be given to a political caucus of the Legislature.

Initiative 134 also places restrictions on mailings by incumbents (now codified in RCW 42.17.132). During the final twelve months of a state legislator's term, the incumbent is prohibited from any mailings at public expense except those in response to a constituent's request for information. That includes letters, newsletters, and brochures. There are two exceptions: one mailing is permitted within thirty days of the start of the regular session and a second mailing is allowed within sixty days of the end of the regular session. The statute also requires the House and Senate to place a specific limit on the total cost of mailings allowed per member.

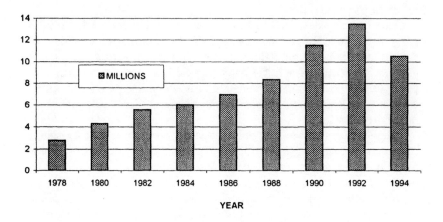

Fig. 11.1. Spending by Legislative Candidates: 1978-1994

Spending on legislative campaigns declined in 1994 for the first time since the PDC started collecting data (see Fig. 11.1) to just over $10 million. Initiative 134 deserves at least a part of the credit. However, more money is being spent by independent groups on behalf of candidates and that is also the result of Initiative 134.   All parties involved—candidates, lobbyists, political parties—have been in agreement for years that too much money is being spent on campaigns. Disagreements are only over the means to reduce spending, particularly over whether public funds should be used.

The average winning legislative candidate in 1994 spent $51,340 and the average losing candidate spent $29,959. Interestingly, even though the Republican version of campaign reform succeeded in 1992, Democratic candidates outspent Republicans by $42,491 to $41,936 in 1994, the first election following passage of the initiative.   However, Republicans outspent Democrats in five of the nine even-year elections from 1978 through 1994. The top contributor to legislative campaigns in 1994 was the Washington State Republican Party with $241,104 doled out to 27 candidates. Second in giving was ARCO, which gave $112,400 to 140 candidates, followed by the Senate Republican Campaign Committee ($103,059 to 12 candidates), the Washington State Dental PAC ($90,799 to 121 candidates), and US West ($80,569 to 136 candidates). Contact the PDC or look in a public library for the *1994 Election Financing Fact Book* for more information.

12

A History of the 1991-1992 Sessions

Every legislative session has some things in common with previous sessions and some things which make it stand apart from the others. The essence of the legislative process at its basic level is really little changed over the last one hundred years. What sets one session apart from others are the key issues or events.

I have chosen to present the 1991 and 1992 sessions in detail as a case study to illustrate the legislative process because those sessions are marked by particularly memorable external events, while at the same time remaining typical of the overall process common to most sessions in reaching agreement on the budget and other major issues. The information is presented in chronological order. It is taken mostly from daily reports in the state's major newspapers, with a few personal observations to give the reader a feel for what it was like to be on the legislative campus at that time. I have tried to report the events in an objective and unbiased manner, but take full responsibility for any opinions that seeped into the work.

1991

The general election of November 4, 1990, produced little change to the political climate in Olympia. The Democrats' majority in the House slipped somewhat from the previous sixty-three to thirty-five to a still comfortable lead of fifty-eight to forty; Democrat Governor Booth Gardner was in the second half of his second term; and Republicans clung to the same one-vote majority they had in the Senate since the end of 1987. Senate Democrats replaced Senator Larry Vognild (D-Everett) with Senator Marc Gaspard (D-Puyallup) as Minority Leader. Otherwise the leadership remained the same: Senator Jeannette Hayner (R-Walla Walla) as Senate Majority Leader, Representative Joe King (D-Vancouver) as House Speaker, and Representative Clyde Ballard (R-Wenatchee) as House Minority Leader.

Governor Gardner's Budget
December 17, 1990. On Monday, December 17, 1990, Governor Gardner, as required by law, reveals his proposed 1991-93 biennial operating budget. Despite the fact that it totals $15.4 billion, an increase of almost 15 percent over the previous biennial budget, it is portrayed as a "lean" budget because it contains no tax increase and preserves the state's rainy day fund of $260 million. A *Seattle P-I* editorial calls the governor's budget proposal "austere."

Gardner proposes to increase a variety of user fees to raise $303 million and to spend most of this on environmental programs, costs associated with growth management, increased social service caseloads and higher school enrollment. Keeping the promise he made in the summer of 1990, most of the increased spending goes for salary increases for teachers and state employees: 4.4 percent the first year and 3.8 percent the second. Higher education takes an overall 5 percent cut but Gardner proposes to let school presidents decide how to do it.

Gardner's budget proposals are criticized from the left and from the right. Gary Moore, director of the Washington Federation of State Employees, AFL-CIO, calls the budget "unacceptable." He and two dozen state employees parade outside the governor's office chanting "Keep the pressure on Booth." Thelma Jackson, president of the School Directors' Association, says it "will seriously impair the progress we've been making in our public schools." Superintendent of Public Instruction (SPI) Judith Billings says Gardner's school budget is "inadequate." Senate Ways and Means Chair Dan McDonald (R-Bellevue) says the governor shouldn't raise salaries at the expense of higher education and human services.

President William Gerberding of the University of Washington says "we are hopeful that by next spring, when the Legislature adjourns, a substantially better budget will have been developed." House budget chief Representative Gary Locke (D-Seattle), who will write the first legislative budget proposal says, "It's a good starting point."

December 21, 1990. Representative Locke predicts "The budget will be the big battle of the session." He says not to expect the House to produce a budget before April. Senator McDonald good-naturedly vows to trash the House budget when he gets it and write a Republican plan from scratch. Governor Gardner, perhaps stung by the negative reaction from the state employees' unions, suggests that if legislators don't like his budget cuts or fee increases, they should look first at reducing his teacher and state employee salary and benefit proposals. All three leaders are well aware that the governor's budget is only the first step in a long journey. Locke and McDonald will have the benefit of the later revenue forecasts before they must show their hands.

War

January 8, 1991. Senator Mike Kreidler (D-Lacey) is called to active duty as part of a mobilization of U.S. reserve and National Guard forces after Iraq invaded Kuwait. Thurston County commissioners invoke a never-before-used state law that allows them to name a temporary replacement. They pick his wife, Lela Kreidler. She will serve in his place for the entire 1991 session.

January 14, 1991. The 1991 Regular Session of the 52nd Legislature opens at noon amid much uncertainty. The prospect of war in the Persian Gulf makes state issues seem small by comparison. Dr. Chang Mook Sohn, chief state economist, says higher oil prices as a result of a Mideast war could knock a $400 million hole in his December revenue forecast.

January 15, 1991. Governor Booth Gardner delivers his state of the state message to a joint session of the Legislature. He urges a bipartisan approach to government and a no-new-taxes budget. The speech is generally well received. Even Senator Jeannette Hayner, the Senate Republican leader, finds it inspiring and thought-provoking.

In another part of Thurston County, North Thurston School District teachers become the first local in the 50,000 member Washington Education Association (WEA) to authorize their leaders to call a strike in the spring. There is little press coverage of the event and few political leaders take it seriously.

There is a large anti-war demonstration in the plaza between the Legislative Building and the Temple of Justice. Afterwards, several hundred demonstrators enter the Legislative Building and get onto the House floor (the Senate sergeant at arms locked them out of the Senate). They shout slogans and raise a ruckus. Six remain overnight until about 8:00 A.M. when they voluntarily agree to leave the House chamber. There is little floor action at this early stage of the session, so the disturbance has little effect on legislative proceedings.

January 16, 1991. At 4:00 P.M. Pacific time, the United States and its allies launch a full-scale air offensive against Iraqi occupation forces in Kuwait and military targets inside Iraq. People are glued to TV sets watching in amazement as wave after wave of jets take off in Saudi Arabia and then are sighted again as they arrive over Baghdad, broadcast live from both places.

At 4:30 P.M. the Secretary of the Senate announces over the loud-speakers that the doors to all buildings on campus will be locked at 5:00 P.M. for security reasons. Everyone who can do so should go home immediately. Americans everywhere watch the Gulf War on CNN. Legislators and staff huddle around TV sets, mesmerized by the incredible show of American military power. Legislative leaders consider but decide against cancelling or postponing the session. Senator Hayner says, "Sometimes you have terrible things happen in your life, but all you can do is work."

Property Tax Relief Plan
January 23, 1991. Senate Republicans push their property tax relief plan through the Ways and Means Committee. Senator Dan McDonald is the architect. His plan is simple: it will roll back property assessments to 1989 levels, subject to approval in each county. Total revenue collected would remain the same. It will shift the property tax from those whose property values went up the most to those whose values did not increase so much.

Democrats are cool to McDonald's plan. They say it hurts low-income property owners. The business lobby opposes it because of the effect on business property. Counties oppose it because of additional paperwork.

Republicans press ahead anyway. They hurry the bill (SB 5195) through Rules Committee and, on January 28, it passes the Senate 34-15 on a mostly party-line vote. Only three Republican senators vote no. Few expect the bill to actually become law, although it creates a dilemma for House Democratic leaders. Should they kill it in committee or on the floor or should they pass it and let Governor Gardner veto it and take the heat? The bill eventually dies in the House Revenue Committee.

The session is off to a slower-than-usual start because of the Gulf War, but also because everyone knows the real battle will not be joined until after the March revenue forecast and House Democrats and Senate Republicans reveal their proposals. Meanwhile, committees meet to hear and discuss matters such as where Washington teachers rank nationwide in pay, whether guns should be banned in schools, whether Gardner's appointee Curt Smitch should be confirmed as head of the Wildlife Department, campaign finance reform, term limits, and whether the governor or a commission should appoint the director of the Department of Transportation.

Republican Priorities

January 31, 1991. Senate Republicans release their legislative priorities for the 1991 session. This is preceded by a lengthy process of caucus discussions to arrive at the final list. For 1991 they hope to institute merit pay for teachers, with the specific method left up to individual school districts; eliminate the requirement for a master's degree for teachers; make job searches mandatory for adults on welfare; cut off the per diem pay of legislators on a gradual basis during special sessions; pass property tax relief; curb campaign contributions; and shorten the time for deciding whether to make a foster home placement for dependent children.

Meanwhile, House Democrats move a measure not on the Republican list. It is an initiative to the Legislature that would put the Supreme Court abortion decision in *Roe v. Wade* into state statute. Senate Republicans, deeply divided on the abortion issue, say they will hold no hearings and take no vote. They will let the initiative go on the ballot as is, just as they did two years earlier with the Children's Initiative.

Several legislators make headlines by donating blood to show their support for U.S. troops in the Persian Gulf.

The secretary of state certifies the initiative to the Legislature to permit physician-assisted suicide. The Legislature does not act on the measure so it goes to the voters in November when it will be narrowly defeated.

How Do Washington Teachers Rank?

February 7, 1991. Last year the House, Senate, governor's office, superintendent of public instruction and the Washington Education Association jointly hired a consultant to do a thorough study and tell them exactly where Washington State teachers rank nationally in terms of salary, benefits and class size. The WEA has been claiming that Washington teachers rank twenty-third or worse in pay. Since this is a joint project agreed to by all, no side can claim bias. The findings could go a long way in determining the level of teachers' salary increases in the 1991-93 budget.

The consultant reports that Washington ranks 12th in the nation overall in teacher salary and benefits, with an average of $44,551 per year. The national average is $40,154. However, Washington is 40th in student-teacher ratio and 40th in length of teaching contract (Washington also has the best educated teachers in the country).

The report seriously damages the credibility of the teachers' organization and chances for anything more than the cost-of-living raises proposed by Governor Gardner. It strengthens the positions of the governor, Senator McDonald, and Representative Gary Locke who have all said no to WEA demands for higher salary increases. Meanwhile, WEA locals continue to vote district by district whether to authorize their leadership to call a strike. Renton teachers become the thirteenth district organization to authorize a spring strike if called by WEA leaders.

Adopting Rules
February 27, 1991. On the forty-fifth day of the Regular Session, Senate Republicans have all twenty-five of their members present so they finally move to adopt Senate rules. It is unusual to wait this long but not critical because members spend most of their time in committee meetings during the first half of the 105-day session anyway, plus they are governed by the previous rules until new ones are adopted.

Rules debates receive relatively little publicity but can be very important to the eventual outcome of issues. The minority typically argues for rules to open up the process and the majority advocates for efficiency. The minority Senate Democrats offer amendments to eliminate the rule which requires 60 percent approval for any amendments to the budget once on the floor. This rule, along with stacking the membership of the Ways and Means Committee and the Rules Committee, allows a one-vote majority to wield more power than their numbers might suggest. Without the supermajority provision, the minority can offer "hero" amendments on the floor which might attract enough majority party members to turn the budget into a Christmas tree full of goodies for everyone. The 60 percent rule has been defended by both Republicans and Democrats when in the majority, and attacked by both when in the minority.

Senator A. L. "Slim" Rasmussen (D-Tacoma) reminds the Republicans that he voted against his own party in 1987 to defeat the 60 percent rule and claims that it cost him a seat on the Ways and Means Committee and the Legislative Budget Committee as punishment. He says he did it as a matter of principle that the majority should rule. But the plea falls on deaf ears. When the vote is taken, the 60 percent rule is retained. The Republicans also beat back amendments to the Senate rules by Democrats to subject the Senate to the state Open Public Meetings Act, disclose gifts of more than $25 by lobbyists and ban guns at legislative gatherings. All fail 25-24 on straight party votes.

The 100 Hour War Ends
The "100 hour war" came and went last week as Allied troops swept aside Iraqi opposition and freed Kuwait. The war is starting to share some news space with other issues. Some legislators are joining in the general spirit of what has turned out to be a highly popular and successful operation. There are measures to thank our troops, to offer tuition breaks to returning Gulf War veterans, to require the state's public and private colleges to grant tuition refunds to students called up to the military, to freeze tuition levels for Gulf War veterans (one at 1990 rates and one at 1977 rates), and a bill to provide compensation to children of Washington State veterans killed in any war, as well as tuition and fee waivers.

Bonds for Schools and Poor
February 28, 1991. Governor Gardner proposes raising the statutory debt limit from 7 percent (statutory limit) to 8 percent (the constitutional limit) of average general state revenues to allow issuance of one billion dollars in bonds. The money would be divided equally between higher education, K-12 education, preservation lands acquisition, and public housing. Gardner's proposal combines some very powerful forces and popular causes. For example, Washington State University would get a new veterinary hospital, the University of Washington would build new fisheries and computer sciences buildings, and public schools all across the state would be built soon after being approved by local voters rather than being on a waiting list for years. Hunting and fishing groups would welcome more habitat. And there would be more low-cost public housing.

The theory is to combine some of the most powerful interest groups in the state—higher education, teachers, parents, construction and labor, environmentalists, local government—and they will all get behind the plan and push for the higher bonding level.

But Representative Gary Locke and Senator Dan McDonald, the budget leaders for the two houses, are skeptical. Increased bonding in the capital budget means increased annual debt payments and increased costs in future operating budgets.

The day after Gardner releases his proposal, former Governor Dan Evans, former Congressman Mike Lowry, and Jim Ellis, godfather of

Metro, appear before a House committee to lend their support for the increased debt limit. A couple of days later they appear before a Senate committee. The proposal is like a starburst in a Fourth of July fireworks display. It burns with a sudden brilliant light and produces many ooo's and aaa's at the moment of explosion, but fades quickly and is forgotten.

March 6, 1991. This is the fifty-second day, the midway point in the Regular Session, and the cutoff for own-house bills out of committees. Half of all the bills introduced die, but nothing major is lost. The session has yet to find its legs.

Competing Education Reform Proposals

Both the House and Senate Education committees pass major "reform" bills but they have little in common. The Senate Republican bill provides $171.6 million, mostly through grants which must be matched by local school districts; it waives the requirement for time to be spent by students studying certain subjects; it requires students to pass a uniform exam to graduate from high school; it allows districts to institute teacher merit pay; it allows people with expertise in other fields to teach without the usual certification requirements; it requires new teachers to pass basic tests before teaching; and it allows special levies 5 percent above the existing levy lids.

The Democratic House/governor bill is heavy on local control. It frees schools from state regulations, such as the 180-day year, and mandatory subjects and hours, and in its place it sets up a commission to establish standards of knowledge and skills and how to test for them.

The battle between the two political parties over differing concepts of "school reform" is deep and will go on until almost the last minute of the last special session.

Campaign Finance Reform

In early March both houses pass very different versions of campaign finance reform. Everyone agrees there is a problem. It has become so bad that in one Seattle Senate race the two candidates spent nearly $300,000 each for a job that pays only $20,000 per year. That kind of money does not come from the candidates' pockets and it does not come without strings. Everyone acknowledges the situation has gotten out of hand and everyone wants to do something about it. The problem is that the solution depends largely on whether a politician is getting money from business or labor. Business can collect contributions in large checks while unions depend on a small involuntary "taxes" on the wages of their members.

Both Republicans in the Senate and Democrats in the House pass their campaign reform bills on almost straight party-line votes ahead of the first cutoff. The Republican plan says no individual contribution can exceed $500 to any one candidate (good if the campaign has lots of wealthy contributors); the Democrats' plan says legislative candidates can take up to $1,000 and statewide candidates $5,000 (good if the campaign has some big organizations like teachers and state employees behind it); the Republicans ban contributions from labor unions and corporations and PACs; the Democrats treat PACs the same as individuals.

But the key difference is in spending. Democrats impose a voluntary spending limit. Republicans have no spending limit at all. Under the Democrats' bill, if one legislative candidate stays under $55,000 and the opponent doesn't, the candidate would get partial matching funds from higher filing fees.

The courts have said that spending limits are constitutional only if there is public funding. That is the sticking point. Republicans adamantly oppose any form of public funding of political campaigns, and Democrats just as firmly oppose campaign reform that leaves out spending limits.

Long Term Care
March 14, 1991. House Democrats, led by Representative Dennis Braddock (D-Bellingham) on this issue, by a vote of 55-43 pass a long-term health care bill (HB 1569) funded by a payroll tax split between employers and employees that will raise $700 million over five years. By the fifth year an employee and employer would share payment of a tax equal to one-half of 1 percent of an employee's gross income up to the first $53,400. The money goes to support the state's estimated 200,000 functionally disabled citizens. The bill "is the sleeper of this session," claims Speaker Joe King. "There is such a need for this. The Senate will not be able to ignore it." Senator Jim West (R-Spokane) says he will give the bill a hearing in his Senate Health and Long-Term Care Committee, but called the bill "a cruel hoax." Governor Gardner is neutral.

Elusive Revenue Projections
March 18, 1991. The Economic and Revenue Forecast Council makes its March projection for the 1991-93 budget. Dr. Sohn says there is about $200 million more than he projected last December when the governor submitted his budget. Governor Gardner announces he will revise his earlier budget proposal to include the additional money.

While more money is generally good in terms of reaching a budget agreement, there are also plenty of worthy places to put the funds:

continuing to fund the full cost of health care benefits for state employees would cost about $169 million; restoring the governor's cuts in higher education—that is, the amount he reduced from higher education requests would take about $100 million; restoring cuts to K-12 in the governor's budget would take another $100 million; eliminating the governor's proposed accounting shifts would take $150 million; not passing the governor's proposed fee increases would take $150 million; and paying for Senator Cliff Bailey's education reform bill would cost $171 million.

True to his word, two days after the revised forecast was released, the governor announces his revised budget proposal to spend an additional $226 million (there was about $26 million in unanticipated savings in addition to the $200 million). Gardner proposes to restore $68 million in earlier cuts to higher education plus another $21 million in other higher education programs; he allocates another $35 million to state employees in health care benefits; $17 million in cost-of-living increases for retired teachers and state employees; $26 million for regional mental health programs; $33 million into the reserve account; and lesser sums for other human services and natural resources programs.

While the governor obviously tries to split the baby (albeit giving higher education the bigger piece), most groups are still not happy. They argue the additional money just restores cuts from their original requests or even, in a few cases, from the amount they said they need to run current programs. The Olympia Education Association President says, "The Governor is always saying that education is his top priority but he's clearly not living up to it." Washington Public Employees Association Director Eugene St. John says, "We're very disappointed." Karen Davis, representing the WEA, says "What's not adequate is the whole picture of compensation for teachers." Presidents of the WEA locals will meet in Seattle on April 13 to decide whether and when to strike.

The next move in the process is up to the House Appropriations Committee and Representative Gary Locke. According to *The Olympian*, he plans to announce his version of the budget by April 2, the seventy-ninth day. In 1989, the Senate had passed its first budget on the eightieth day, so even if the House meets this deadline it will be behind in the process.

A few days after the governor releases his budget, Senate Majority Leader Jeannette Hayner tells the *Seattle P-I* that Republicans plan to provide more money for higher education and K-12 in their budget than the governor has proposed. She doesn't say how much, but it is widely known that Senator Jerry Saling, the Senate Higher Education chair, wants another $88 million for higher education, and Senator Cliff Bailey (R-Snohomish) wants $171 million more for K-12. She will need the vote of every Senate Republican in order to negotiate. As she explains to *The Olympian*: "When you have a slim majority you try to accommodate everybody's wishes as best you can."

Republican Education Reform Passes Senate

March 19, 1991. Senate Republicans pass their version of education reform by a slim 25-24 straight party line vote. The bill (SB 5919) beefs up student achievement testing, provides permanent block grants, expands counseling in early grades, provides grants for vocational education and gives extra aid to urban and small districts. The bill costs $170 million but there is no funding in the bill. The chief sponsor, Senator Cliff Bailey, vows to "fight till the last day of session" to get full funding. Senator Nita Rinehart (D-Seattle), the leading Democrat on Bailey's Education Committee, says the bill "is a U-turn on the way to reform."

One of the key points in Bailey's bill would give performance-based raises above regular salaries to teachers based on how their students do on standard tests. Republicans argue it is a fair measurement. Democrats oppose, saying it rewards the high achievers only and that it would penalize teachers of slow learners.

Property Tax Relief Dies

March 20, 1991. With seven Republicans joining most of the Democrats, the Senate defeats Senator Dan McDonald's property tax bill 27-22. The bill would have rolled assessments back to the 1989 level. Some eastern Washington Republicans fear it would shift the property tax burden from west to east where values have not gone up as fast.

Adding Sexual Orientation to Hate Crimes

The House passes 77-21 a bill to add sexual orientation to the categories of people covered by existing state malicious harassment laws. Current laws protect persons from harassment based on race, color, religion, ancestry, national origin, or handicap. Gay rights activists and religious leaders have been advocating for the inclusion of gays and lesbians for several years. Its future in the Senate is in doubt.

Growth Management or Else

March 21, 1991. The House passes a 120-page growth management bill, a pet project of Speaker Joe King and of Governor Booth Gardner. The bill is a continuation of a growth management measure passed in 1990. It directs counties to set up ten and twenty-year urban growth boundaries and limit most growth to these areas, directs the state to issue guidelines for the formulation of local comprehensive plans, sets up state hearings boards to rule on appeals, and requires the governor to approve any appeals by state agencies.

Business interests are somewhat successful in watering the measure down in the House but are still not happy with the plan. The bill goes to the Senate Government Operations Committee where the chair, Senator Bob McCaslin (R-Spokane), says that all parties must come to an agreement before he will move it. He says he does not want a repeat of 1990 when a conference committee went further with growth management than he thought necessary.

House Majority Leader Brian Ebersole (D-Tacoma) says "Our commitment is to stay here" as long as it takes to get a growth management bill.

Term Limits Rejected by Senate
March 23, 1991. By a 28-21 vote the state Senate rejects a bill to limit to twelve years the terms of all state legislators and the nine statewide elected officials such as governor, lieutenant governor, SPI, etc. Chief sponsor, Senator Jack Metcalf, warns that voters will pass much more harsh term limits if the Legislature does not act first. His prediction is right. Voters pass an initiative in 1992 which allows senators to serve only eight of the last fourteen years and House members six of the last twelve years.

Rules Change
March 25, 1991. Senator Marc Gaspard, the minority leader, gives the required twenty-four-hour notice of a proposed rule change. He is ominously joined by Republican Senator Peter von Reichbauer, which clearly sends a signal to Senate Republican leaders that he has a majority on this issue. The new rule requires members of the Senate and staff to disclose to the Public Disclosure Commission on a quarterly basis any gifts they receive from lobbyists of a value over $50 or the value of entertainment if over $100. A similar amendment was offered by the Democrats on February 27 when the Senate Rules were adopted, but the Republicans held fast to defeat it. With von Reichbauer now on board, the Democrats are suddenly in the driver's seat if they can hold their own twenty-four members on the issue. This particular rule is similar to a PDC request bill that died earlier in the Senate Law and Justice Committee. On March 20, the twenty-five Republicans had locked up to block an attempt by the Democrats to pull it out of committee to the floor.

For the past several years Senate Republicans have been operating on the basis of the "rule of thirteen." They take votes inside their own caucus and whatever a majority decides there, all will support on the floor. This unity is the source of their power against the Democratic House and governor and is the crowning achievement of their leader, Senator Jeannette Hayner. The significance of the proposed rule change is whether this marks the end of unity on other, larger issues.

Two days later, March 27, the rule change comes up for a vote. After listening to Senator Gaspard and Senator von Reichbauer speak for the new rule, Republican leaders Hayner and Senator Irv Newhouse (R-Mabton) decide to join them rather than fight a losing battle. They point out, however, that it would apply only to the Senate. Senator Gary Nelson (R-Edmonds), who is responsible for killing the PDC-request bill in his Law and Justice Committee, now says it would be better to pass the bill (SB 5149) than a rules change. He does not explain why he killed the bill in committee. Senator A. L. "Slim" Rasmussen, an old foe of Senator von Reichbauer's from when he switched parties in 1981, wonders aloud why von Reichbauer (he always mispronounced the name as von Rickbur) had earlier voted against pulling the bill to the floor, but now co-sponsored a rules change to accomplish the same thing. When the fun and polite jabs are over, the proposed rules change is approved by voice vote with no recorded nays.

Threats From the Speaker of the House
House Speaker Joe King tells the Tacoma *News Tribune* editorial board he will hold up passage of the state operating budget until the Republican Senate comes to grips with the growth management issue and campaign finance. Speaker King wants to expand planning requirements for local governments, add Spokane County to those counties that come under the act, define the role of state government and provide sanctions for the state to force compliance. The House campaign finance reform bill limits both contributions and spending. The Senate bill limits only contributions.

King's linkage strategy is not new. He tried it without success in 1989 when he linked the gas tax increase to growth management. Gardner will try it next year when he links tax reform (the income tax) to an increase in the gas tax. Democrats use the strategy because it is all they have. Since Republicans generally want less from government, it is hard to trade bills with them. The ultimate weapon for Democrats is to threaten to keep the Legislature in session.

Locke's Budget
April 2, 1991. Representative Gary Locke, House Appropriations Committee chair, reveals his budget at a press conference at 9:00 A.M. on the

seventy-ninth day of the Regular Session. This is the first legislative budget proposal for the 1991-93 biennium. Locke holds committee hearings the same night and next day.

Locke assumes the same amount of money available to spend as the governor: $15.6 billion. The major differences are that Locke lifts the enrollment lids at colleges and universities to allow about 5,000 more students to enroll and adds $10 million to pay for it; he adds $27 million of a $54 million block grant for K-12 the Republicans favor; he reduces the governor's proposed K-12 teacher raises but puts more money into first-year teacher salaries; he adds money for developmental disabilities programs; and he reduces the natural resources, general government, and human resources areas to fund the increases.

Locke makes only slight changes in Gardner's proposed state employee raises, lowering the overall amount slightly in order to pay more to those furthest behind their private sector counterparts. He also proposes a two-tier system of welfare grants with larger increases going to recipients in five Puget Sound counties.

Governor Gardner calls Locke's effort a "go home budget" and his budget chief, Len McComb, describes it as "the Governor's priorities with some slight differences."

Senator Dan McDonald says that he and Locke were "miles apart in 1990 and 1989 but in 1991 I don't see us that far apart in philosophy or direction."

The Washington Education Association praises the level of funding for education programs but expresses disappointment over salary increases. They are not excited about paying more to beginning teachers, as their membership obviously includes fewer of those. They previously had set April 13 as a strike deadline and make no change in that threat.

State employee union leaders criticize the low level of salary increases in Locke's budget and the failure to fully fund health benefits.

Of the $15.6 billion expected in 1991-93, Locke's budget spends all but $30 million. It also assumes passage of $135 million in fee increases and the use of $104 million in interest earnings previously retained in their respective dedicated funds. Locke's very low reserve will obviously be a point of contention for the Senate Republicans.

Bill to Protect Homosexuals Loses
April 3, 1991. Despite heavy lobbying by Governor Gardner and appeals from prominent Republicans, including Lieutenant Governor Joel Pritchard and United States Senator Slade Gorton, HB 1037 which would extend malicious harassment protection to gays and lesbians, fails in the Senate

Law and Justice Committee on a tie vote, 4-4. Republican opponents say it will give special protection to homosexuals.

House Passes Budget

April 6, 1991. On Saturday, April 6, 1991, the eighty-third day, the full House passes an operating budget for 1991-93. It provides pay raises for state employees of 3.6 percent in each year, lower than the governor's proposed 4.4 percent and 3.8 percent, but it puts more money in health care benefits.

Teachers and education administrators get 4 percent and 3.5 percent, classified education employees (janitors, bus drivers, etc.) get 4.4 percent and 3.8 percent. The House also adds a $2,000 bonus per year to first, second and third-year teachers, less than Locke's original proposal.

Higher education faculty would receive 3.9 percent each year. Enrollment increases are provided but less than what colleges want.

The House budget passes on a party-line vote. One of the things most criticized by Republicans is the use of interest from dedicated funds to pay for operating budget programs. As expected, they also don't like the fact that it leaves very little money in reserve.

Republicans Reveal Their Budget

April 11, 1991. Five days after the House Democrats pass their budget, Senate Republicans reveal their spending plan. The major differences are: Republicans spend $15.54 billion instead of $15.61 billion; Republicans keep $326 million in reserve instead of $265 million; Republicans give teachers the same across-the-board salary increases as House Democrats but put an additional $10 million in the budget for merit pay; Republicans give about 1 percent more in salary increases to higher education faculty; Republicans give slightly more than the Democrats to state employees; and Republicans almost completely eliminate the House's $34.1 million in welfare grant increases, and erase $51.5 million in vendor rate increases.

Newspaper headlines report that the Senate Republicans reduce funding for human services and increase spending for education, higher education and for the budget reserve.

The Senate Republican budget gives teachers a 7.5 percent pay raise and a 17.5 percent increase for new teachers over two years. Ironically, only hours after Senator Dan McDonald reveals his budget, about 500 western Washington teachers march through the capitol campus demanding higher pay and smaller class sizes.

Governor Gardner says the Republican proposal will prolong the session. He calls it "a meaner and crueler budget" than his own or the House's.

Representative Locke says "the Senate proposal is way out of balance" between the young and old, rich and poor.

The Republicans slash $254.7 million from the Department of Social and Health Services. They take it from welfare increases, Medicaid, mental health, developmental disability programs, drug and alcohol abuse programs, long-term care, children's services and juvenile rehabilitation.

Phil Kaplan, a lobbyist for the poor and homeless, says: "We're horrified."

Senate Budget Out of Committee

April 12, 1991. ESHB 1330, the House operating budget, now carrying a Republican striking amendment, is signed out of the Senate Ways and Means Committee on April 12 on a straight party-line vote.

The Senate Republican budget is viewed by some as a political document brilliantly crafted to create havoc in the ranks of the Democrats. Republicans increase spending for education, a traditional Democratic constituency in which Republicans hope to score some gains, and take it out of welfare and poverty programs, where people either didn't vote or are solid Democrat. Democrats may be forced to choose between funding for education, their major political base, and restoring cuts to programs for the poor and homeless, their moral base. The governor is right. The stage could be set for a very long session.

WEA Threatens Action

April 13, 1991. Carla Nuxoll, head of the WEA, says the state teachers union will strike unless the Legislature antes up hundreds of millions of dollars more for teacher salaries and school funding. "They [legislators] can solve the problem by stepping up to it and getting the revenues necessary to fund schools." A strike could force closure of many schools and cancellation of many school-related events. However, a state law requires that time lost to a strike be made up so striking teachers will not lose pay unless schools attempt to operate without them.

Republicans Pass Their Budget

April 15, 1991. Senate Republicans run their budget on the floor. The Democrats had placed a proposed rule change on the desk the previous week to abolish the requirement for 60 percent approval to amend the budget. They decide it is hopeless, however, and withdraw all their amendments.

After only an hour, the vote is taken. It is a tie, 24-24, on straight party lines because Senator George Sellar (R-Wenatchee) was excused when he checked into Providence Hospital with heart problems. The Democrats agree to provide the necessary twenty-fifth vote just to keep the process moving. Minority Leader Marc Gaspard says that in return for this gesture he hopes the Senate Republicans will negotiate in good faith. One other Democrat, Senator Brad Owen, also votes for the Republican budget because he says he was threatened by a House Democrat that if he voted with the Republicans, an important bill of his would die in the House. He wants to show he will not be intimidated. There is no doubt as to Senator Owen's sincerity but it is noted that he voted with the Republicans on budgets in 1987 and 1989, so his vote in 1991 is consistent with his independent, conservative previous actions.

Following passage by the Senate of the Republican version of the budget, Senator McDonald tells the press, "We're a lot closer [to the House budget] than we've been the past two years."

The House immediately rejects the Senate budget and asks for a conference committee to start working out the differences. Representative Locke says, "I'm disappointed to see how far apart we are." Conferees begin meeting to iron out differences.

Teachers' Strike Begins
April 18, 1991. On the ninety-fifth day of the scheduled 105-day session, the teachers strike of 1991 begins. About 21,000 of the state's 50,000 teachers put down their chalk and take up picket signs. Although teachers in most of the state's school districts have rejected the strike and remain on the job, some striking teachers vow they will remain out as long as it takes for the Legislature to give them what they want, which is higher pay (usually defined as a 10 percent raise over the next two years) and smaller classes. There is a push during the days preceding the strike deadline to get legislators to tap the rainy day fund to provide the money, but all the principals in the budget negotiations say no deal. WEA President Carla Nuxoll emerges from a last-minute meeting with Governor Gardner saying "There's no solution in sight." She rules out the creation of a task force or a blue ribbon panel as a way out. Speaker Joe King says "The strike is well intentioned but will have no effect on the Legislature."

Coincidentally, on the same day, Senator Bailey's education reform bill comes back from the House to the Senate, amended to reflect the Democrats' priorities. Senate Republicans amend Bailey's original bill back on as a striking amendment and fire it right back asking for a conference. House leaders agree and conferees are appointed.

April 19, 1991. It is a rare, sun-drenched spring day in Olympia. When legislators and staff trudge to their offices, the only signs of something amiss are the bright blue porta-potties placed at strategic points on campus and on sidewalks along Capitol Way. Soon there is the sound of carpenters' hammers erecting a speakers' stand near the Tivoli Fountain. By mid-morning the green campus is filled with thousands of teachers carrying pre-printed signs. Many are wearing brightly colored T-shirts to designate their school districts: purple for Bellevue, orange for Seattle, etc. Most arrive around 10:00 A.M., many in big yellow school buses (what else?) which are then parked in rows along Capitol Way, others in private cars parked along Water Street. Most are in their thirties or forties. A number of them have brought along their children. They are Nordstrom-casual in dress, tasteful but conservative, the kind of people who live quiet lives in suburbs and that one feels safe with. They seem uncomfortable, maybe a little embarrassed, with their picket signs.

Despite the large number of participants, the strike seems benign, almost pleasant, more like a company picnic. There is little or no anger, no vandalism, few harsh words. The teachers gather first around the temporary wooden platform, listening to speeches and sometimes singing songs. After some time they form into a long line which snakes past the war memorials, around the Legislative Building, past the governor's mansion and the Temple of Justice, and back to the fountain. They stay on the sidewalks whenever possible, keep polite distances between themselves, are neat and orderly. They leave no litter behind.

Legislators and staff peek at these interlopers warily at first from their third and fourth floor offices in the Cherberg and O'Brien buildings, surprised at the numbers, not sure what to expect. A few old-timers tell about the raucous timber workers and labor rallies of years ago. Later in the day, legislative staff and lobbyists will stand at the edges of the crowd so they can listen to the speeches. Within a few days, some legislative staff will get to know the strikers well enough to politely discuss and debate issues. There is no report of any argument or altercations. Uniformed State Patrol standing around the edges look bored.

Next day a group of teachers from the Peninsula School District jogs the thirty-nine miles to Olympia. There is a large picture of them in the morning Tacoma *News Tribune* looking happy, smiling and cheering. One carries a picket sign almost like an Olympic torch, another is wearing a DARE TO SAY NO TO DRUGS T-shirt. They look like they are having fun.

Back to the Budget
April 22, 1991. With one week to go in the Regular Session, the operating budget is still unresolved with the conferees reporting little progress. Other issues are also unresolved. Democrats are insisting on stricter growth management, campaign spending limit reform and clean air legislation. Republicans want a ban on casino-style gambling (at that time allowed only as part of Reno-night for charities and on some Indian reservations), performance-based pay incentives for teachers, and campaign finance contribution (as opposed to spending) limits. All of these matters are in conference committees. There is the potential for resolving them all in the last week of the session but that seems highly unlikely.

A special session seems a certainty either immediately following the regular session or soon thereafter. If the budget disagreements drag on, members might even wait until after the June revenue forecasts to resume talks.

Teachers Continue to Rally
There has been much in the press about the teachers' strike, mostly positive at first. Some districts have talked about going to court to force teachers back, but seem reluctant to act hastily. The daily demonstrations appear to have little impact on legislators. Some members who favor the teachers appear as speakers and a few even become cheerleaders. Those against simply go about their business and ignore the whole matter.

April 23, 1991. Superintendent of Public Instruction Judith Billings holds a press conference to present her views on the strike. She is clearly on the side of the teachers, as she has been from the beginning of the session. She advocates immediate creation of a blue ribbon panel to come up with a long-term fix, legislation to raise the levy lid to pay for non-basic education programs, and for all parties to sit down immediately to work out a solution to the current problems. She says she is concerned because the parties are not talking together.

Ms. Billings makes no mention of any effort by her office to force teachers back to their classrooms or to make them comply with their contracts. She is unable to respond to press questions about how her proposal for a second-tier levy would affect teachers' salaries. Ms. Billings even lapses into the "we" pronoun when referring to the teachers' positions. Governor Gardner and Speaker Joe King, answering press questions, say lifting the levy lid and spending the rainy day fund have no support in the Legislature and reject Billings' proposals.

The following day two school districts in Pierce County, Franklin Pierce and Peninsula, seek and are granted injunctions against the striking teachers requiring them to honor their contracts and return to the classrooms. Instructors at Highline Community College agree to end their walkout in the face of possible fines. Teachers in the North Beach School District in Grays Harbor return to their classrooms, dropping the total number of districts on strike to thirty-three. The school boards of Edmonds, Everett and Sultan school districts authorize legal action if teachers do not return. Several districts say they are holding off until next Monday, as there is a general feeling the strike will end by then.

Budget Negotiations Stalled
April 25, 1991. Thursday, the 101st day of the Regular Session. Budget negotiations continue to go nowhere. The negotiations began technically over a week earlier but conferees have actually spent only about three hours together thus far. Each side is waiting for the other to make a new offer. Neither seems in a hurry, even though only three days remain in the Regular Session. The teachers' strike is now a week old and seems to have had little impact on budget negotiations. If anything, it has made the House Democrats a little nervous about appearing to give in and the Senate Republicans more determined than ever not to reward the strikers. Nearly everyone assumes a special session is inevitable.

Strike Continues
April 26, 1991. Teachers continue to picket the Legislature in even larger numbers as Olympia and Tumwater vote to join them for one day. A vigil is planned for Saturday night in the rotunda of the Legislative Building with organizers predicting 20,000 persons in attendance.

Court actions by districts to force teachers to return are mostly delayed until Monday. The WEA says it will decide on Sunday whether to continue the strike. Only Sequim School District and Highline Community College District have been ordered back to work. There seems to be a consensus in most districts that the strike will be tolerated until Monday but after that school directors will all go to court. Monday would also be the first day of a special session if one is called immediately.

Teachers flood members' offices and the legislative hotline with messages, stop members whenever they find them in public areas, and provide a constant visual reminder of their cause. But it appears that few minds are changed.

On the Inside
Meanwhile, inside the Cherberg Building, with only two days remaining in the 1991 Regular Session, Senator Bob McCaslin, chair of the Senate

Governmental Operations Committee, finally agrees to hold a hearing on Speaker King's cherished growth management bill, long-since passed by the House and languishing in committee. McCaslin has his own bill—dubbed "growth lite"—which Democrats claim is a retreat from growth management.

Speaker King has informed the press on several occasions that an "acceptable" growth management bill is a prerequisite for the passage of the budget and the end of the session. Senator McCaslin says he doesn't want to pass any bill, not even "growth lite" because that might lead to a conference committee with the House and a compromise which would only make matters worse from his perspective.

At the hearing in McCaslin's committee, it is apparent that the issue is so complex and so controversial that it needs more than just one hour's hearing. There appears little chance that a growth management bill can pass the Senate in the remaining two days of the Regular Session.

The Governor Has a Surprise
About 3:00 P.M. on Friday, April 26, 1991, Governor Gardner surprises almost everyone when he announces that he will not call a special session of the Legislature until June 15, seven weeks from the end of the Regular Session on Sunday. He says the Senate Republicans' proposal to increase funding for education is right, the House Democrats' position not to take the money from children's and social programs is right, and his arguments for a "sense of balance" is right. But it has produced "a situation for which there is no seeming solution." He says the dilemma cries out for a cooling-off period to let tempers subside and to seek a fresh solution. His reason for picking June 15 is so there would be another revenue forecast and "only then will we have the possibility for a win for all concerned." In other words, he is praying for an increase in the revenue forecast.

The governor calls on teachers to return to their classrooms on Monday and he congratulates the Legislature on what he calls "the most successful environmental session in our state's history." To support his claim he cites the clean air bill, the oil spill prevention bill, and the energy strategies bill (he could also have cited the recycling bill). He says if these are joined by a growth management bill and a decent level of funding for outdoor recreation, it will be even better.

Reaction to Governor's Call
Reaction to the governor's delaying a special session until June 15 is loud and almost universally negative. It becomes apparent he didn't consult

with his own party's legislative leaders before announcing the decision. It is reported that House Speaker King had only two minutes' prior notice. Senate Democrats, who seem not to have been consulted at all, are overwhelmingly in favor of sooner rather than later. Their leader, Senator Marc Gaspard, says "We do feel like the rug has been cut out from under us." Representative Gary Locke calls the governor's announcement "crazy."

Leaders of the striking teachers are furious. With legislators about to depart, there seems little point in continuing to picket in Olympia. Carla Nuxoll, the union leader, says they might continue the strike by picketing legislators at their homes or businesses. She warns, "It's not over." Teresa Moore, a WEA spokesperson, says "In Texas, where I come from, it's called turnin' tail and runnin'."

April 27, 1991. Shortly after noon on Saturday, the 104th day, the Senate votes 48-0 to call themselves back into session immediately on Monday (SCR 8414). Not one single member, not one single Democrat, votes to support the position of the governor.

The Senate does little work the rest of the day while waiting to see if the Democratic House will follow their lead or support the governor. Striking teachers lobby House members to support the resolution and stay in Olympia. There are angry speeches on the steps of the Capitol Building aimed at Booth Gardner. One can hear chants of "GET BUSY NOW" from blocks away.

The weather is incongruous with the demonstration and the angry speeches. It is 65 degrees on Saturday afternoon, partly sunny, with the campus glowing with pink and white-blooming cherry trees, yellow daffodils and red tulips. Despite the angry rhetoric of their leaders, teachers still seem mainly in a festive mood. It is hard to be otherwise on such a glorious day.

It is rumored that many strikers intend to spend the night in sleeping bags inside the rotunda. Security personnel are instructed to let as many in as the fire code allows.

Sine Die
April 28, 1991. Sunday, the final day of the 1991 Regular Session, and the weather has reverted to the normal gray and overcast with intermittent drizzle. Only a couple hundred strikers show up and they leave early. Half a dozen high school-age students dressed in black caps and gowns march around the striking teachers with signs saying: "YOU MADE YOUR POINT—NOW WHAT ABOUT US?"

At 2:30 P.M. the House puts itself under the call (lock the doors and require all members to be present). They take up the Senate resolution to call themselves back into special session the next day. Democratic Floor Leader Brian Ebersole speaks for the resolution, arguing legislators need to stay to deal with the issues. Republican Minority Leader Clyde Ballard speaks against, saying it will send the wrong message. Then they take the very unusual procedural action of a roll call vote, rather than the electronic machine. The measure (SCR 8414) needs sixty-six votes to pass. House Republicans lock up against it and it fails by 57-41.

Shortly afterward, the WEA announces teachers will voluntarily return to work on Monday if the governor will call a special session immediately. Representative Gary Locke suggests on KIRO radio that the governor should call a special session in return for this pledge from the WEA. But Governor Gardner holds fast in his insistence that there has to be progress on the budget before a special session is justified. House Republicans also stay firm in their conviction that coming back on Monday would be giving in to the WEA strikers.

There is a second House vote on Sunday night on the resolution for the Legislature to call itself back into special session with the same result, short of the two-thirds required. It is highly unusual that of the four caucuses, the only one that supports the Democratic governor's position is the House Republicans. Right or wrong, this odd coupling forces a delay in the calling of the first special session. It is also ironic that in the end, the only thing the WEA demands for returning to work is calling a special session on Monday and they can't even get that.

With a special session promised on June 15, the Regular Session dies a quiet and unlamented death on Sunday night.

The Day After
April 29, 1991. Many of the teachers return to their classrooms on Monday. Others take formal votes on Monday and return on Tuesday or Wednesday. Many district administrators claim they were ready to go to court to force a return if the teachers didn't do it on their own. The unanswered question for some parents is why that wasn't done earlier.

Legislators and staff dribble in to work Monday morning, faces drawn and clothing wrinkled. Many have been working late for days or weeks now and show the strains of long hours and prolonged stress. There is a kind of universal weariness typical of the end of every long session. Session is like a cacophonous sound that grows louder and louder each day. When it seems almost intolerable, it suddenly stops and there is a sense of relief and calm. The strikers are gone, many of the session employees have departed. It is a time-out in the game, a chance for the sides to huddle, think things over. The first signals of the strike are the last to leave as trucks load up and haul away the blue porta-potties.

All the striking teachers return to work by Tuesday. By the end of the week the papers carry nothing more about the strike and little about education issues.

WEA leaders threats to move their pickets from Olympia to the homes of the Republican legislators who opposed an immediate special session fail to materialize. They declare the strike a success because it increased awareness of education issues and galvanized teachers as a political force.

Meanwhile, school districts scramble to make up for the weeks of missed classes. They use a variety of means such as lengthening the school year, Saturday classes, longer days, etc. to satisfy the state requirements. No teacher loses any wages because of the strike although they, like the students and parents, are clearly inconvenienced.

Winners and Losers So Far
Press summaries of the 1991 Regular Session make everyone look bad. House and Senate Democrats are generally portrayed as groveling at the feet of the WEA, trying to outdo one another in pandering to the crowds of striking teachers. Senate Republicans are portrayed as anti-education despite their proposals to add money for education to the biennial budget. House Republicans, with only forty votes, finally get to play in the game but only as a negative force to halt an immediate special session.

Governor Gardner, who wants to be remembered as the "Education Governor" and indeed can legitimately claim the title by virtue of long-standing interest and efforts, ends up being vilified by WEA leaders (who supported him in the 1990 election) and by some fellow Democrats because he won't give in to WEA demands to keep legislators in session. One wonders if Gardner's decision not to seek reelection to a third term was formed during the last few weeks of the Regular Session of 1991.

Post-Session Talks
Two days after the end of session, Gary Locke and Dan McDonald have lunch together and the budget conferees begin meeting. The focus turns from arguing about specific spending items to speculation about the June revenue forecast. Both sides want to add funds for K-12. The question is whether to wait for the June forecast, as Gardner prefers, or work off current estimates and get it done sooner.

May 2, 1991. Governor Gardner announces that the special session may need to start June 1 rather than June 15 in order to pass budget adjustments needed to complete the current fiscal year. The governor's staff forgot about the current budget when Gardner announced the June 15 date. The second supplemental budget had been agreed to and was ready to go at the end of the Regular Session but Len McComb, the governor's budget chief, said he didn't think they needed it, so it was put off. Now, some agencies are saying they might run out of money and might have to close if funding isn't provided by June 15 for the balance of the current year. Normally, there are a few minor adjustments to the biennial budget rolled together in a second supplemental budget and passed before the end of regular session of odd-numbered years.

Budget conferees continue to meet in the weeks immediately following the Regular Session with varying stories coming out of the meetings. With the Democrats boxed in between cuts in education and cuts in social programs (actually they are not cuts but reductions in the rate of in-creases), they pin their hopes on a healthy increase in the June 14 revenue forecast.

Governor Says Get To Work

May 9, 1991. At an informal press conference in his office, Governor Gardner criticizes the House and Senate budget negotiators for being no closer to an agreement than they were a month earlier. Gardner says he came back from a meeting in San Francisco and "found we had the second work stoppage of the spring. First the teachers went on strike and now the budget conferees have done pretty much the same." Gardner says the conferees met only fifty minutes this week. "What we are seeing is a lack of will," he concludes.

Representative Gary Locke shoots back, "I don't think we lack any will. We're talking about some very tough choices here. A lot of things are going on that Booth isn't aware of. I think we're making progress. I think we're going to surprise Booth."

A Proposal From House Democrats

May 13, 1991. True to Locke's word promising a surprise, four days later House Majority Democrats hold a press conference to propose taking $130 million out of the rainy day fund as a way out of the budget stalemate. They would match the Republicans proposal for K-12 and higher education and maintain their own higher levels for welfare and social programs and the environment. They (Ebersole and Locke) say the rainy day fund would be replenished from increased revenues in the June and September forecasts. In other words, they want to borrow against hoped-for optimistic revenue projections, an idea similar to that proposed by Senate

Democrats weeks earlier. At that time, both Speaker King and Governor Gardner had rejected it.

At their press conference, Locke says this is the only way out. Carla Nuxoll, the WEA President, cries out "Yea team." She later says it proves legislators have gotten the message from the teachers' strike.

Senate Republican budget chief Dan McDonald gives an emphatic no to the idea and accuses House Democrats of caving in to the WEA. McDonald says he agrees with the governor's earlier statement that using the rainy day fund now would be "shortsighted and foolhardy." Gardner is in Washington D.C. and has no comment on the latest proposal of the House Democrats.

The Forecast Council moves its next forecast up to June 12. Most staff and members expect there to be about $130 million in increased revenue projections, enough to satisfy everyone.

A few days later Governor Gardner names a blue-ribbon commission to study the state's education system. The 21-member panel includes Boeing President Frank Shrontz, Seattle Mayor Norm Rice, Carla Nuxoll, president of the WEA, SPI Judith Billings, eight legislators and almost everyone who is anyone in the current education establishment of the state. Gardner is chair. The commission is to come up with recommendations for the 1993 session.

Locke Takes A Fall

On the weekend of May 18, Representative Gary Locke, the chief negotiator for the House Democrats, falls from the roof of his Seattle home and breaks his back. He is taken to the hospital where, on Monday, he is listed in satisfactory condition. Renowned as a workaholic, he vows gamely not to let the injury interfere with budget negotiations.

The next week, negotiators, without Locke, meet with the governor. Rumors abound in Olympia that a deal is close and that Gardner will call a special session to start on June 3, but it is just another false start. Things have actually deteriorated. By the end of May all reports are negative. Senator McDonald reportedly walked out of one meeting in disgust. At another, the conferees go all the way back to square one, arguing over the process.

On June 4 an article in *The Olympian* says that in the thirty-six days since the end of the Regular Session (April 28), the budget negotiators have met only fourteen times, once for as little as forty-five minutes. OFM Director Len McComb is quoted as criticizing legislators for not working harder. He points out that the Legislature is in violation of state law which requires a budget thirty days before the end of the biennium.

At one point it appears that not only are Democrats and Republicans in disagreement but the three Democrats on the budget conference have begun fighting with one another. It is reported that on June 4 the Democrats left the conference to go into their own private session to try to come to agreement before continuing discussions with the Republicans.

Second Special Session
June 10, 1991. The Legislature reconvenes at the call of the governor. There are only twenty days left in the biennium, after which state agencies will have no money to operate.

Despite the fact that time is short and budget negotiations continue to be stalled, there is no sense of urgency or alarm. The hope is that the Economic and Revenue Forecast Council, now scheduled to meet next day, on June 11, will forecast enough additional money to resolve the differences. Another $100 million might cover things.

Growth management is also stalled. Negotiations have been taken over by the four caucus leaders but produced nothing thus far.

The education reform bill is the third major piece thought to be needed for 1991. Negotiators have been going in circles. Democrats want more local control and more money, Republicans want accountability, testing and merit pay.

Gardner's appointment of a blue-ribbon commission probably undercut efforts at education reform, even though Republicans continue to insist their reforms (testing and merit pay) are a prerequisite for increased funding in the current budget.

While not much is actually done, education issues are certainly debated more than usual in the 1991 session. The main areas of contention are:

- Testing as a requirement for students to advance. Republicans favor it as quality control, Democrats say it will increase the dropout rate and work against teachers of slower students, whose job is already difficult enough.
- Merit pay. Republicans favor it as a common business practice, Democrats oppose it as impractical and demoralizing in the education field.
- Mandatory master's degree for teachers. Democrats favor it because it is thought to produce better trained teachers, Republicans oppose it as driving up costs and unnecessary.
- Probationary periods for beginning teachers. In 1991, it was one year whenever a teacher started new in a district. Republicans want it to be longer.

- Teacher testing. Republicans favor, Democrats oppose.
- Parent councils. Mixed politically. Probably more Democrats oppose and Republicans favor.
- Alternative certification of teachers. Democrats oppose because it will water down qualifications, drive down teacher salaries and possibly weaken the union. Republicans favor.

New Forecast

June 11, 1991. On Tuesday, the second day of the First Special Session, the Economic and Revenue Forecast Council meets to examine the state economy for the next two years. Two days later the chief economist, Dr. Sohn, will release his much anticipated estimate of the state revenues available for the next two years.

The game plan for the Democrats is to argue for a higher revenue estimate based on a stronger economy. That way there will be enough money to cover all the needs. A study by Dick Conway, a Seattle economist, is released showing that Dr. Sohn had been too conservative in twenty-six of the last twenty-seven forecasts (he is affectionately called "Doctor Doom" by some staff).

At the Forecast Council meeting, Len McComb, Gardner's budget chief and a member of the Forecast Council, argues that Sohn's economic estimate, the basis for the revenue forecast, is too low in terms of growth in average wages, the level of Boeing employment, and the level of new construction. Dr. Sohn agrees to move up his estimate of wage growth but resists changes in the other factors. McComb says he might vote against Sohn's proposed forecast, which needs approval of the council. It appears likely that Revenue Director Dennis Okamota, another Gardner appointee, will support McComb, while Republicans Senator Dan McDonald and Representative Bruce Holland will back Sohn. That would leave the decision in the hands of Democrats Senator Marc Gaspard and Representative Art Wang, both considered likely to back McComb and a higher estimate. This would be the first time there has been a partisan disagreement on the council, if it occurs.

June 13, 1991. At a packed meeting of the Economic and Revenue Forecast Council in the Senate Rules Committee room, potential political division over the amount of revenue available dissipates when Dr. Sohn estimates there is another $73 million available to spend in the coming biennium. He passionately denies giving in to political pressure. The council unanimously adopts his new forecast. Senator Dan McDonald, the only budget negotiator on the council, says afterwards that he is now optimistic for a budget agreement.

Prospects for a resolution of the budget get even better the following Wednesday, June 19, when the governor's office announces it has "found" $55 million it didn't know it had coming from the federal government for Medicare. This, plus the $73 million causes the Democrats to abandon their demand to use the rainy day fund. Representative Locke says he thinks there is now enough money to fund all the state's needs. So, the size of the pie is finally defined and it only remains to carve up the pieces.

Giving Up On Growth Management
House Democrats announce they are giving up hope for a growth management plan for 1991. They say they will ask for a special session later in the year if they think an agreement can be reached. Otherwise they say they will try to get an initiative to the people on the ballot in 1992.

Agreement at Last
June 25, 1991. Tuesday, House and Senate budget conferees announce they have an agreement on the 1991-93 budget to begin July 1. The draft is given to the Code Reviser's Office to be put into bill form. It is expected that there will be a hard copy to take to the four caucuses on Thursday with a final vote on Friday, although that schedule seems overly optimistic to some.

Meanwhile, the growth management bill which had been given up for dead, comes back to life when negotiators meet until Tuesday midnight, then schedule further meetings for the next day. The education reform bill dies in a different way—it is compromised into nothing.

In a flurry of activity, Senate Republicans push through two "morality" bills on Tuesday: one to regulate nude dancing and the other to outlaw casino-style gambling on Indian reservations. Both face difficulties in the Democratic House and with the governor, but appeal to right-wing constituencies important to some Republican members.

Another Sine Die
June 30, 1991. On Sunday, the Senate passes the operating budget by 36-11 and the House by 82-13. It could have passed on Friday but the Senate Democrats held it up to try again to make something of education reform. Even though in the minority, Senate Democrats can do this because Senator Jerry Saling is in Hawaii, thus causing a 24-24 tie in the Senate. Governor Gardner has to personally ask the Democrats to let the budget go. He signs it at 11:30 P.M.

The final budget agreement is pretty much as many observers predicted months earlier. Republicans keep their proposed increases to K-12 with $570 million earmarked for class size reductions and block grants. Democrats get a 6.5 percent welfare grant increase and more money for foster parents. State employees and teachers get 8.2 percent raises over two years, .08 percent below Governor Gardner's original proposal.

Education reform finally bogs down over the elimination of the master's degree requirement and raising the local levy lid. Senate Republicans refuse to pass the bill, even though the House passes it 87-3.

One interesting final note to the 1991 session. Abortion ends up in the budget by Senate oversight, despite the best efforts of some Republicans to avoid the issue. Representative Gary Locke wants to include money for clinics that provide abortions to low-income women. In the House draft of the budget there is funding for these family planning clinics, but Senate negotiators miss it. The conference report is already signed and on the members' desks when pro-life Senator Ellen Craswell (R-Bremerton) discovers this funding and demands that it be removed. Embarrassed Senate Republican leaders ask House leaders to help. Locke initially agrees but two hours later comes back with a list of things he wants in exchange. The final budget is passed with a proviso eliminating funding for abortions and with Locke's new programs. The governor is having none of this and vetoes both.

So the 1991 legislative session finally closes, having set a new record for lateness: June 30. The previous latest finish was June 22, 1977.

Disappearing Revenues
September 16, 1991. Barely two and a half months after the legislators completed their work on the 1991-93 budget, dark clouds begin to appear over the sunny forecast of revenues on which the final compromise had been fashioned. Dr. Chang Mook Sohn reveals at the September meeting of the Forecast Council that revenues are down $26.5 million from the previous quarter. He predicts there could be as much as a $200 million hole in the just-passed budget. The *Bellevue American*, in an editorial on September 18, 1991, says this "does call into question those rosy forecasts of just three months ago that enabled Governor Booth Gardner and state lawmakers to pass a budget that pleased just about everybody but now probably won't have staying power beyond next January's legislative session." A prescient comment.

Other Matters
October 3, 1991. About a month to go before the general election and campaigns are heating up. There are four major initiatives to be decided by voters: I 119, Death with Dignity; I 120, Abortion Rights; I 553, Term Limits; and I 559, Property Tax Reform.

Later in the month, Booth Gardner quietly announces he will not be a candidate for a third term as governor. Speculation immediately begins that Gardner will seek the United States Senate seat of Brock Adams should he decline to run again.

Off-Year Election Results
November 7, 1991. In the off-year election, the Death with Dignity, Term Limits and Property Tax Reform initiatives all fail. United States Congressman and Speaker of the House Tom Foley (D-Spokane) is given much of the credit for defeating the term limits initiative. Backers of all three initiatives say they will try again. The Abortion Rights initiative, which puts into state statute the *Roe v. Wade* Supreme Court decision, passes very narrowly.

Just before the election, Republicans State Senator Dan McDonald and Congressman Sid Morrison announce they are candidates for governor in 1992, and shortly after the election Democrat Speaker Joe King announces that he, too, is a candidate for governor. A few days later Republicans State Senator Jack Metcalf and Attorney General Ken Eikenberry also jump into the governor's race.

Budget Crisis Worsens
November 8, 1991. The budget crisis is deepening. It now appears the state will have at least a $500 million deficit, more than double that announced in September. Chief forecaster Chang Mook Sohn blames the bad news on a stubborn national recession, disappointing growth in aerospace jobs and consumer fear of spending.

Governor Gardner at first rules out raising taxes but as the crisis deepens, he leaves all options open. He says the sudden sea of red ink means "everything is on the table." Earlier he had ordered agencies to prepare contingency plans for 2.5 percent across-the-board cuts (to save about $205 million) by December 1 and he tells them now to plan for another cut of the same magnitude. Senator Marc Gaspard, chair of the Forecast Council, says "I fully expect that 2.5 percent cut to be implemented."

December 6, 1991. Gardner's budget chief, Len McComb, testifying before a legislative panel, says he believes the state's revenue shortfall for the current biennium will reach $900 million. He blames sporadic economic recovery from the recession, slow growth in new jobs and wages, and continued growth in demand for state services like schools and welfare programs. Governor Gardner orders across-the-board cuts of 2.5 percent, hitting social services and higher education particularly hard. McComb warns that when the governor releases his proposed supplemental budget later in December it will include some combination of deeper cuts, fee increases, tax-loophole closures, canceled raises for teachers and state employees, and a dip into the state's $260 million reserve.

December 16, 1991. At the meeting of the Economic and Revenue Forecast Council, Dr. Sohn again revises his estimate down. Instead of being $200 million short, he predicts the state budget will be short by about $700 million. In addition, another $200 million is needed to cover unexpected increases in welfare costs, thus agreeing with the earlier prediction of McComb. Legislators and the public are shocked. There hasn't been a negative supplemental budget since 1982, and never one of this proportion.

Gardner's 1992 Budget Proposals
Governor Gardner responds to the increasingly bad news with a tough share-the-pain 1992 supplemental budget proposal in which he proposes to eliminate the 1993 salary increases for state employees (saves $16 million), teachers (saves $78 million) and higher education faculty (saves $17 million). He proposes eliminating welfare increases, increasing college tuition to raise about $44 million, raising the tax on cable television users for about $21 million, cutting block grants to K-12 schools by $31 million, capturing and spending about $43 million in overpayments to the pension fund, closing a loophole in the real estate title transfer tax for $9 million, creating a gambling tax worth about $11 million, reducing state workers by 1,100 positions, and spending all of the $260 million rainy day fund.

Gardner's proposal for dealing with the $900 million problem is a real potpourri—there is something for everyone to hate. In its defense, Gardner points out that it contains only $40 million in new taxes and another $44 million in tuition increases. The rest is done by cuts.

In keeping with the Christmas season, the Washington Federation of State Employees calls Gardner "the Grinch who stole Christmas." Gary Moore, the executive director, says "We're not going to sit still and simply give up those salary increases."

Senate Republican budget chief Dan McDonald is critical of depleting all of the rainy day fund. He wonders what will happen if things get worse? McDonald says he thinks state employment can be cut more. He offers no specifics at this time but promises he will when his Senate Ways and Means Committee hears the supplemental budget.

It is astounding to legislators how the revenue forecast has turned sour so quickly when outwardly the state seems much the same. In June the governor and the Democrats had openly pressured Dr. Sohn to raise his forecast to help break the budget impasse. Sohn steadfastly insisted politics was not a part of his forecast. Still, he did add $73 million at just the right time to resolve the budget impasse in June 1991. By August Sohn had to admit that the critical June forecast had indeed been somewhat rosy. And by December it was clear he had missed in a big way on the high side.

In Sohn's defense one should remember that President Bush had declared the recession to be over in the spring of 1991, and many economists shared the administration's view that the economic engine was about to surge forward. In fact, the Bush Administration waited until Thanksgiving to concede that the recession was still on and Sohn had that part figured out by the end of summer.

Another factor in Dr. Sohn's overly optimistic June projection might have been an attempt to compensate for earlier projections he made which were too pessimistic. In 1990 Dr. Sohn had missed by over a billion dollars on the low side. It is perfectly reasonable to assume that he made some adjustments to his economic model to prevent that from happening again. The life of an economic forecaster is not an easy one.

1992

Uncertain Political Landscape
Going into the 1992 Regular Session, Washington State has a political landscape riddled with uncertainties, an economy that is faltering and arguably still in recession, and the largest budget deficit in the state's history.

Health Care Reform or Not
As if overcoming the budget problems was not enough, Governor Gardner decides to make health care reform a top priority in the upcoming session. Of course, the two are more than a little related as health costs are the fastest rising part of both the state and federal budgets. Republicans show little interest. Gardner announces his health care proposals on December 16, 1991. Senate Republicans admit they have no health reform plan of their own—they are waiting for Senator West, the chair of the Senate Health and Long-Term Care Committee, to develop one. They suggest it would be prudent to wait for the final report from the Health Care

Commission, due at the end of 1992, before taking any action. This theme of caution and delay in health care reform by the Republicans versus a sense of urgency and alarm by the Democrats will surface again and again during the legislative session. In retrospect one can see the health care debate in Washington State as a precursor for the one to follow nationally in 1993 between President Clinton and congressional Republicans.

Of course, politics might have a little to do with it. Democrats believe that health care reform is the hot issue with the public. United States Senator Harris Wofford (D-PA) had unexpectedly defeated former U.S. Attorney General Dick Thornburgh for the U.S. Senate seat in Pennsylvania in November on this single issue. Governor Gardner and legislative Democrats are united in wanting to do something to expand access and cut costs, even if they don't agree on specifics. Republican state senators and representatives are just as determined to preserve the private health care system and fight against more government intrusion. There are some very large and powerful special interests involved on both sides. Some cynics say the best of all worlds is for the Republicans to defeat attempts at reform, thereby winning substantively, but giving the Democrats a strong campaign issue for '92.

Beyond health and the budget, the only other major legislative issue on the horizon in December is mass transportation in the Puget Sound corridor. A federal court judge had held the current structure of METRO unconstitutional, there is substantial money available in the federal budget for mass transportation, and there is a growing impatience by the public with highway gridlock in the I-5 corridor.

Term Limitations, Part II
In November 1991, the term limits initiative was defeated 46 percent to 54 percent. Backers believe the loss was caused because the provisions were retroactive and were poorly drafted. They vow to return with a new version which will not be retroactive; where the congressional limits would only be triggered if ten other states join; which will allow persons to run for reelection after six years' absence; and which will provide an absolute limit of fourteen years service in the state Legislature and eighteen years in Congress. They begin to gather signatures for a second try in November 1992.

Campaign Finance Reform
In 1990, a record $12 million is spent by the 286 candidates for the Washington State House and Senate. The average Senate candidate spent $111,183. The average House candidate spent $34,869. These figures are

up 38 percent over the previous election. The ten biggest contributors to the 1990 state legislative campaigns are: United for Washington (business), the Washington Federation of State Employees (labor), Washington Medical PAC (mostly doctors), the Washington State Labor Council (labor), Senate Republican Campaign Committee (biggest contributors are Norton Clapp, Republican National Committee and Philip Morris Co.), Washington Education Association (teachers and administrators), Senate Democratic Caucus Committee (biggest contributors are three unions and Philip Morris Co.), State Trial Lawyers Association, the Boeing Company and the Realtors Association. Everyone, including the lobbyists, believes the amount of money spent on campaigns has become a shameful and disgraceful aspect of politics. But attempts by the two parties to come together to solve the problem have thus far failed. Republicans will not accept public financing of campaigns and Democrats see no way to reduce spending without it.

In January 1992, Republican backers turn in 220,000 signatures for Initiative 134 and qualify it for the November ballot. It focuses on limiting contributions rather than spending. Contributions from any one source are limited to $500 for legislative candidates and $1,000 for state offices. Those limits include political action committees, political parties, caucuses, labor unions, and businesses as well as individuals. Initiative 134 also prohibits transfers of money between candidates, restricts taxpayer-funded mailings by state officeholders, prohibits public funding of campaigns (as already in existence in King County), prohibits fund raising during legislative sessions, prohibits the state employees union from using a voluntary payroll checkoff, and restricts out-of-state contributions.

Initiative 134 receives heavy financial support from big corporations like Weyerhaeuser, PACCAR and Philip Morris. Officially, the chief sponsors are Republican Senate Majority Leader Jeannette Hayner and Republican Senator Linda Smith. The initiative is designed and written to benefit the Republicans because, as one Republican leader said, "We rely on individuals more." Democratic candidates rely on heavy support from teacher and state employee unions which collect money from their members as part of their dues. Under Initiative 134, these unions will be limited to $500 per legislative campaign.

Democrats had been working with the League of Women Voters to come up with an alternative initiative. They hope to get Republicans to agree on a compromise to place on the ballot with Initiative 134, but few think this will happen. The Republicans' version of campaign reform has the signatures and is already qualified. They have no incentive to offer an alternative.

The dilemma for the Democrats is that the courts have held there can be no campaign spending limits without public financing. And public financing of political campaigns is not popular with voters. Thus, even if the Democrats can gather the signatures for their version of campaign reform to include public financing, most expect it to lose to the Republican proposal which specifically bans public funding of political campaigns. So, there is no progress on campaign finance reform during the 1992 session. That issue will await the decision of the voters in the November election.

The Budget Battle Resumes

January 7, 1992. With the start of the 1992 session still a week away, Senator Dan McDonald holds a press conference in Olympia to outline his views on the state's massive budget deficit. He says he is disappointed in the governor's proposals since he wants deeper cuts in state government spending, citing a 25 percent increase in state employment since 1985, and he wants to retain the rainy day fund. He says he wants to protect funding for education, especially for starting teachers; he wants no tax increases of any kind; he wants a constitutional rainy day fund that would require the governor to declare an emergency and have approval by two-thirds of both houses to spend; and he wants to eliminate about 1,300 state jobs and halt most state spending on travel, furniture and equipment.

Next day, Len McComb, Governor Gardner's budget director, counters McDonald's claim that the number of state employees has grown by 25 percent since 1985. He doesn't deny the numbers but claims that any growth is due to increased population and the demand for more services. McComb says the 25 percent increase in higher education programs was supported by McDonald. He adds there was another 25 percent in social services staffing for children and the mentally ill, 10 percent increase in staffing at state prisons, and 12 percent in natural resources and the environment due to new programs approved by the Legislature. Representative Gary Locke, echoing McComb, says only 7,000 of the 18,000 new jobs that Senator McDonald claimed were created under Gardner were funded by the state, with the remainder federally funded.

Session Begins

January 13, 1992. The 1992 Regular Session begins quietly at noon. There are few meetings scheduled. As usual, newspaper editorials urge legislators to get to work and finish the job within the allotted sixty days. They are generally favorable to Gardner's proposal to share the pain by cutting spending by $560 million, using up the $260 million rain-day fund, imposing new taxes on gambling and cable TV, raising college tuition, and shifting interest earnings from the state transportation fund to the general fund.

House Democratic leaders say they plan to pass both the budget and health care reform bills by the end of January. Senate Republicans say no to health care reform and no to most of Gardner's proposals, especially the new taxes and using the rainy day fund.

State of the State Message and Health Care

At 5:15 P.M. on January 13, Governor Gardner gives his state of the state message to the 1992 session of the Legislature. It is carried live on several Seattle TV stations. It lasts only ten minutes. The governor focuses almost entirely on a sweeping "play or pay" health care proposal, barely mentioning the $900 million budget deficit. The play or pay name refers to a requirement for employers to either provide a basic level of health insurance to their employees (play) or pay the state to do so. Gardner's plan would create a health care commission to limit costs and set the basic coverage to the 550,000 Washington residents without health insurance. He says details and funding will be provided when he submits the bills. He urges citizens to call their legislators to demand action and even gives the legislative hot line number. The governor is clearly trying to go over legislators' heads directly to the people. He did this before with tax reform and the gas tax and failed. It is surprising to many observers that he would try again on health care and more so that he would try for such a costly issue in a session already saddled with a huge deficit.

Next day, Senator Jim West holds a hearing on the Republican version of health care reform, called the "Good Health Care" bill. It focuses on preventive health measures like immunizations. It appropriates $130 million to public health departments and clinics but makes no mention of where the money will come from. Democrats and pro-reform groups see West's bill as merely an attempt to deflect efforts from "real" health care change. West's bill does nothing to provide access to persons not already insured or to hold down health care costs. Some who testify in favor of West's bill say it is good but they want health care reform, too.

Climbing the Ladder of Political Offices

As of January 16, 1992, there are eight current state senators running for Congress, two for governor, two for the United States Senate and one for state lands commissioner. This is just in the state Senate. There are roughly twice as many state House members seeking higher office. Senate Minority Leader Marc Gaspard is quoted in the Kent newspaper as saying that "Every morning, all across the state, lawmakers are waking up, looking in the mirror, and seeing a U.S. Senator, a Governor or a Congressman." Steve Lansing, head of the Lutheran Public Policy Center, says, "We're a little worried that this Legislature is going to turn into a political convention without the balloons and confetti."

House Speaker Joe King says, "Dan McDonald and I have two things in common. One, we both want to be Governor. And two, we know that if we are in Olympia in May or June, neither of us is going to be Governor."

Jim Erickson, in an article in the *Seattle P-I* on January 17, 1992, says: "The first week of the 1992 legislature has been much like the last week of the 1991 session—teachers hinting of strikes, Republicans eyeing welfare cuts, and Democrats wishing it were all over."

Locke Responds to McDonald's Budget
January 20, 1992. Representative Gary Locke holds a press conference in the O'Brien Building to release his supplemental budget proposal. Locke's job is made somewhat easier by the discovery of $77 million in federal Medicaid money that Gardner didn't have available when he released his budget proposal a month earlier. Basically, Locke cuts almost every area of state spending in order to restore 3 percent salary increases for state employees, teachers and faculty and to beef up a few selected areas in education and human services.

The key new points in Locke's proposal are:

• 10 percent reduction in travel, printing, equipment and personal service contracts for all but education and human services for savings of $9 million.
• reduction of 4.5 percent in the budgets of most agencies and 5 percent in administrative costs for higher education and some others.
• second year raises of 3 percent for all state employees, teachers, and higher education faculty.
• an early retirement program to save $15.9 million.

Locke's proposed budget cuts a total of $286 million from the 1991-92 budget; eliminates 1,869 state jobs; and raises taxes $40.4 million on gambling, cable television and real estate transactions.

Speaker King says, hopefully, that the early release of the House (Locke's) proposal should boost chances of finishing the session in sixty days. Senate Majority Leader Hayner says the House package is "definitely encouraging," although the Senate might balk at the tax increases and use of the entire rainy day fund. Karen Davis from the

WEA gives Locke's budget qualified praise. Gary Moore from the state employees union says "it's 100 percent better than the governor."

While initial reaction to Locke's budget is mostly favorable, there are a few dissident voices. Bruce Wishart of the Sierra Club criticizes cuts in environmental programs. Jeff Parsons of the National Audubon Society complains that cuts in natural resources are too much. Spokespersons from the Department of Ecology and from the Department of Natural Resources say cuts will harm good programs. The governor remains ominously silent.

The Rainy Day Fund Controversy
There is an interesting debate in the Senate Ways and Means Committee on January 20 over Senator McDonald's bill to require the state to have a 5 percent rainy day fund that would take a governor's declaration of emergency and two-thirds vote of each house to spend. It would build up by putting aside 1 percent of the total operating budget each year. Democrats argue it is like a new tax or an across-the-board reduction in spending. They challenge McDonald to say where the extra money would come from. They also argue it is undemocratic to require more than a majority to spend money. They say it is nothing more than taxing people to put money into a savings account.

Republicans respond that if the state had done this five or six years earlier, it wouldn't be in the financial bind it is now.

McDonald's bill passes the committee on a straight party-line vote. Senator Phil Talmadge cryptically remarks that McDonald is merely using the bill as campaign rhetoric since he knows it will never pass.

McDonald and Drivers' Education
The 1991 budget put high school drivers' education classes on a pay as you go basis. It cut funding for the biennium by $10 million, paying only for those who couldn't. It seemed like a good idea to require those parents who could afford it to pay for drivers' education programs since this wasn't really part of basic education. Senator Dan McDonald had proposed it as a cost-cutting measure and the Democrats agreed. McDonald would rue the day.

Parents all over the state became incensed at the new costs. They blamed McDonald and many wrote him letters. By August he acknowledged it was a political error. He correctly pointed out that other legislators had voted for the budget and by implication were also to blame but the issue had become synonymous with him. In any case, he promised to restore the funding in the 1992 supplemental budget so school districts could continue to provide drivers' education classes without charge.

But Governor Gardner and the House Democrats said not so fast. If Senator McDonald wants to restore that $10 million, it will cost him. For a few days in January they enjoyed watching McDonald squirm. McDonald did put the $10 million back in his budget proposal, though. In the final budget that was reduced to $5 million, fully funding drivers' education only for the second year of the biennium. School districts either ate the costs for the first year or extracted them from the parents. No one is likely to propose reducing funding for drivers' education again for a long time.

The Budget Moves Out of House Committee

January 24, 1992. On Friday evening, the twelfth day of the 1992 session, the House Appropriations Committee passes Representative Locke's supplemental operating budget on a straight party-line vote. It restores most of Gardner's cuts in education block grants, developmental disabilities programs, mental health funding and payments to nonprofit vendors such as foster homes. It does this by taking $77 million from the federal government through a tax on Medicaid bills and by reductions in management costs throughout state government.

Governor Gardner is reported by the Tacoma *News Tribune* (January 25, 1992) to be "livid" with Locke and the House Democrats. He is said to have scolded Representative Locke and Speaker King for reversing many of his proposals and avoiding his cuts. Len McComb calls Locke's proposal a "have your cake and eat it too" budget. Locke's budget makes general cuts in staff to be carried out after the Legislature has left town, while Gardner's cuts are more specific. House Majority Leader Brian Ebersole defends Locke's budget by saying they didn't want to tell agency heads how to manage. "They know best how to reduce spending with the least effect on programs. Hopefully, [the cuts] will be in management," Ebersole said. The House tentatively schedules a vote on Locke's budget by the full body for the middle of the next week.

Senator McDonald, meanwhile, says he won't present his budget until the House passes bills fully implementing their budget costs, specifically by raising taxes $40 million and appropriating the rainy day fund. Locke reacts with surprise. He maintains that implementing legislation is traditionally passed after an agreement is reached. House Democrats argue that McDonald is just trying to force them to take an unpopular tax-increase vote. Locke says McDonald "should put up or shut up. Let's see him balance the budget without using the rainy day money and without the gambling tax, without cutting higher education, without raising tuition, and still give teachers their pay raise."

The Governor Reacts to Locke's Budget Proposal
January 27, 1992. Governor Gardner calls a press conference to discuss his reaction to Locke's budget on Monday, one week after Locke's announcement. There have been hints all week that the governor is angry about cuts in the natural resources and environment areas. Gardner is reported to be surprised at how much his fellow Democrat's budget deviated from his own proposal. The reports prove to be true. Gardner blasts the House Democrat/Locke supplemental budget as being based on shaky revenue assumptions and overly optimistic savings predictions. He calls it "a re-election budget." Gardner says that Locke's budget will make the budget problems of the next biennium worse because of the "bow wave" effect from teacher and state employee salary increases. He says that even without the raises, projections put the 1993-95 budget out of balance. The governor sides with McDonald and the Republicans that the House should pass the gambling and cable TV tax increases and rainy day fund along with their budget and not separately. House Democrats have admitted they won't pass tax increases until a deal is made since they don't want to be on the record for new taxes until absolutely necessary and everyone else is on board.

The fact that Gardner sides with the Senate Republicans shows just how angry he is with the House Democrats for not consulting him before releasing their budget and for taking such a divergent position. Speaker King and Appropriations Chair Locke are quick to defend, however. Locke stands by all of the assumptions underlying his budget. He says, "If anything, we have been very conservative and underestimated our estimate of savings. It certainly wasn't written for re-election."

Right-to-Die Moves
The House Health Care Committee passes a right to die measure, HB 1481, by 10-1. Surprisingly, the chief sponsor is conservative Republican Fred May of Mercer Island. The measure allows patients to reject food and water machines in order to die. Current state law allows patients to be taken off life support machines but doesn't define whether that includes food and water.

The state Catholic Conference supports the bill, even though it opposed Initiative 119 to allow physician-assisted suicide in the last November election. The Catholics hold that food and water devices are "artificial life supports" that people have a right to reject.

Human Life of Washington, an ally of the Catholic Conference in last year's battle, opposes HB 1481 and most observers have given it little chance of passage. The lopsided committee vote and sponsorship by a conservative Republican get everyone's attention and indicate the issue has strong support.

House Budget Moves

January 29, 1992. On Wednesday night, the seventeenth day of the 1992 Regular Session, the House passes the supplemental operating budget (HB 2470) by a vote of 56-41. House members claim it is a record to have done it so early. Every House Democrat except outgoing Representative Joanne Brekke (D-Seattle) votes for the budget and every Republican votes against it. House Republican Leader, Clyde Ballard says: "A very troubling part of this process is passing a budget without the revenue stream to support it." Senator Dan McDonald restates his position that he won't propose a budget until the House passes the tax measures to fund their budget. Locke challenges McDonald to unwrap his budget proposal now so the process can move forward. He says: "There will be no tax increase unless Republicans join in." About a week later the whole issue becomes moot when House Majority Leader Ebersole announces that the proposed taxes on cable TV, punchboards and pull tabs that were included in both the governor's budget and assumed in the House's budget are dead. He says the proposals simply don't have the votes to pass the House.

Back to the Battle Over Health Care Reform

January 29, 1992. Governor Gardner steps into the lion's den as he presents his health care reform plan to the Senate Health and Long-Term Care Committee. He and the committee chair, Jim West, trade blows. "Governor, I think you're sincere in what you're trying to do. I applaud you. My concern really is whether you're going to promise people something we're not going to deliver," West says. Gardner refers to West at one point as "obstructionist." Two days later the Senate Health and Long-Term Care Committee passes the governor's "Health Care Reform Act of 1992" as a committee substitute bill. West is playing hardball. He strips the governor's bill and makes it his own. West's bill calls for more study, expansion of existing health care plans, and voluntary enrollment in the plan by small businesses.

Senator Mike Kreidler, the ranking Democrat on the committee, calls West's plan "smoke and mirrors." Representative Braddock, the House Democratic leader on health issues, says it is "an insult to our intelligence." West's bill moves to Senate Rules on a straight party vote.

The central issue in the health care debate is the creation of a state commission with the power to set rates for medical services and the level of benefits. That is what West objects to and what the state medical association dislikes. It is removed from the bill that is signed out of West's Senate committee. A few days later, though, the Democratically-controlled House Health Care Committee passes a bill on a straight party-line vote which includes a five-member panel appointed by the governor with power over rates and benefits. Braddock's bill is similar to the governor's except it drops Gardner's "play or pay" financing in favor of a payroll tax on all business and employees.

Another Player in the Budget Game
February 5, 1992. Minority Senate Democrats call a press conference to release their own budget. They say they are doing it because Senator McDonald refuses to consider the House budget and has yet to release his own. Their budget contains no new taxes, no tuition increases, and restores $18 million in welfare cuts. Otherwise it is modeled after the House Democrats' budget. They make up the revenue loss by spending the reserve fund. Senator Marc Gaspard says that revenue collections are on a pace to be up $70 million over the November forecast (which formed the basis for the governor's budget). In a shot at Senate Republicans, he says it would be wrong to raise tuition just to put money into a reserve fund. This move puts Senate Democrats squarely on the side of House Democrats as opposed to the governor and Senate Republicans. It spells the likely end of talk about tax increases or raises in tuition—leaving only the rainy day fund to fight about.

More Money to Spend
February 11, 1992. Dr. Chang Mook Sohn announces that there will be $100 million more to spend than he predicted last December. The Economic and Revenue Forecast Council meets in one week to formally approve the projection.

Health Care Reform Takes a Pain
February 12, 1992. In a surprising development, the Democratic House defeats the Braddock/Democrat health care reform proposal, HB 2590, by a vote of 55-39. This is the plan that includes a commission to regulate costs and benefits and a payroll tax. All the Republicans vote no and a sizable number of Democrats join them. This is a major setback for Governor Gardner and for Representative Braddock who says he will try again next week.

Health care reform appears dead for the session after this vote. It needed a strong push from the Democratic House to have any chance in the Republican Senate. If the Democrats can't get their reform through the House where they have 60 percent of the members, that is likely to be the end of it this year.

The McDonald Budget Proposal Arrives

February 14, 1992. Senator Dan McDonald unveils his much-anticipated supplemental budget proposal. He does it in a classroom-style setting where he makes a presentation, then takes questions from the press.

McDonald shows pictures of twenty-nine state employee-occupied buildings in Thurston County as proof of the growth of state government in the area. He promises elimination of 10 percent of these employees as part of an overall reduction of 3,600 state employees, 1,500 of whom would come from mid or upper management jobs. He wants to keep all of the $260 million rainy day fund, give no salary increases to state employees, but give a 3.6 percent increase to teachers. He cuts money from the state's new Growth Management Act and from wetlands programs.

When pressed by reporters for specific programs to be cut, McDonald offers up the 114 "public information officers" scattered through the various state agencies and colleges as examples. Like the House Democrats, he would let managers figure out the rest.

McDonald says his budget is partly based on a Republican poll taken earlier in the year which showed 58 percent of voters support raises for teachers but only 26 percent favor raises for state employees.

There is criticism of McDonald's budget from every Democratic quarter. The governor's press secretary claims that McDonald voted for all twenty-nine of the buildings he showed and the budgets to support them. He says McDonald's figures are distorted because Thurston County "is the headquarters of state government so, of course, there are going to be more managers here." The governor's press secretary calls McDonald's budget "fiscal chaos." Representative Gary Locke says "I was just very disappointed. I felt it [the budget] was really nothing more than political grandstanding. It is not a bona fide good faith proposal." Locke is particularly upset that McDonald refuses to spend the rainy day fund. "What is his obsession with the rainy day account? If it's not raining now, how many people must be thrown out on the streets?" Locke calls McDonald's budget "heartless, unfair and unwise." Tony Lee, spokesman for the Washington Association of Churches, says that up to 8,000 mentally ill and destitute people will lose vital state services under McDonald's proposal.

Quick Action on McDonald's Budget
Senator Dan McDonald's budget is written in the Senate Republican caucus and is based on the reality that it has twenty-five votes. Senate Republicans waste no time in moving it along. They hold a Ways and Means Committee meeting in the Senate Republican Caucus at 3:00 P.M. on the same day it is announced, Friday, February 14. Democrats object that there is not the required five-day meeting notification required under Senate rules and there isn't space for the public in the small caucus. McDonald replies there has already been enough testimony on the budget and he is ready for executive session.

The McDonald/Republican budget quickly passes out of the committee but since the Senate has already adjourned to Sunday, the bill cannot be read in on the floor until then. Technically, the Republicans will need help from the Democrats to suspend the rules in order to act on the bill the same day it is read in.

The Senate comes into session on Sunday at noon and members go into their respective caucuses. They emerge back on the floor at 1:30 P.M. and begin to debate the budget bill, ESHB 2470, without objection. The Democrats offer some small amendments, then offer a major striking amendment which basically substitutes their version. It is defeated 24-24 (one Republican is absent). On the vote to add McDonald's striking amendment to the House bill, Lieutenant Governor Pritchard is needed to break the tie. The Democrats then permit the Republican leaders to suspend the rules so the bill can be bumped to third reading and it is passed on a straight party vote. Lieutenant Governor Joel Pritchard sums up the situation at this point: "This doesn't mean a damn thing. It's just a way to get the negotiations going."

A general pall settles over the Legislature after the budget preliminaries are completed. Two years earlier the Senate passed the supplemental budget on the forty-fifth day and the House on the fifty-first day. This year, 1992, the House passes it on the seventeenth day and the Senate on the thirty-fifth day. While the two sides are miles apart in what they want to do, they at least have allowed themselves more time than usual to do it.

Where Things Stand
February 19, 1992. It is Wednesday, the thirty-eighth day of the Regular Session. Yesterday, in New Hampshire, Pat Buchanan stunned President George Bush by getting 37 percent to the President's 53 percent in the

Republican primary. The Democratic field is reduced to ex-Senator Paul Tsongas, who received 35 percent, and Arkansas Governor Bill Clinton who got 26 percent.

The Forecast Council predicts an increase of $144 million over the December figure. Dr. Sohn says it was a very good Christmas for stores, producing more sales tax revenue. Democrats, already committed to a 3 percent increase for state employees and teachers, say they want to use the extra funds to increase the raises back to last year's 3.6 percent, reduce college tuition increases and boost college financial aid. Republicans say they are wary about the economy and would rather protect the rainy day reserve fund.

The First Cutoff

The first cutoff of the session, that for considering own-house bills in committees, is on Tuesday, February 18, the thirty-seventh day. Senate Republicans pass four bills which weaken the power of local governments to regulate wetlands use (SB 6096, 6201, 6254 and 6255). They also pass McDonald's measure to establish the rainy day fund in the Constitution. It would require the treasurer to remove one-half percent of the general fund in 1993-94, 1 percent in 1995-96 and 1 and a half percent thereafter until the rainy day fund gets to 5 percent, then place excess monies in the school construction fund (SB 6470), which currently relies exclusively on sales of state timber.

The Democratic House passes a bill creating a regional transit authority in King, Pierce and Snohomish counties with the power to levy voter-approved local option taxes and issue bonds for mass transit.

It's Over for Health Care

Despite furious lobbying by Governor Gardner and Speaker King, the health care reform bill can't get the votes to pass the House. They, along with Representative Braddock, blame the medical industry lobbyists. Braddock predicts the medical industry will be "buying legislators by the bushel basketful" in next year's elections.

In the end, House Democrats can't even get enough votes to pass a commission to design a health care plan and determine its costs. Wednesday, February 19, Speaker King has the House sitting idly at ease while he summons one after another member into his office to plead for their vote. He offers to add members of the health care industry to the commission and to exempt businesses with less than twenty-five employees, but he can get no closer than forty-seven votes.

Fourteen House Democrats will not go along. They fear that if they vote for health care reform, the Republicans will hammer them in the next election for approving another tax-and-spend bill. One Democrat says the polls show constituents want health care but are unwilling to pay for it.

The debate over health care reform in the 1992 session is a portent of how the issue will be dealt with politically in the future. Democrats focus on the inadequacy and unfairness of the current health system, its high cost, its failure to reach a large portion of the population. Republicans talk about taxes and a basic distrust of government at any level to manage the health care system.

Budget Barbs

February 21, 1992. House and Senate budget conferees meet for the first time on Friday, the fortieth day.

The day before, Gardner and his budget chief McComb blast the Republican budget as containing $120 million in "dubious revenue assumptions." Representative Locke says it is "fiscally reckless and lacking in fairness." McComb surprisingly says the Senate budget is also unconstitutional because it gives too much authority to his own boss, the governor.

McDonald responds to these attacks by calling them just so much posturing. He predicts a budget agreement will be reached by the end of the Regular Session.

Two Bills That Won't Die

February 24, 1992. The House passes a health care reform bill similar to the one that failed 39-55 just two weeks earlier. The major change is that the new bill requires a separate vote by the public on paying for it and it expands the membership of the commission. All but two House Democrats vote for it. Senator Jim West immediately condemns the bill as a "political document" and says it will not pass the Senate. He characterizes it as government-run health care.

Governor Gardner, clearly elated, says he will call the top Republicans handling the health issue, West and Hayner, to his office to try and work something out.

About this same time the Senate Transportation Committee is getting bogged down over the regional transportation bill. It is generally considered near death when Chairman Senator "Pat" Patterson (R-Pullman) expresses the view that we "may need to study it another year."

Budget Infighting

February 26, 1992. The Regular Session is three-fourths finished. Senator Dan McDonald walks out of the budget negotiations in disgust. Republicans accuse the Democrats of wanting to raise three different taxes. Democrats counter that McDonald wants to preserve all of the $260 million rainy day fund, so they just gave him a list of taxes to choose from to pay for it.

Despite the stormy breakup almost everyone believes there will be agreement on a supplemental budget by the end of the sixty-day session. Hayner and King are meeting regularly with McDonald and Locke to check on progress. They are reported to have said that if the conferees can't get it done in another ten days (about March 7), they will take over.

The outline of a final agreement has seemed clear to many insiders for weeks already: no new taxes, spend about $150 million of the $260 million rainy day fund, give raises of about 2.5 or 3 percent to teachers and state employees, perhaps a little more to higher education. Some legislators wonder aloud if it is so obvious why the conferees can't get it done.

The Puzzle of Mass Transportation

March 3, 1992. The Legislature continues to be unable to deal with mass transportation. A month earlier, the House passed HB 2610, which authorizes Pierce, King and Snohomish counties to create a regional transit authority to plan, build and operate a high-capacity transportation system. This authority, made up of a variety of elected local officials and state government executives, has the power to levy taxes and issue bonds if the voters approve.

The day before, the Senate Transportation Committee adds a 60 percent requirement for voter approval and other restrictions. They also postpone until 1993 the Regional Transit Authority's (RTA) power to seek taxes. At best, under the Senate bill, construction couldn't even begin for three years.

Natural Death Act

March 4, 1992. On Wednesday afternoon Senator Jerry Saling moves to pull HB 1481, the Natural Death Act, to the floor from Senate Rules. With mostly Democrats supporting, it passes 33-15. Saling is rumored to have told his fellow Republicans that they either let the bill out of Rules for a vote on the floor or he will switch sides and go with the Democrats.

HB 1481 really doesn't do much. It simply allows dying and comatose people to be taken off food and water if they have a written will requesting to do so. Even the Catholic Church, which had worked so hard and so successfully against the 1991 initiative to permit physician-assisted suicide, is for this bill.

Senator Linda Smith has succeeded in holding the bill in Rules because of the "rule of thirteen," which means a majority within the Senate Republican caucus of twenty-five can determine how all twenty-five will vote. But Saling, in his last days as a senator and with nothing to lose, breaks the rule. Smith (along with Senator Ellen Craswell) fights the bill with amendments and speeches on the floor, but in the end the Natural Death Act passes the Senate by 28-21. The House accepts the bill as amended by the Senate and swiftly moves it to the governor's desk for a sure signature. It is interesting to note that Smith and Craswell, who are the primary opponents of choice in abortion, are also the leaders in the fight against "death with dignity."

More on Health

As the Regular Session enters its last week, there is action in many areas.

Senator West's Republican health care bill, with no funding (leaves it to be funded in the budget), survives minority Senate Democrats' attempts to expand it on second reading. However, the bill fails on final passage. Before the final vote is announced, however, Democrats begin changing their votes to yes in order to get some bill, any bill, into a conference committee with the House. Republicans quickly realize what's going on, and each time a Democrat stands to announce a change from no to aye, a Republican senator stands to do the opposite. Finally, Senator Snyder moves to reconsider the whole matter so it can be talked about and fought over at a later date. Next day the bill is passed 27-22 and is put in conference.

Education Reform, Two Versions

Near the end of the Regular Session, the Senate passes its version of education reform by 28-21. The main features are competency testing, three-year probation for new teachers, and a required exam at the end of the twelfth grade for graduation. The House earlier passed its version which provides for more deregulation of the local school districts. The only thing the two versions have in common is the elimination of the master's degree requirement for teachers. Few believe the final version will do much more than that.

It is a real surprise when, a few days later, the House and Senate conferees agree on a bill that does much more (SB 5953). House Democrats get the decentralization they want and Senate Republicans get testing and accountability. Local districts can, in the future, get exemptions from state requirements like classroom hours. A state panel is established to determine which skills all graduating students should have and to recommend a system to measure performance. Probation for new teachers is doubled to two years. Students must obtain a "certificate of mastery" before graduating from high school. Local school boards get more leeway in designing courses and structuring school days. And, of course, the master's degree requirement for teachers is repealed.

While nothing is done in the area of parents' rights, there is still more "education reform" in 1992 than almost anyone expected.

Mass Transportation Gets On Track

The Senate continues to have a problem coming to grips with a regional transit agency bill. Republican Senators "Pat" Patterson and Leo Thorsness (R-Renton) want a requirement for 60 percent approval of bonds, rather than a majority, before the three counties can move forward on any construction. King County threatens to go it alone if that is in the bill. After much jockeying, a bill is passed (HB 2610) without this additional burden, sent on to the House and then to the governor.

The RTA has taxing and bonding authority. A vote of the public in Snohomish, King and Pierce counties could come as early as 1993. [The vote didn't occur until 1995 when it was rejected by the voters. It was put back before the voters in 1996.] The cost of building the three-county rail system is believed to be about $7.5 billion by 2020. Another $11.5 billion will go for park-and-ride lots, high occupancy vehicle lanes, etc. The only thing not in the final bill that was in the original House bill is authority for the RTA to force local governments to plan regionally.

To get mass transit moving, the three county governments would first need to agree to be part of the RTA. The county executives then appoint persons to the RTA board. The board would put the RTA membership to a vote which would need to be approved by all three counties (if two approved they could go without the third). Voters would be asked to vote to pay additional taxes (additional penny on the sales tax, .08 percent motor vehicle excise tax and $2 per month head tax on employers). If all had gone according to plan, there could have been rail mass transit from Tacoma to Everett by the end of the Twentieth Century.

The End of Health Care Reform

When health care reform was last seen, the Democrats had reluctantly agreed to provide the votes for Senator West's Good Health bill just to get something into a free conference committee with the House. Once there, they try to rewrite the whole thing to get their version of health care reform. There is some suggestion that after a budget agreement is reached between the House and Senate, the governor might refuse to sign the deal and keep the Legislature in session until they pass health care reform. Gardner's top aides, Wayne Ehlers and Dean Foster, have held discussions with House Democrats about blocking an override of a veto if he goes that way. But the will for health care reform just isn't strong enough in 1992. Legislators are more determined to finish the session on time and go home. An overwhelming majority of the members have political campaigns on their minds. And, to be fair, the public still hadn't coalesced behind any particular concept. To be sure, the polls show people want universal health care access and cost containment. But they can't agree on how to do it and, more importantly, on how to pay for it.

Senate Republicans block creation of a conference committee on health care so House Democrats add a striking amendment to Senator West's Good Health bill and send it back. Senate Republicans refuse to recede and return it to the House, where it dies for the session.

Throughout the summer and fall of 1992, various Republican members meet with Governor Gardner to try and work something out. There are occasional rumors of progress. The governor even considers calling a special session to try and force legislators to deal with this issue. But reason prevails. After all, Gardner is a lame duck, as are many of the legislators. Besides, the only thing there is a consensus on is that there is a serious problem. The solution isn't clear yet. As one old senator would say, "That dog just won't hunt."

Juvenile Justice

The juvenile justice bill was touted by some as the possible big issue of the 1992 session. But there are huge costs to do anything in this area and so it dies in the Senate Ways and Means Committee for lack of funding. In the end, the Senate Republicans decide to pass everything they can in the area of juvenile justice reform that doesn't have a price tag. The final bill contains broad policy statements; allows judges more flexibility in sentencing juveniles; gives counties the option (but not the funding) of creating "boot camps;" and allows transferring children from crisis residential centers to other group homes. Senator Gary Nelson sums it up: "Anything that won't end up costing a lot of money will stay in the bill."

Senator Phil Talmadge adds, "The persistent problem the Legislature has is making policy and rhetoric about juvenile justice but then not providing any funding." Early in the 1992 session Talmadge had announced he would no longer vote for "hypocritical bills" that contain high-sounding goals and policy but provide no money or resources to accomplish them.

Budget Agreement

March 9, 1992. An agreement is reached on the budget on Monday night, the fifty-seventh day of the sixty-day Regular Session. It is not much different from what many observers have guessed all along: 3 percent raises for teachers and state employees; spending $160 million of the $260 million rainy day fund; and cutting about 2,000 state jobs (Locke wanted 1,800, McDonald wanted 3,600). These cuts are to be done through attrition and an early retirement program, also included in the budget.

Actually, the budget agreement didn't go quite as smoothly as that. There was supposed to be a press conference on Tuesday, following the Monday night agreement, to announce the details. This press conference is cancelled, however, when the agreement begins to unravel. Speaker King on Tuesday morning tells the press "we're here for a special session."

The problem is that some members of the Republican caucus in the Senate decide at the last minute that they won't support an agreement unless there is at least $1.5 million to fund property rights and wetlands mapping. Bills to accomplish this had died in the House and had not been part of the budget negotiations. At the last moment, however, Senator Scott Barr (R-Colville), dug in his heels. He says, "We are willing to do whatever it takes to get this issue." With her slim one-vote margin in the Senate, Majority Leader Jeannette Hayner has little room to maneuver insider her own caucus. To compound matters, Senate Democratic leaders announce they will also vote against the budget agreement because it doesn't contain enough money for teachers' salaries. Some suggest that what really irks them is that they weren't consulted on the final agreement. It was made by the House Democrats and the Senate Republicans because they are the parties with the majorities in their bodies.

March 11, 1992. Despite these indications of trouble, Locke and McDonald go ahead with a press conference on Wednesday, the fifty-ninth day. Each puts his own best twist on the final agreement. McDonald emphasizes savings and reductions, Locke says how much good the money will do for those in need. Locke can't resist adding how close the final agreement is to his original House proposal. McDonald admits that the Republicans had indeed tried to hold up the budget to get SB 6201, property rights, and SB 6255, mapping of wetlands, as part of the deal, but Locke and the House Democrats wouldn't give in. He says that he gave it his best shot and would be back later to try again. There is no mention of whether he is also speaking for Senator Barr.

March 12, 1992. The sixtieth and final day of the 1992 Regular Session is a glorious feast of sunshine and blue skies. By mid-afternoon, it has reached the unseasonable high of 70 degrees.

The previous night at about 10:00 P.M. the Senate votes down, by a margin of 18-28, a key part of the budget agreement—SSB 6286, which spends $39 million "extra" in the pension fund. A combination of all the Democrats and some of the Republicans gang up to defeat what they view as a raid on the pension fund. Next morning it is thought that the Senate leadership has worked out the problem and has the votes to move this piece of the puzzle, but it will be tight.

Meanwhile, the indefatigable seventy-six-year-old senator from Colville, Scott Barr, along with Senator Ann Anderson (R-Acme), fights on to hold up the budget agreement until the House passes wetlands mapping and compensation of private landowners for "taking" private property. To add to the division, Senator Jerry Saling asserts the position that he won't vote for the budget because of the raid on the pension funds and perhaps other bills.

The harried Senate majority leader, Jeannette Hayner, is in danger of losing her one-vote majority from several quarters as her members insist on one thing or another as a price for their vote on the budget. In order to keep things on track and pass the budget without a special session, she seeks help from the previously-ignored Senate Democrats. She confers with Minority Leader Marc Gaspard and others and finds that the price of their cooperation will be dear, but that is the only way out.

Adding to the uncertainty, the governor's office makes threatening sounds about the budget. They, too, have been left out of the negotiations. They say final figures are based on "funny money," false or shaky assumptions such as the amount of savings from the early retirement bill (no one could really say how many teachers and state employees will take advantage of the opportunity to retire early). They imply that the governor may veto many parts of the budget or even the entire document.

Hayner is threatened, then, on the right by Barr and others in her own Republican caucus over property rights, and on the left by the Democrats over health care reform, and in the center by the governor over revenue projections. All the while, she knows that if she can't bring the session to conclusion on this last day and there is a special session, the list of demands will only grow longer and the process of resolution even more difficult. After many years of holding her one-vote majority of Senate Republicans together by patiently listening to and working with each member of her caucus, Hayner watches it disintegrate in the final hours of the 1992 session. The policy differences within her caucus that she managed to subordinate to the will of the majority for so long are too great. Perhaps the growing rift between the traditional rural Republicans and the new urban Republicans is just too wide to bridge.

In the end, the long-ignored Senate Democrats emerge as the key players. With the Republican caucus fractured and some in open rebellion, the Senate Democrats are suddenly and uncharacteristically united. Behind their leader, Marc Gaspard, they force the Republicans to reduce the amount to be withdrawn from the pension fund from $40 million down to $25 million, restore $4 million in college tuition waivers, add $2 million for foster care, and make the transfer of the $160 million from the rainy day fund without recourse—it doesn't have to be paid back as McDonald had won in the earlier negotiations.

Senator Barr and his dissident property-rights champions won some-thing, too. The $350 million already in the capital budget for cities and counties could now be used to help pay for identifying and mapping wetlands and warning property owners of a potential loss of use.

And so it ended. History will record that the 1992 Legislature completed its work in the allotted sixty days and without a special session. It was messy, but it was done.

Winds of Change
One can only wonder whether the collapse of the formerly-impenetrable Senate Republican front and the newly-discovered Democratic unity in the Senate would translate in the next election to a change in the majority for either body. In hindsight, we know that Washington voters in November 1992 did give the victory to Democrats and that the Democrats enjoyed a majority in both Houses as well as control of the governor's chair for the first time in many years. But just as the Democrats were getting comfortable, those same voters in 1994 threw out the House Democrats and gave that body overwhelmingly to the Republicans.

Health care reform, which Governor Gardner and the Democrats tried to pass in 1992, came back and was passed in 1993. That, too, didn't last, however. It was mostly undone by Governor Lowry and Republicans in the Legislature in 1995.

1992 marked the end for one of the strongest and most effective leaders to ever grace the Washington State legislative chambers. In July, Republican Senate Majority Leader Jeannette Hayner from Walla Walla, still sprightly and schoolgirl slim at age 73 but with twenty years in the

Legislature, announced she would not seek reelection. She quietly left the scene she had dominated for more than a decade.

Nor would Hayner be alone. Fifteen of the forty-nine senators would either resign or not seek reelection, including the greatly respected third-ranking Senate Democrat, Pat McMullen from Sedro-Woolley, and the beloved, long-time Transportation chair, "Pat" Patterson from Pullman. Ten senators would retire, two would seek seats in Congress, two in the U.S. Senate, and one for the Pierce County Commission. Twenty-eight House members would leave or seek other offices, including the Speaker of the House, Joe King from Vancouver, and the popular second-ranking member of the House Republican caucus, Eugene Prince from Thornton (he moved to the Senate). Fourteen House members sought seats in the state Senate, nine retired, three ran for Congress, one for governor, and one for lands commissioner.

Before the 1992 election was ever held, the 1993 Legislature, both House and Senate, was assured the largest number of freshmen since the end of the second world war. And it would be topped again by the even-greater turnover in the state House in 1994.

Gardner Gets the Last Word

The last legislator is the governor. Governor Gardner uses his veto to resist cuts in the budget to social programs and growth management. He also vetoes the "gang bill" as too vague and aimed at minorities, and the pesticide bill as unnecessary. The "gang bill" would have allowed judges to extend the sentences of youths convicted of crimes if they were part of street gangs—this was watered down from the original bill making gang membership itself a crime. The pesticide bill would have made the state Department of Agriculture (as opposed to the Department of Ecology) the supreme authority over pesticide regulations and prevented cities and counties from writing their own rules.

The governor signed the Regional Transit Authority bill, a bill to permit the governor to negotiate casino gambling with the Indian tribes, tougher penalties for child abuse, and an "anti-stalker" bill making it illegal in some circumstances to follow a person.

The governor "reluctantly" signed the $15.3 billion supplemental operating budget using his veto to restore funding for some environmental and children's programs. When he finished, there was $100 million left in the rainy day fund and a mere $44.6 million in reserve (left over at the end of the biennium). His largest vetoes were to restore $2.1 million for building regional and local state offices; $2.5 million for food and nutritional counseling to low-income mothers and children; $1 million to continue growth management planning; and $785,000 in water resources programs.

The governor also vetoed a bill prohibiting employers from discriminating against workers who smoke or use lawful but harmful products off the job.

Death of a Common Man
On April 8, 1992, John A. Cherberg died. He was eighty-one years old. He had been the lieutenant governor of the state from 1957 until 1989. He was formerly the head football coach of the University of Washington Huskies. He was fired, sued the University, then used the ensuing publicity to propel himself into state office. Once there, he used his position to represent the common people of this state. Through much of the seventies and eighties, he was easily the most popular politician in the state, either party. He seriously considered running for governor in 1976, and probably would have won if he had, but in the end he thought he was not worthy.

Cherberg always viewed himself as an outsider, the champion of the "little guy." Typical of him was the time in 1984 when the Department of Social and Health Services was about to move into new office buildings on Plum Street in Olympia. Cherberg and his faithful aide and friend, "Ole" Scarpelli, drove down to look over the new buildings. Cherberg noticed there was plenty of reserved parking around the buildings for state employees, but only three time limited spaces for the public, and those at some distance. He went back to his office and called the head of the Department of General Administration and "suggested" that more parking be provided for the public and that the public spaces should be the ones closest to the main entrance.

As lieutenant governor, Cherberg served on the State Capitol Committee along with the governor and public lands commissioner. For over thirty years, Cherberg insisted on preserving open space around the state capital buildings in the face of repeated requests by various agencies to build their offices on the broad green areas. Washington State's capitol campus is one of the most beautiful in the country because of his vision.

Cherberg was a humble, honest, decent man who was extraordinarily gracious toward everyone, without exception. He literally had no enemies, even though privately he was highly critical of many of the state's public officials, especially those who had high opinions of themselves. He presided over the Senate during the sixties, when it was popular not to care; the seventies, when there was a lax attitude toward public funds; and the eighties, when greed was considered a virtue, but he never changed.

There is no better model for a public official or for those who work in the public sector than John A. Cherberg.

Glossary of Legislative Terms

act. A bill adopted by the Legislature.

actuary. The state Actuary is a legislative staff officer appointed by the Joint Committee on Pension Policy to prepare actuarial analyses of pension proposals and other items as directed by the Legislature. Serves as staff to the Joint Committee on Pension Policy, which reviews proposed changes to retirement laws and recommends changes.

ad hoc committee. A committee formed for a short duration, usually to study a specific issue.

adjourn. To conclude a day's session with a time set to meet again, or to conclude a meeting.

adjourn sine die. To conclude a regular or special session without setting a day to reconvene.

adopted. To approve formally.

agency request bill. A request for legislation proposed by an agency of the executive branch of government.

agenda. The proposed order of business for a meeting.

amend. To modify, delete or add to a proposal.

amendment. Any change in a bill, resolution or memorial. A committee amendment is an amendment proposed in a committee meeting. A floor amendment is an amendment proposed on the floor of a legislative chamber.

appeal from decision of the chair. A parliamentary procedure for challenging the decision of a presiding officer by asking the members to uphold or reject the decision.

apportionment. The division of the state into districts with distinct geographic boundaries and the allocation of the number of legislators or congressmen to be elected to represent each district. Also known as redistricting.

approach the bar. Refers to a legislator's physical movement from any place on the floor of either house to the rostrum.

appropriation. A legislative allocation of money for a specific purpose.

at ease. A pause in the proceedings of either house, usually for an indefinite time.

Attorney General's Opinion. A formal expression of legal reasons and principles regarding statutory or common law questions from state agencies or legislators.

Baby Book. Popular term for the Pictorial Guide to the Washington State Legislature.

bar of the House or Senate. This generally refers to the rostrum within both houses behind which sit or stand the President of the Senate, the Speaker of the House, and others as designated, for presiding over the body, recording and processing legislation being considered by the houses.

bicameral. Composed of two chambers or two legislative bodies. The Washington State bicameral legislature is made up of a House of Representatives and a Senate.

biennium. Two-year period. The Washington State fiscal biennium is from July 1 of odd-numbered years to June 30, two years later.

bill. A proposed law presented to the Legislature for consideration.

bill books. Binders located adjacent to the chamber or in committees containing all bills and amendments currently before or passed by the Legislature or committee.

bill clerk. A legislative employee who keeps the bill books up to date with newly introduced bills as well as with amendments, or provides bills to the public in the Bill Room.

bill digest. Section-by-section summary of a bill, prepared by the Code Reviser's Office.

bill drafting office. Office located on the first floor of the Legislative Building in the Code Reviser's Office. A legal staff is employed to draft legislation consistent with a legislator's intent, thereafter to be introduced to the Legislature. (Officially named the Statute Law Committee.)

bill history. A record of the action taken on bills, resolutions and memorials.

bill index. A list of legislative measures by subject matter.

bill report. Summary of background and effect of bills, prepared by committee staff.

Bill Room. A room on the first floor of the Legislative Building in which copies of all bills are kept during the session. Bills are sorted in the Bill Room and are available to the public.

bills on calendar. Printed volumes with yellow covers distributed to each member's floor desk. Includes the full text of bills and proposed committee amendments on the pending calendar.

budget. Bill appropriating funds needed to carry out state programs for a fiscal period.

bumping. Slang term for suspending the rules to allow a bill to be advanced from second to third reading without having the bill revert to the Rules Committee.

calendar. A list or schedule of pending business.

call of the House or Senate. A procedure used to compel attendance of members.

call to order. Notice given indicating the Legislature is officially in session. Also used to restore order during a legislative session.

capital. Olympia, Washington.

capital budget. Appropriations made to state and local agencies for building and construction projects.

capitol campus. The grounds and group of buildings surrounding the domed Legislative Building, holding the offices of most of the state's elected officials.

caucus. A meeting of members of a body who belong to the same political party.

chair. Presiding officer.

chamber. Official hall for the meeting of a legislative body.

chapter number. A chapter number, in numerical order, is given to each bill enacted. The chapter number is the number of the law. When "codified" the chapter is inserted in the appropriate section of the statutes known as the Revised Code of Washington (RCW).

Cherberg, John A. Building. The four-story building directly southeast of the Legislative Building, houses offices for senators and staff and hearing rooms. Formerly known as the Public Lands Building.

Chief Clerk. A person elected by the members of the House of Representatives to record the official actions of the House and to be the chief administrative officer of the House.

Code Reviser. Operating under the supervision of the Statute Law Committee, this person codifies into the appropriate sections of the RCW those measures enacted into law by the Legislature and also codifies administrative rules adopted by executive branch agencies.

committee. A portion of a legislative body charged with examining matters specifically referred to it.

committee legislative assistant. Employee designated to keep records of committee action and perform such other responsibilities as the committee chair or staff supervisor may dictate.

Committee on Committees. Committees in each house that select the chairs and members of standing committees.

companion bill. A bill introduced in the same form in both the House and the Senate.

concurrence calendar. A list of own-house bills amended by the opposite body and returned for possible concurrence.

concurrent resolution. A resolution relating to the internal operation of the Legislature, in which one house concurs in the action of the other; it may originate in either house.

conference calendar. A list of bills to which both bodies have appointed conferees to discuss differences and seek resolution.

conference committee. A committee which may be appointed to discuss specific differences of opinion between the House and Senate on bills which have passed each house but with differing positions on one or more amendments.

confirmation. Approval by the Senate of gubernatorial appointments.

conflict of interest. Any interest, financial or otherwise, any business or professional activity, or any obligation which is incompatible with the proper discharge of duties.

consent calendar. Bills with little or no known opposition which are placed on a special calendar by the Rules Committee.

constituent. A person residing within the boundaries of a district that is represented by an elected official.

Constitution. The written instrument embodying the fundamental principles of the state that establishes power and duties of the government and guarantees certain rights to the people.

constitutional amendment. Proposed change in the Washington State Constitution which has been approved by two-thirds of both houses of the Legislature. To be enacted, the proposed amendment must be placed on the next general election ballot and secure a simple majority of votes in favor of adopting the measure.

constitutional convention. Assembly of citizens for the purpose of writing or revising a constitution.

constitutional majority. A majority of members elected to either the Senate or the House. In the Senate a constitutional majority is 25; in the House it is 50.

convene. Assemble for an official meeting.

co-sponsor. Two or more persons proposing any document.

cutoff dates. Time certain set by a legislative body for specified action such as bill introduction, committee action, or passage of bills by either house.

Daily Clips. Compilation of print media articles about legislative matters. Also called the Media Digest.

day certain. Adjournment with specific day to reconvene.

debatable. Open for discussion or argument.

debate. Discussion of a matter following parliamentary rules.

department request bill. A request for legislation proposed by a department of state or local government (also known as agency request bill).

dilatory. Deliberate use of parliamentary procedure to delay or slow up proceeding.

discharge. What happens to an elected official who has been recalled. Occasionally used as a reference to the motion on the House or Senate floor to relieve a committee of a bill; called a "discharge petition" in Congress.

dispute calendar. Bills amended by one body where the second body refuses to concur and asks the first body to recede.

dissent. Difference of opinion.

district. Area encompassing citizens represented by a legislator. There are currently 49 legislative districts, each having two House members and one senator.

division. A method of voting by standing.

division of question. Consideration of each item separately.

effective date. The date a bill, once passed, becomes law. Unless a different date is specified, bills become law ninety days after sine die.

election. The act of selecting by ballot a person to fill an office in government.

emergency clause. A provision in a bill that allows a measure to become effective immediately upon the signature of the governor.

enactment. The passage of a bill by both houses and the signing by the governor.

engrossed bill. A bill which reflects all amendments made in the house of its origin.

enrolled bill. A bill passed by both houses, which incorporates all amendments, and to which has been attached a certificate of enrollment indicating the date passed, votes cast on the bill, and the certifying officers' signatures. It is presented to the governor for signature.

ethics. Standard of moral conduct. Legislative ethics standards are set forth in Chapter 42.52 RCW and House and Senate rules.

excused. Absent with permission from the legislative body.

executive action. This can refer to two distinct concepts: 1. Executive action of a standing committee refers to final consideration of a bill by the committee. 2. Executive action on a bill already passed by both houses refers to action taken by the governor.

executive order. A directive or command from the governor to agencies in the executive branch.

executive request bill. Request for legislation proposed by the governor.

Executive Rules. See Facilities and Operations.

executive session. A meeting of committee members to discuss and vote on bills they wish to report out of committee. These meetings are open to the public but no testimony is taken. Note that in other contexts executive sessions are closed to the public.

ex officio. Holding one office by virtue of or because of the holding of another office. Ex-officio members of a committee have voice but may not vote.

expulsion. The act wherein a body removes one of its members as provided under its rules.

Facilities and Operations Committee. The Senate leadership committee that oversees matters relating to staff, the physical plant and equipment, and operational matters. The corresponding House committee is called Executive Rules.

first reading. First of three readings required to pass measures. Bills on first reading are introduced and referred to standing committees.

fiscal. Relating to financial matters. The state fiscal year (FY) is July 1 through June 30.

fiscal note. An estimate of the expected cost of a measure to state and/or local government.

flash calendar. A listing of bills on the second or third reading calendar for the next day's agenda.

floor of the House or Senate. The actual floor space, committed primarily to legislators' desks, on which the business of the Legislature is conducted.

floor resolution. A written motion calling for action, which may be offered from the floor of either house.

gallery. Areas of both chambers where public visitors may observe the Legislature in session.

germane. Relating directly to a question.

gerrymandering. Legislative district boundary lines drawn to obtain partisan or factional advantages.

governor. The chief executive officer of a state.

grandfather clause. Inserted in a bill making provisions nonapplicable to activities or personnel involved prior to the enactment of the new legislation.

green sheet. The list of bills eligible for action by the Senate Rules Committee. Green sheet bills can be placed directly on the floor calendar, if approved by a majority of the members of the Rules Committee.

gubernatorial appointment. Designation by the governor to fill an office or position.

hearing. A legislative committee meeting at which witnesses present testimony on matters under consideration by the committee.

honorary page. A young person who is acting as an unpaid short-term page for either house.

hopper. Box located in the bill drafting area in which legislative measures are deposited for introduction.

hotline. This is a toll-free number by which citizens can communicate their concerns to a legislator. The number is 1-800-562-6000. It was initiated during the 1972 session.

House of Representatives. Lower chamber of a two-body legislature.

indefinitely postpone. To postpone without setting a definite time for consideration.

initiative. A legislative power vested in the people. An initiative is proposed through a petition containing signatures of 8 percent of the number of voters voting in the last preceding regular gubernatorial election. There are two types of initiatives: 1. Initiative to the people. Original legislation by the voters, proposing a new law (or changing existing laws) without consideration by the Legislature. 2. Initiative to the Legislature. Original legislation by the voters, proposing a new law (or changing existing laws) for consideration by the Legislature at its next regular session. If not enacted, it is placed on the next general election ballot.

Institutions Building. A two-story building southeast of the Legislative Building, it houses office space for senators and staff.

Insurance Building. Lying directly to the east of the Legislative Building, the Insurance Building houses the Insurance Commissioner and the Office of Financial Management.

interim. Time between regular legislative sessions.

interim committee assembly. A legislative practice during the interim of having some days devoted to committee hearings and caucuses in Olympia or another location within the state.

intern. A college or university student from a higher education institution within the state, working with the Legislature, who receives stipend and credit hours. Legislative interns are assigned to members' offices during session and to committee staff during the interim.

introduction of bills. An order of business during which new bills are read into the record.

invocation. Prayer given prior to a session. The schedule for persons offering prayer is determined by the presiding officer.

JARRC. Joint Administrative Rules Review Committee. Reviews agency rules to ensure consistency with legislative intent.

JLARC. Joint Legislative Audit and Review Committee. (Formerly Legislative Budget Committee.) A joint, bipartisan committee which conducts performance audits, program evaluations and other oversight duties assigned by the Legislature.

joint committee. Committee which consists of members from both houses.

joint memorial. A message or petition addressed to the President and/or Congress of the United States, or the head of any other agency of the federal or state government, asking for consideration of some matter of concern to the state or region. Proposed amendments to the U.S. Constitution are also in the form of joint memorials.

joint resolution. An act of the Legislature which proposes an amendment to the state Constitution for reference to the people for acceptance or rejection. To pass, joint resolutions must receive a two-thirds affirmative vote of the members elected in each house.

journal. Official record of action of legislative session.

judicial impact note. An estimate of the impact of a measure on the workload and administration of the courts of the state.

law. Common law is law set by precedent in court and by interpretation of the Constitution and statute law. Statute law is governing action or procedure approved through the legislative process.

leadership. The officers elected by their respective caucuses.

LEAP. Legislative Evaluation and Accountability Program. A computer-based program developed by the Legislature to monitor the budgetary process. Administered by a joint committee and staff.

legislative auditor. Staff director of JLARC.

legislative budget notes. Document providing detail about the biennial operating budget.

Legislative Building. The domed capitol building of the state of Washington containing both the House and Senate chambers and the offices of the Governor, Lt. Governor, Treasurer, Auditor and Secretary of State.

Legislative Council. Joint legislative committee that dealt with legislative business during the interim periods between sessions from 1947 to 1973.

Legislative Digest and History of Bills. A publication issued periodically containing the sponsors, titles, short digest of content, legislative actions, and veto messages of the governor for each bill, memorial, resolution and gubernatorial appointment.

Legislative Ethics Board. Nine-member board with four legislators and five nonlegislators. Authority to interpret and apply the state ethics law for legislators and staff by training, advisory opinions, and complaints.

legislative intent. If the words of a law cannot be clearly interpreted as written, the court may refer to the journal and bill reports to establish the "intent" of the Legislature in passing certain bills.

Legislative Manual. Biennial publication that contains the rules of each body, joint rules, biographical and other information about the Legislature and state government. Also called the "Red Book."

Legislative Report. Summary of legislation passed during one or more legislative sessions.

legislator. Elected member of either the House of Representatives or Senate.

Legislature. The body made up of the members of both the House of Representatives and the Senate.

LEGLink. The electronic link to legislative information.

lieutenant governor. Presiding officer of the Senate.

lobbyist. A person who tries to get legislators to introduce or vote for measures favorable and against measures unfavorable to an interest that he or she represents.

LSC. Legislative Service Center. An organization which provides planning, data and information processing services, equipment and training in support of the Legislature and legislative agencies. Policy and administrative supervision are provided by the Joint Legislative Systems Committee and the Legislative Systems Administrative Committee.

LTC. Legislative Transportation Committee. A joint committee composed of eleven senators and twelve representatives which conducts transportation studies between legislative sessions.

majority leader. Leader of the majority party in the state Senate. In the House, second in command to the Speaker. Elected by the majority caucus in each body.

majority party. The party numbering the most members in a legislative body.

majority report. Document bearing the signatures of a majority of the members of a committee recommending a particular action on a measure.

mansion. The official residence of the governor, located directly west of the Legislative Building.

measure. Any matter before a body such as a bill, memorial or resolution.

Media Digest. Compilation of print media about legislative activities for a certain period. Also called Daily Clips.

members. Legislators having taken the oath of office.

message from the governor. Official communications from the governor.

message from the House. Official communication to the Senate from the House.

message from the Senate. Official communication to the House from the Senate.

minority party. A party numbering less than a majority of members in a legislative body.

minority report. Document carrying signature(s) of a minority of the members of a committee recommending an action different from the majority.

moot. A term indicating that a motion is not timely because it can no longer affect an action or event.

motion. A proposal that the Senate or House take a certain action.

motion to reconsider. A motion which, if it succeeds, would place a question in the same status as it was prior to a previous vote on that question.

move. A formal request for action.

null and void clause. Language specifying that a measure is invalid unless funding is provided in the budget by a specified date.

oath of office. Oath taken by members-elect of the Legislature prior to being seated.

O'Brien, John L. Building. The four-story building southwest of the Legislative Building, contains House members' and staff offices, hearing rooms, and other House facilities. Formerly known as the House Office Building.

OFM. Office of Financial Management. The chief executive agency for evaluating the budget, preparing fiscal notes, and providing fiscal policy analysis to the governor.

operating budget. Two-year plan for funding ongoing activities of state agencies, except transportation.

OPR. Office of Program Research. The House nonpartisan research and committee staff located in the John L. O'Brien Building. Equivalent to Senate Committee Services.

order of business. The usual order of daily activities of a body, set out in its rules.

order of consideration. A list of measures anticipated to be acted upon by the House or Senate on a particular day.

page. High school students who assist the House or Senate during regular legislative sessions. Each page is appointed by a member for one week for which they receive a stipend.

parliamentary inquiry. Question posed to chair for clarification of a point in the proceedings.

passage of bill. The act of passing a bill by either or both houses of the Legislature.

PDC. Public Disclosure Commission. Oversees the reporting of information filed by lobbyists, state agencies, legislators, candidates and political committees on the amount of money spent on the political process and enforces the campaign laws.

penalty clauses. Sections of bills which lay out criminal or civil penalties for violation of the law.

Pension Policy, Joint Committee. Committee which reviews proposed changes to retirement laws and recommends changes.

petition. A formal request.

per diem. Payment in lieu of living expenses.

Pictorial Directory. Publication containing pictures and biographical material about the statewide elected officials and members of the Legislature. Known as the "Baby Book."

plurality. The person or alternative with the most votes between two or more choices; as opposed to a "simple majority," meaning 51 percent or more of those present and voting. A "constitutional majority" is 51 percent or more of those elected to the House or Senate.

pocket veto. Causing a measure to die by inaction of the chief executive within a specified time. Available to 37 state governors, but not Washington.

point of order. A demand or request by a member for a legislative body to adhere to its rules of procedure.

postpone to a day certain. To defer consideration until a later time or day.

prefiling. The act of introducing a bill prior to the beginning of session. Prefiling starts on the first Monday in December prior to the commencement of the session, or twenty days prior to a special session.

president. Presiding officer of the Senate and lieutenant governor of the state.

president pro tempore. A senator elected by the Senate to discharge the duties of presiding officer in the lieutenant governor's absence.

previous question. A motion to close debate and bring the pending question or questions to an immediate vote.

prime sponsor. The originator or first name on a bill or amendment that has been introduced.

proclamation. An order issued by the governor, such as a proclamation calling a special session of the Legislature.

proposal. A plan of action or a proposed bill which has not been formally introduced.

proviso. A clause in a bill that sets out specific exceptions to the general law.

pull. Slang term for moving a bill. For example, Rules Committee members may move (pull) bills from the green sheet to the floor for action by the full Senate or from the white sheet to the green sheet, or members may vote to pull a bill from a committee to the floor.

put the question. When the presiding officer instructs the body what it is about to vote on.

quorum. A majority of members of the group concerned. This means a majority of those elected to either house; in a committee, this means a majority of members assigned to the specific committee.

RCW. See Revised Code of Washington.

recall. The recall is the vote of the people which, in effect, tries the elective public officer on charges brought against the officer. All elective public officers except judges of courts of record are subject to recall and discharge from elective offices.

recede. To withdraw from an amendment in which the other house refused to concur.

recess. Intermission of a daily session, usually to a specified time.

recommitted bill. A procedure whereby a bill is referred back to a standing or conference committee for further consideration by the committee. A bill may be recommitted at any time, usually on second or third reading. A bill need not be recommitted to another committee to study a different aspect of the bill. Recommitment of bills can be used to "kill" a bill during the final days of a session.

reconsider. To vote again on a question previously before the body.

Red Book. The Legislative Manual.

redistricting. Redrawing the boundaries of areas of representation to make them equal in population. Generally done once each decade.

refer. To send a measure to a committee for study and consideration.

re-refer. To reassign a measure to a different committee.

referendum. Recently passed legislation referred by the Legislature to the voters for their rejection or enactment.

referendum measure. The legislative power whereby the electorate may call back recently-enacted laws for voter consideration. It originates in a petition containing signatures of 4 percent of those registered and voting at the last preceding regular gubernatorial election.

relieved. A committee may be "relieved" of further consideration of any bill in either house by a majority vote of the members of the particular house.

reorganization meetings. Meetings of legislative caucuses to select leaders. Generally held in even-numbered years shortly after the general election.

repeal. To revoke or abrogate by legislative action.

repealer clause. The section of a bill that lists which RCW sections and chapters of law are revoked and abrogated by the proposed legislation.

reporting out. Action by a committee on a measure which moves the measure out of the committee. Committee reports include do pass, do not pass, amend, substitute, refer to another committee, or no recommendation.

representative. Member of the House of Representatives.

resignation. The act of voluntarily leaving office.

Revised Code of Washington. This is a codification of current statutes as enacted and amended.

roll call. Record of how members voted on a particular issue or question.

rule suspended. To temporarily set aside a rule.

rules. Regulating principles used in the conduct of legislative business.

Rules Committee. Committee responsible for setting the daily calendar of the Senate and House. The President of the Senate and Speaker of the House serve as chair of these committees.

scope and object. A parliamentary ruling by the presiding officer as to whether a proposed amendment fits within the subject matter of the bill under consideration. Senate and House rules prohibit amendments which change or expand the scope and object of a bill.

Secretary of the Senate. A person elected by the Senate members to record the official actions of the Senate and to be the chief administrative officer of the Senate.

second reading. The reading of a bill for the second time, in full, in open session, opening it to amendatory action.

select committee. A committee appointed to consider a particular topic for a limited time. Used interchangeably with special committee.

Senate. Upper chamber of a two-body legislature.

Senate Committee Services (SCS). The Senate nonpartisan research and committee staff located in the John A. Cherberg Building. Equivalent to House Office of Program Research (OPR).

senator. Member of the Senate.

Sergeant at Arms. Enforces protocol of the House or Senate and provides security for the legislative offices.

session. Official meeting of the Legislature. The Constitution provides for one 105-day regular session during odd-numbered years and one 60-day regular session during even-numbered years each biennium.

severability clause. A section of a bill which instructs the court that if one section of the act is found unconstitutional, the remainder of the act will remain intact.

short title. An abridged description of the bill.

sine die. To conclude a regular or special session without setting a day to reconvene.

Speaker. Presiding officer of the House of Representatives.

special order of business. A motion to take up a specified measure at a specific time.

special session. A session of no more than 30 days, convened by the governor or the Legislature, following adjournment of the regular session. The Legislature, upon two-thirds vote of all members, may call itself into special session.

sponsor. Member offering a bill, amendment, resolution or memorial.

standing committees. Committees set up by the Legislature to last for the entire length (two years) of a Legislature.

state budget. The biennial operating budget.

state officials. The state of Washington elects nine administrative officers statewide: Governor, Lieutenant Governor, Attorney General, Secretary of State, Treasurer, Auditor, Commissioner of Public Lands, Insurance Commissioner, and Superintendent of Public Instruction.

status sheets. A daily publication during session giving status of bills pending or acted upon by the Legislature.

statute. A law enacted by the Legislature.

Statute Law Committee. See Code Reviser.

strike out. To delete language from a bill or resolution.

striking amendment. Amendment removing everything after the title and inserting a whole new bill.

subcommittee. Selected members of a committee designed to study a special area of concern and then report to the whole committee their findings and recommendations.

substitute. A bill which replaces an entire bill or resolution.

sunset. A program for review of state agencies, programs and statutes by JLARC and OFM.

sunset provision. A date certain for a law to automatically be repealed unless renewed by the Legislature.

supplemental budget. Changes in the second year of the biennium to funds allocated in the original capital, operating, or transportation budgets.

Supreme Court. The highest court of the state is made up of nine elected justices serving staggered six-year terms.

suspension calendar. Special calendar of noncontroversial bills created by the House Rules Committee. The only question on the floor is acceptance of committee recommendations and advancement to third reading. Closely related to the consent calendar occasionally used in the Senate.

table. To set aside a matter for possible consideration at a future time.

Temple of Justice. The building directly north of the Legislative Building, housing the Supreme Court and offices of the Supreme Court Clerk, Commissioner, Reporter of Decisions, and the Law Library.

term. Duration of office of an elected official.

term limits. Restrictions on the length of service for elected offices.

third house. An association whose membership includes most of the professional lobbyists in the state.

third reading. The final consideration of a bill before either house. The bill can be debated, tabled, referred, but not amended. Final passage takes a "constitutional majority."

title of bill. Description of bill or act which encompasses the intent of the bill.

title-only bill. A bill which contains nothing more than a title and a number. It is introduced in order to have a vehicle on which to amend substance at a later time.

transportation budget. Appropriations for highways, bridges, ferries, transit, vehicle licensing, and traffic enforcement.

TVW. Washington State version of C-SPAN,® broadcasting state government meetings and activities.

ulcer gulch. Slang term for area in the Legislative Building used by lobbyists and general public for telephone calls and messages.

unfinished business. Business which has been laid over from a previous day.

unicameral legislature. A legislative body having only one house, such as a city council. Nebraska has the only unicameral state legislature.

veto. Rejection of legislative bill by governor. Governor has power to veto sections of bills but cannot make any additions. The governor can also veto appropriation items. To pass a bill over a governor's veto takes a two-thirds vote of both houses and is known as overriding a veto.

vote. Formal expression of will or decision by Legislature or citizen.

WAC. Washington Administrative Code. States how state agencies shall organize and adopt rules and regulations. "WACs" and "rules and regs" refer to agency guidelines adopted pursuant to the Administrative Procedure Act.

WALIS. Washington Legislative Information System. A number of different types of services, including a data processing system, which provides accurate up-to-date information on legislative actions.

Washington State Register. A monthly publication which lists all proposed new agency WAC "rules and regs" as well as proposed amendments, meeting notices, etc.

Ways and Means. The chief revenue and appropriations committee in the Senate. The committee is responsible for deciding the "ways" in which state monies will be spent and the "means" that will be used to raise the tax revenues.

whip. An assistant to the majority or minority leader, the duties of the whip include counting votes, checking attendance and maintaining caucus discipline on partisan issues and procedural questions.

white sheet. The list of bills eligible for consideration to be moved to the green sheet by the Senate Rules Committee. "Pulls" from white to green do not require a vote.

withdraw a motion. To recall or remove a motion according to parliamentary procedure.

within the bar. Refers either to a legislator's presence within the bar of the house or to his or her physical presence on the floor of the Legislature.

work room. Area behind the rostrum of each house where the bills are processed, roll call information retained and bills engrossed, enrolled, etc.

work session. Informal discussion of a measure or topic by a committee. No executive action or amendments are permitted.

yield. To relinquish the floor of the House or Senate to allow another member to speak.

Bibliography

GENERAL

Bish, Robert L., *Governing Puget Sound*, Puget Sound Books, distributed by University of Washington Press, Seattle, WA, 1982.

Bone, Hugh, Hart-Nibbig, Nand E., and Pealy, Robert H., *Public Policymaking, Washington Style*, Institute of Governmental Research, University of Washington Press, Seattle, WA, 1980.

Final Legislative Report, published annually, contains a summary of legislation passed in preceding session(s), published by the Washington State Legislature, Olympia, WA.

Legislative Manual, published biennially by the Washington State Legislature, Olympia, WA, contains the joint rules, rules of the House and Senate, biographical information on legislators, and other interesting and useful information.

Members of the Washington State Legislature, 1889-1991, revised periodically and published by the Secretary of the Senate and the Chief Clerk of the House, Olympia, WA.

Nice, David C., Pierce, John C., and Sheldon, Charles H., *Government and Politics in the Evergreen State*, Washington State University Press, Pullman, WA, 1992.

Senate Reference Manual, a continually updated compilation of legislative reference materials published by the Washington State Senate.

Swanson, Thor, Mullen, William F., Pierce, John C., and Sheldon, Charles H., *Political Life in Washington*, Washington State University Press, Pullman, WA, 1985.

Washington State 1995 Data Book, published by the Office of Financial Management, Olympia, WA, 1996.

CHAPTER 1: THE STATE CAPITOL

The Botany of the Washington State Capitol Campus, published by the Office of the Governor and others, Olympia, WA, 1986.

"The King of Domes," *Valley Daily News*, January 15, 1995, author unknown.

A Tour of the Washington State Legislative Building, published by the Legislative Building Tour Office, Olympia, WA, 1995.

Washington State Capitol, A Guide through the Legislative Buildings of the Washington State Capitol Campus, published by the Office of the Governor and others, Olympia, WA, 1986.

The Washington State Capitol Campus, published by State of Washington, Senate and House of Representatives, Olympia, WA, 1990.

Washington State Yearbook, A Guide to Government in the Evergreen State, published annually by the Office of the Governor and the Office of the Secretary of State, Olympia, WA.

CHAPTER 2: LEGISLATIVE SESSIONS

"1995 Legislative Session Calendar," *State Legislatures*, February 1995, p. 37.

"1996 Legislative Session Calendar," *State Legislatures*, February 1996, p. 35.

"Legislative Sessions: Legal Provisions," *The Book of the States, 1994-95*, National Conference of State Legislatures, Denver, CO.

Members of the State Legislature by Districts, published by the Washington State Legislature, January 1991.

Kurtz, Karl L., "Understanding the Diversity of American State Legislatures," *Extension of Remarks*, June 1992, pp. 2-6.

CHAPTER 3: BILLS

Behnk, William E., "California Assembly Installs Laptops for Floor Sessions," *Journal of the American Society of Legislative Clerks and Secretaries*, Spring 1996, pp. 10-12.

"Bills In and Out of Committees," *Washington Legislative Service Center*, February 27, 1996.

Brummel, Jack, "Emergency Clause Material in Bill Drafting Guide," a memo to the Code Reviser, Olympia, WA, December 9, 1991.

Colorado Legislators Handbook, Legislative Council Research Publication No. 311, December 1987.

Cooper, Dennis, "Updating Phrases and Clauses," Code Reviser's Office, Olympia, WA, April 2, 1996.

Fiscal Update: May 1996, a memo published by the Senate Ways and Means Committee.

"Initiatives to the People and to the Legislature, 1914-1994," a chronological listing provided by the Office of the Secretary of State, Olympia, WA, April 1996.

"Introductions and Enactments," *The Book of the States, 1994-95*, published by the Council of State Governments, Lexington, KY, pp. 148-150.

"Leadership Report," *Washington Legislative Service Center*, Olympia, WA, April 5, 1996.

"Measure Numbering," a briefing paper published by the Washington State Code Reviser's Office, Olympia, WA, August 1, 1989.

Munro, Ralph, *Initiative and Referendum*, a pamphlet published by the Secretary of State's Office, Olympia, WA, undated.

Rhyme, Nancy, and Mackey, Scott, "This Year's Do-it-Yourself Laws," *State Legislatures*, October 1994, pp.23-25.

Richter, M.J., "Technology on the Front Lines," *Governing*, May 1996, pp. 69-80.

CHAPTER 4: COMMITTEES

Chi, Keon S., "State Trends," *State Government News*, January 1996, p. 38.

Jones, Steve, and others, "Fiscal Note Process," a memo produced by the Senate Ways and Means Committee, Olympia, WA, January 3, 1996.

O'Donnell, Bob, "How to be an Effective Committee Chair," *State Legislatures*, January 1996, pp. 27-29.

Petty, Janice, *A Chairman's Guide to Effective Committee Management,* National Conference of State Legislatures, Denver, CO, May 1981.

CHAPTER 5: MANAGEMENT OF LEGISLATION THROUGH CUTOFFS

Brown, Marty, and Hendrickson, Brad, "Amendments R Us," a memo from the office of the Secretary of the Senate, Olympia, WA, February 21, 1994.
Brown, Marty, "How Rules 'Pulls' Work," a memo from the Secretary of the Senate, Olympia, WA, January 31, 1995.
"Cutoff Calendars," annual, prepared by Senate Committee Services, Ed Seeberger, Director, Olympia, WA.
Inside the Legislative Process, a survey of the American Society of Legislative Clerks and Secretaries in cooperation with the National Conference of State Legislatures, Denver, CO, 1988.
"Joint Rules, 1993-94," adopted and published by the Washington State House and Senate, Olympia, WA, January 1993.
Karras, Dennis, "Conference Committees," a memo published by the House, office of the Chief Clerk, Olympia, WA, April 5, 1989.
Leos, Kate Julin, *The Legislature and the Legislative Process in the State of Washington,* Institute of Governmental Research, University of Washington, Seattle, WA, 1973.
McQuery, Elton, *Lawmaking in the West,* Council of State Governments, Chicago, IL, 1967.
Pritchard, Joel, "Rules Committee Procedures," a memo from the office of the Lieutenant Governor, Olympia, WA, January 19, 1988.
Reed, Thomas, *Reed's Parliamentary Rules,* first published by the U.S. House of Representatives, 1889, reprinted by the Washington State Legislature, Olympia, WA, 1971.

CHAPTER 6: THE BUDGETS

Agency Descriptions and Historical Budget Information, Office of Financial Management, Olympia, WA, 1990.
Comparative State/Local Taxes - 1987, Washington State Department of Revenue, Olympia, WA, December 1988.
Introduction to the Washington State Budget for Legislators, prepared by Senate Ways and Means Committee, Olympia, WA, December 1992.
Jones, Steve, "Decision in Initiative 601 Litigation," a memo to Senate members and staff, Olympia, WA, August 31, 1994.

"Key Facts - A Summary of Useful Transportation Data," published by the Washington State Department of Transportation, Olympia, WA, January 1996.

Legislative Budget Notes, 1995-1997, prepared by the House and Senate fiscal committees, Olympia, WA, 1995.

"Overview of Washington's Tax Structure," a memo prepared by the Senate Ways and Means Committee, Olympia, WA, December 1, 1995.

"Outline of Major Taxes in Washington State," a memo prepared by Washington State Department of Revenue, Olympia, WA, January 1993.

"Passing Tax Increases the Hard Way," Randall, Sharon, editor, *State Legislatures,* July/August 1996, p. 9.

Walker v. Munro, 124 Wn. 2nd 402 (1994).

Washington State Legislative Budget Fact Book, prepared by House and Senate fiscal committees and the LEAP Committee, Olympia, WA, 1994.

Washington State Taxes in a Nutshell, prepared by Senate Committee on Ways and Means, Olympia, WA, 1984.

Ziegler, Brian J., *Transportation Planning and Performance Measurement in Washington State,* a memo presented to the Transportation Research Board Conference, December 3, 1995.

CHAPTER 7: THE GOVERNOR AND THE LEGISLATURE

Crew, Robert E., and Hill, Marjorie, "Gubernatorial Influence in State Government Policy-Making," *Spectrum,* Fall 1995, pp. 29-35.

Cook, Tony, "Veto Lawsuit," a memo, Olympia, WA, May 2, 1995.

Eichstaedt, Peter, "No, No, Two Hundred Times No," *State Legislatures,* July/August 1995, pp. 46-49.

Erickson, Robert, and others, *Statehouse Democracy,* Cambridge University Press, New York, 1993.

Hodgins, Randy, "Governor's Budget and Tax Vetoes," a memo to Senate members, Olympia, WA, April 3, 1996.

Pharris, James K., *Veto - Legislature - Governor,* Attorney General Opinion 1995 No. 12, October 4, 1995.

Rosenthal, Alan, "Governors and the Legislature," *Congressional Quarterly Press,* Washington, D.C., 1993.

Sabato, Larry, "Goodbye to Goodtime Charlie," *Congressional Quarterly Press,* Washington, D.C., 1983.

Washington State Legislature v. Lowry, Complaint for Declaratory Judgment, No. 94-02725-2, in the Superior Court of the state of Washington, September 1994.

CHAPTER 8: LEGISLATORS

Barcellona, Miriam, and Grose, Andrew, "Term Limits: A Political Dilemma," *WESTRENDS*, Council of State Governments, August 1994.

Bazar, Beth, *State Legislators' Occupations: A Decade of Change*, National Conference of State Legislatures, Denver, CO, March 1987.

Chi, Keon, S., "State Trends," *State Government News*, January 1996, p. 38.

"Death Takes J. H. Ryan," *Tacoma News Tribune*, January 21, 1943.

Ehrenhalt, Alan, "A Coup in Connecticut: The Unmaking of a Leader - And Its Consequences," *Governing*, August 1990, pp. 74-79.

Gurwitt, Rob, "The Strains of Power," *Governing*, February 1995, pp. 17-22.

Hodson, Timothy, and others, "Leaders and Limits: Changing Patterns of State Legislative Leadership Under Term Limits," *Spectrum*, Summer 1995, pp.6-15.

Hurley, Margaret, *An Oral History*, interviewed by Laurie Mercier, Office of the Secretary of State, Olympia, WA, 1995.

"Mailing/Franking Policies in Various State Senates, October, 1989," compiled by Senator Mary George, Minority Leader, Hawaii State Senate.

McCord, Robert S., "Revival in the Arkansas House," *State Legislatures*, July/August 1995, pp. 40-45.

"Method of Setting Legislative Compensation as of January 31, 1989," compiled by National Conference of State Legislatures, Denver, CO, 1989.

Neal, Tommy, "Recall of State Officials," *NCSL Legisbrief*, July 1994.

Peery, George, "Transcending Term Limits," *State Legislatures*, June 1996, pp. 20-25.

Renstrom, Mary, "1996 State Legislator Compensation and Living Expense Allowances During Session," National Conference of State Legislatures, April 29, 1996.

Rhyme, Nancy, "Term Limits Updates," *NCSL Legisbriefs*, Denver, CO, September 1994 through February 1996.

Schwarz, Christopher, "From the Ivory Tower to Political Power," *State Government News*, September 1994, pp. 6-9.

Simon, Lucinda, "The Legislative Pay Puzzle," *State Legislatures*, July 1987, pp. 14-19.

Washington State Register, "Proposed Rules: Redistricting Commission," July 12, 1991.

CHAPTER 9: THE GENDER REVOLUTION

Biemesderfer, Susan, "Political Women Give Even Cowboys the Blues," *State Legislatures*, October 1990, pp.21-23.

Cox, Elizabeth M., "The Three Who Came First," *State Legislatures*, November 1994, pp. 13-19.

Dahlkemper, Lesley, "Growing Accustomed to Her Face," *State Legislatures*, July/August 1996, pp. 37-45.

Edwards, G. Thomas, *Sowing Good Seeds*, Oregon Historical Society Press, Portland, OR, 1984.

Gooding, Barbara, *Women in the Washington State Legislature, 1913-1983*, a senior thesis submitted to The Evergreen State College, 1983.

Gordon, Diane, "Republican Women Make Gains," *State Legislatures*, February 1995, p. 15.

Hinsch, Kathryn, *Political Pioneers*, a publication of Elected Washington Women, Eleanor Lee, Founder, Olympia, WA, 1983.

Roberts, Mary Helen, Quantock, Ann, and Swift, Earlyse Allen, *Impact: A Woman's Guide to Legislative Action*, Washington Women United, Olympia, WA, 1982.

"Sexual Speculations," *The Economist*, April 20, 1996, p. 21.

CHAPTER 10: LEGISLATIVE STAFF

"Agency Descriptions and Historical Budget Information," published by the Office of Financial Management, Olympia, WA, 1990.

Balutis, Alan P., "The Role of the Staff in the Legislature: The Case of New York," *Public Administration Review*, Washington, D.C., July/August 1975.

Chi, Keon S., "State Trends," *State Government News*, Lexington, Kentucky, January 1996, p. 38.

Kurtz, Karl T., "Understanding the Diversity of American State Legislatures," *Extension of Remarks*, Boulder, CO, June 1992.

Loomis, Burdett, "Being There: Research in a State Legislature," *Extension of Remarks*, Boulder, CO, June 1992.

Simon, Lucinda, *A Legislator's Guide to Personnel Management*, funded by grants from the U.S. Office of Personnel Management and the National Science Foundation, National Conference of State Legislatures, Denver, CO, July 1979.

Simon, Lucinda, *A Legislator's Guide to Staffing Patterns*, funded by grants from the U.S. Office of Personnel Management and the National

Science Foundation, National Conference of State Legislatures, Denver, CO, August 1979.

Simon, Lucinda, *Legislative Staff Services: 50 State Profiles,* funded by a grant from the U.S. Office of Personnel Management, National Conference of State Legislatures, Denver, CO, Spring, 1979.

"Washington State Legislative Internship Program," a publication of the Washington State Legislature, Olympia, WA, 1995.

Weberg, Brian, "1986 State Legislative Staff Salaries and Personnel Policy," *State Legislative Report,* May 1987.

CHAPTER 11: ETHICS, DISCLOSURE AND CAMPAIGNS

1994 Election Financing Fact Book, Washington State Public Disclosure Commission, Olympia, WA, January 1996.

"Advisory Opinions of the Legislative Ethics Board," published periodically, Olympia, WA.

Boulard, Gary, "Pluperfect Purity," *State Legislatures,* January 1995, pp. 29-33.

Boulard, Gary, "Lobbyists as Outlaws," *State Legislatures,* January 1996, pp. 20-25.

Bowman, Editor-in-Chief, *Public Integrity Annual,* Council of State Governments and American Society for Public Administration, Lexington, KY, 1996.

Brown, Marty, "Mailing Restrictions," a memo from the Secretary of the Senate, Olympia, WA, December 14, 1995.

Collins, William B., "Basic Questions and Answers about the 1994 State Ethics Law," Office of the Attorney General, Olympia, WA, June 1994.

Commission on Ethics in Government and Campaign Practices, "Final Report," Olympia, WA, January 6, 1994.

Ensign, David, "Tests of Strength," *State Government News,* April 1996, pp. 20-22.

Golob, Gordon, "Gift Reporting," a memo from the Secretary of the Senate, Olympia, WA, July 12, 1991.

Hull, William B., "The Eleven Commandments: Colorado Adopts Legislative Staff Ethics," *States West,* Council of State Governments, May 1996.

"Lobbyist Reporting," and "Employers of Lobbyists," pamphlets published by the Washington State Public Disclosure Commission, Olympia, WA, 1995.

Mallory, Carol, and Hedlund, Elizabeth, *Enforcing the Campaign Finance Laws: An Agency Model,* The Center for Responsive Politics, Washington, D.C., 1993.

Money in Western Politics, A study of campaign finances by the Money in Western Politics Project of the Western States Center, Portland, OR, October 1992.

Neal, Tommy, "Campaign Contribution Limits on Individuals," *NCSL Legisbrief,* published by the National Conference of State Legislatures, February 1996.

Prochnow, Tyler, *Campaign Finance Legislation 1993,* National Conference of State Legislatures, Denver, CO, 1994.

Rosenthal, Alan, "Administering Ethics to Legislators," *Spectrum,* 1995, pp. 28-35.

CHAPTER 12: A HISTORY OF THE 1991-1992 SESSIONS

"The Daily Clips," a daily collection of articles, features and editorials from Washington's major print media including *The Seattle Times, Seattle Post-Intelligencer, The News Tribune, The Spokesman-Review,* and *The Olympian.*

Index

Printed in the United States
201872BV00001B/148-207/A

9 780295 975726